The Virtual American Empire

The Virtual American Empire

WAR, FAITH, AND POWER

Edward N. Luttwak

Transaction Publishers
New Brunswick (U.S.A.) and London (U.K.)

Library of Congress Catalog Number: 2009018772
ISBN: 978-1-4128-1039-5 (cloth); 978-1-4128-1040-1 (paper)
Printed in the United States of America

Library of Congress Cataloging-in-Publication Data

Luttwak, Edward.
    The virtual American empire : war, faith, and power / Edward N. Luttwak.
        p. cm.
    ISBN 978-1-4128-1039-5 (alk. paper)
    1. War. 2. Peace. 3. International relations. 4. United States--Foreign relations. I. Title.

U21.2.L9 2009
355'.033073--dc22

2009018772

Contents

Introduction

Until the financial and economic downfall of 2008, the power and authority of the United States on the world scene were sustained not only by political prestige, cultural attraction and overwhelming military strength, but also by wealth in all its varied forms, from the investment capacity of American private finance to the purchasing power of the world's largest importer. When the latter finally ruined the former—huge trade deficits passively tolerated for years in the name of free trade must de-capitalize as well as de-industrialize—American diplomacy quite suddenly had to function without much of its former economic leverage.

The consequences were immediately manifest in the ease and finality with which American strategic allies such as France, Germany, Italy, the Netherlands, and others flatly refused to cooperate with the economic measures of the new Obama administration in early 2009. With global activity diminishing, as reduced demand reduced production, reducing employment thus further reducing demand, only a sharp increase in public spending net of taxation could counter the downward spiral.

That much was undisputed even as debate continued between the advocates of tax cuts and of more spending, yet the major European governments but for the United Kingdom flatly refused to join the United States, China, and Japan in either lowering taxes or spending more. Instead they proposed to let others carry the entire burden of increasing public debt and the risk of inflation with it, in the tranquil expectation that their own exporters would still fully benefit from any increase in global demand. American military strength could hurt and intimidate enemies but it could hardly deter or punish such blatant "free-riding" by historic allies. Nor could it be done with tariffs, quotas, capital controls or more subtle measures not prohibited by any international trade treaty, because in the United States there is an elite consensus—not shared by a majority of Americans—that strenuously opposes any form of protectionism, which is viewed as downright sinful and not as a set of possible actions whose costs and benefits should be evaluated rationally. The preferred alternative is to begin international consultations leading to new agreements—but when nothing is agreed, nothing is done about it. That is how China was allowed to continue its long-standing distortion of the yuan-dollar exchange rate that cheapens its exports at the expense of American and other dollar-based competitors. Free-trade ideology and the varied interests that march under its flag inhibited any retaliation, so that loud public complaints by a succession of U.S. treasury secretaries, were ignored and even ridiculed by Chinese officialdom with perfect impunity.

Debtors cannot expect much respect from creditors, especially if they remain captive to ideological fixations even when they ought to act most vigorously. That free trade require freely moving, undistorted exchange rates to yield its plentiful benefits, is perfectly obvious, for imbalances can only be self-correcting through the appreciation of the currency of champion exporters, and the depreciation of the currency of persistent net importers. Moreover, it would have been easy enough to dissuade the purchases of U.S. Treasury bonds and other dollar assets by foreign governments that kept propping up the value of the U.S. dollar against the Chinese yuan and other currencies. No treaty prohibits the imposition of taxes on the earnings of foreign-held securities, including taxes that exceed those earnings by any amount, so that instead of rewarding currency manipulators with interest payments, they would have been forced to pay for the privilege of holding U.S. debt. Such negative interest rates worked very well for the Swiss, when they restored the competitiveness of their exports by discouraging the avalanche of foreign bank deposits that was driving up the value of the Swiss franc.

Characteristically, this perfectly straightforward safeguard against currency distortion was not even considered, while officials and the usual modish columnists instead kept repeating that Chinese and other foreign government purchases of U.S. Treasury paper were necessary to finance the huge and rising U.S. trade deficit. Actually matters stood exactly the other way around: it was precisely those government purchases of U.S. debt that caused the huge trade deficits in the first place—without them, interest rates would have risen to realistic levels dissuading borrowing and preventing the housing bubble, while the dollar would have become cheap enough to narrow drastically if not end the trade deficit, by favoring exports and dissuading imports.

The protracted failure to safeguard the American economy, and more especially American manufacturing from blatant currency manipulation by foreign governments, finally eroded not only America's wealth but also American prestige on the world scene. For such behavior is never attributed to self-restraint or even to ideological rigidity but rather to foolish weakness or worse, the predominance of narrow interests: Swiss bankers were forced to drive away foreign depositors to lower the franc for the sake of Swiss industry, but their American counterparts were allowed to thrive greatly on the packaging and placing of ever-growing debt, thereby directly benefiting from the currency manipulation that was hollowing out the American economy. The outcome was the financial collapse of 2008, which aggravated the American and global economic crisis, and undoubtedly weakened the United States on the world scene.

Some Americans have always been displeased by the magnitude of American power in the world, no doubt because they project onto the entire nation their own discomfort with the exercise of power. For them, as for the few ideological leftists still in circulation, the weakening of the United States is not a problem at all, but rather a most welcome development. For others, including the present writer the events of 2008 amounted to a very unwelcome thought-experiment: how much power can the United States still have if it no longer has its former economic leverage? The results so far are not promising, and there is more: the collapse of American private finance and the severe contraction of the American economy have greatly encouraged the enemies of the United States, from Latin American buffoons to assorted Muslim fanatics, and far more significantly, they have enhanced the relative standing of the Chinese government—not an enemy of the United States to be sure, not even malevolent in most respects, but certainly an enemy of democracy.

The essays that follow venture in many directions, but in their totality they also present a certain vision of the United States, which excludes the possibility that the downfall of 2008 will not be followed by an even greater resurgence. But that will require more than rescue packages and policy tinkering at the edges, for all such would at best restore the pre-crisis economic situation, which was not sustainable—or rather was sustained only by the continuing accumulation of more debt.

A new American economy is indeed emerging in which American households consume less and save more to rebuild their capital base, but the United States as a whole must also export more and import less to start retiring foreign holdings of U.S. debt instead of adding to them. Unless foreign demand increases, the global economy will shrink in proportion to the loss of American demand, and indeed more so because of ricochet effects. It would be worthwhile to avoid that outcome, and perhaps some of the structural ideas presented below could be of some use for that purpose.

What is certain is the impossibility of a new equilibrium if the champion exporters Germany, China, Japan, Korea, and more do not also become champion importers, which is in turn impossible if their populations continue to save up to 50 percent of their incomes. That reflects no excess of frugality but rather the absence or miserable inadequacy of pensions and health care for the poor in China, the relative inadequacy of Japanese retirement funding, the obstacles to family formation in Germany, and similar systemic conditions. Hence a new equilibrium for the United States and the global economy that is not set at a drastically lower level, would require vast reforms all over the place, on which agreement may be politically difficult if not impossible, and which would certainly require an enormous amount of new government activity. In the case of China, already swimming in corruption at every administrative level, that alone is a frightening prospect. But the alternative to a new post-crisis equilibrium that is so difficult to achieve—and which the German government for one does not even want to achieve—is the disequilibrium of global inflation, because the U.S. government will assuredly continue to print money so long as unemployment rates exceed politically tolerable levels.

In the meantime, the security of the American people will not be assured by the enthusiasm for global multilateralism that followed the actual or supposed unilateralism of the past. A great many international organizations, many of them affiliated to the United Nations in some way, work effectively every day to assure all sorts of essential services, from the transmission of epidemic disease warnings to the carriage of the mails. But security is another matter: to stop killers, it is necessary to fight, and only single political communities committed to the mutual defense, and military alliances of the same can do that. The United Nations cannot be such an alliance –and the experiment with its species of international security has already been made once and for all by the different populations of Bosnia-Herzegovina, Croat, Muslim, Serb, or even "Yugoslav" as the broad-minded continue to call themselves. They witnessed the ineffectual visitations of United Nations officials and heard their hollow pronouncements while their agony of rape, murder and destruction continued year after year; they watched the variegated troops sent by countries rich and poor in their baby-blue UN helmets arrive and then depart, and while the rich soldiers drunk and whored and the poor soldiers stole and smuggled, neither ever protected anyone all from brutality or death—for that would have required a willingness to fight, absent in the UN Secretariat where the egregious Kofi Annan was in charge of so-called peace-keeping, absent in almost all home governments that sent troops to Bosnia-Herzegovina, and certainly among almost all officers and men, most of whom could not have fought in any case, being the product of armies that only use their weapons against their own unarmed civilians if at all. Worse still was the failure of the European Union to make Bosnia-Herzegovina its own integrating project, for a European army would have required a European defense ministry and thus a European government, instead the Adriatic summer beach seasons continued in full swing while people were being massacred just across the water. That nothing at all has changed since then, in spite many solemn UN pronouncements, and all manner of costly military programs by the European Union, is proven by the inability of both to respond to the very least of violent threats at this particular time, the piratical attacks of small boat-loads of under-nourished Somalis with their rusty weapons, which handfuls of determined guards repel with ease.

When it comes to providing security for the American people, there is only unilateralism, or collective action with like-minded allies whenever possible. It was ever so, and so it will remain.

Part 1

The Paradoxical Logic of Strategy

1

Give War a Chance

Premature Peacemaking

An unpleasant truth, often overlooked, is that although war is a great evil, it does have a great virtue: it can resolve political conflicts and lead to peace. This can happen when all belligerents become exhausted or when one wins decisively. Either way the key is that the fighting must continue until a resolution is reached. War brings peace only after passing a culminating phase of violence. Hopes of military success must fade for accommodation to become more attractive than further combat.

Since the establishment of the United Nations and the enshrinement of great-power politics in its Security Council, however, wars among lesser powers have rarely been allowed to run their natural course. Instead, they have typically been interrupted early on, before they could burn themselves out and establish the preconditions for a lasting settlement. Cease-fires and armistices have frequently been imposed under the aegis of the Security Council in order to halt fighting. NATO's intervention in the Kosovo crisis follows this pattern.

But a cease-fire tends to arrest war-induced exhaustion and lets belligerents reconstitute and rearm their forces. It intensifies and prolongs the struggle once the cease-fire ends—and it does usually end. This was true of the Arab-Israeli war of 1948-49, which might have come to closure in a matter of weeks if two cease-fires ordained by the Security Council had not let the combatants recuperate. It has recently been true in the Balkans. Imposed cease-fires frequently interrupted the fighting between Serbs and Croats in Krajina, between the forces of the Yugoslav federation and the Croat army, and between the Serbs, Croats, and Muslims in Bosnia. Each time, the opponents used the pause to recruit, train, and equip additional forces for further combat, prolonging the war and widening the scope of its killing and destruction. Imposed armistices, meanwhile—again, unless followed by negotiated peace accords—artificially freeze conflict and perpetuate a state of war indefinitely

3

by shielding the weaker side from the consequences of refusing to make concessions for peace.

The Cold War provided compelling justification for such behavior by the two superpowers, which sometimes collaborated in coercing less-powerful belligerents to avoid being drawn into their conflicts and clashing directly. Although imposed cease-fires ultimately did increase the total quantity of warfare among the lesser powers, and armistices did perpetuate states of war, both outcomes were clearly lesser evils (from a global point of view) than the possibility of nuclear war. But today, neither Americans nor Russians are inclined to intervene competitively in the wars of lesser powers, so the unfortunate consequences of interrupting war persist while no greater danger is averted. It might be best for all parties to let minor wars burn themselves out.

The Problems of Peacekeepers

Today, cease-fires and armistices are imposed on lesser powers by multilateral agreement—not to avoid great-power competition but for essentially disinterested and indeed frivolous motives, such as television audiences' revulsion at harrowing scenes of war. But this, perversely, can systematically prevent the transformation of war into peace. The Dayton Accords are typical of the genre: they have condemned Bosnia to remain divided into three rival armed camps, with combat suspended momentarily but a state of hostility prolonged indefinitely. Since no side is threatened by defeat and loss, none has a sufficient incentive to negotiate a lasting settlement; because no path to peace is even visible, the dominant priority is to prepare for future war rather than to reconstruct devastated economies and ravaged societies. Uninterrupted war would certainly have caused further suffering and led to an unjust outcome from one perspective or another, but it would also have led to a more stable situation that would have let the postwar era truly begin. Peace takes hold only when war is truly over.

A variety of multilateral organizations now make it their business to intervene in other peoples' wars. The defining characteristic of these entities is that they insert themselves in war situations while refusing to engage in combat. In the long run this only adds to the damage. If the United Nations helped the strong defeat the weak faster and more decisively, it would actually enhance the peacemaking potential of war. But the first priority of UN peacekeeping contingents is to avoid casualties among their own personnel. Unit commanders therefore habitually appease the locally stronger force, accepting its dictates and tolerating its abuses. This appeasement is not strategically purposeful, as siding with the stronger power overall would be; rather, it merely reflects the determination of each UN unit to avoid confrontation. The final result is to prevent the emergence of a coherent outcome, which requires an imbalance of strength sufficient to end the fighting.

Peacekeepers wary of violence are also unable to effectively protect civilians who are caught up in the fighting or deliberately attacked. At best, UN peacekeeping forces have been passive spectators to outrages and massacres, as in Bosnia and Rwanda; at worst, they collaborate with it, as Dutch UN troops did in the fall of Srebrenica by helping the Bosnian Serbs separate the men of military age from the rest of the population.

The very presence of UN forces, meanwhile, inhibits the normal remedy of endangered civilians, which is to escape from the combat zone. Deluded into thinking that they will be protected, civilians in danger remain in place until it is too late to flee. During the 1992-94 siege of Sarajevo, appeasement interacted with the pretense of protection in an especially perverse manner: UN personnel inspected outgoing flights to prevent the escape of Sarajevo civilians in obedience to a cease-fire agreement negotiated with the locally dominant Bosnian Serbs—who habitually violated that deal. The more sensible, realistic response to a raging war would have been for the Muslims to either flee the city or drive the Serbs out.

Institutions such as the European Union, the Western European Union, and the Organization for Security and Cooperation in Europe lack even the UN's rudimentary command structure and personnel, yet they too now seek to intervene in warlike situations, with predictable consequences. Bereft of forces even theoretically capable of combat, they satisfy the interventionist urges of member states (or their own institutional ambitions) by sending unarmed or lightly armed "observer" missions, which have the same problems as UN peacekeeping missions, only more so.

Military organizations such as NATO or the West African Peacekeeping Force (ECOMOG, recently at work in Sierra Leone) are capable of stopping warfare. Their interventions still have the destructive consequence of prolonging the state of war, but they can at least protect civilians from its consequences. Even that often fails to happen, however, because multinational military commands engaged in disinterested interventions tend to avoid any risk of combat, thereby limiting their effectiveness. U.S. troops in Bosnia, for example, repeatedly failed to arrest known war criminals passing through their checkpoints lest this provoke confrontation.

Multinational commands, moreover, find it difficult to control the quality and conduct of member states' troops, which can reduce the performance of all forces involved to the lowest common denominator. This was true of otherwise fine British troops in Bosnia and of the Nigerian marines in Sierra Leone. The phenomenon of troop degradation can rarely be detected by external observers, although its consequences are abundantly visible in the litter of dead, mutilated, raped, and tortured victims that attends such interventions. The true state of affairs is illuminated by the rare exception, such as the vigorous Danish tank battalion in Bosnia that replied to any attack on it by firing back in full force, quickly stopping the fighting.

The First "Post-Heroic" War

All prior examples of disinterested warfare and its crippling limitations, however, have been cast into shadow by NATO's current intervention against Serbia for the sake of Kosovo. The alliance has relied on airpower alone to minimize the risk of NATO casualties, bombing targets in Serbia, Montenegro, and Kosovo for weeks without losing a single pilot. This seemingly miraculous immunity from Yugoslav anti-aircraft guns and missiles was achieved by multiple layers of precautions. First, for all the noise and imagery suggestive of a massive operation, very few strike sorties were actually flown during the first few weeks. That reduced the risks to pilots and aircraft but of course also limited the scope of the bombing to a mere fraction of NATO's potential. Second, the air campaign targeted air-defense systems first and foremost, minimizing present and future allied casualties, though at the price of very limited destruction and the loss of any shock effect. Third, NATO avoided most anti-aircraft weapons by releasing munitions not from optimal altitudes but from an ultra-safe 15,000 feet or more. Fourth, the alliance greatly restricted its operations in less-than-perfect weather conditions. NATO officials complained that dense clouds were impeding the bombing campaign, often limiting nightly operations to a few cruise missile strikes against fixed targets of known location. In truth, what the cloud ceiling prohibited was not all bombing—low-altitude attacks could easily have taken place—but rather perfectly safe bombing.

On the ground far beneath the high-flying planes, small groups of Serb soldiers and police in armored vehicles were terrorizing hundreds of thousands of Albanian Kosovars. NATO has a panoply of aircraft designed for finding and destroying such vehicles. All its major powers have antitank helicopters, some equipped to operate without base support. But no country offered to send them into Kosovo when the ethnic cleansing began—after all, they might have been shot down. When U.S. Apache helicopters based in Germany were finally ordered to Albania, in spite of the vast expenditure devoted to their instantaneous "readiness" over the years, they required more than three weeks of "predeployment preparations" to make the journey. Six weeks into the war, the Apaches had yet to fly their first mission, although two had already crashed during training. More than mere bureaucratic foot dragging was responsible for this inordinate delay: the U.S. Army insisted that the Apaches could not operate on their own, but would need the support of heavy rocket barrages to suppress Serb anti-aircraft weapons. This created a much larger logistical load than the Apaches alone, and an additional, evidently welcome delay.

Even before the Apache saga began, NATO already had aircraft deployed on Italian bases that could have done the job just as well: American A-10 "Warthogs" built around their powerful 30 mm antitank guns and British Royal Air Force Harriers ideal for low-altitude bombing at close range. Neither was employed, again because it could not be done in perfect safety. In the calculus of the

NATO democracies, the immediate possibility of saving thousands of Albanians from massacre and hundreds of thousands from deportation was obviously not worth the lives of a few pilots. That may reflect unavoidable political reality, but it demonstrates how even a large-scale disinterested intervention can fail to achieve its ostensibly humanitarian aim. It is worth wondering whether the Kosovars would have been better off had NATO simply done nothing.

Refugee Nations

The most disinterested of all interventions in war—and the most destructive—are humanitarian relief activities. The largest and most protracted is the United Nations Relief and Works Agency (UNRWA). It was built on the model of its predecessor, the United Nations Relief and Rehabilitation Agency (UNRRA), which operated displaced-persons' camps in Europe immediately after World War II. The UNRWA was established immediately after the 1948-49 Arab-Israeli war to feed, shelter, educate, and provide health services for Arab refugees who had fled Israeli zones in the former territory of Palestine.

By keeping refugees alive in Spartan conditions that encouraged their rapid emigration or local resettlement, the UNRRA'S camps in Europe had assuaged postwar resentments and helped disperse revanchist concentrations of national groups. But UNRWA camps in Lebanon, Syria, Jordan, the West Bank, and the Gaza Strip provided on the whole a higher standard of living than most Arab villagers had previously enjoyed, with a more varied diet, organized schooling, superior medical care, and no backbreaking labor in stony fields. They had, therefore, the opposite effect, becoming desirable homes rather than eagerly abandoned transit camps. With the encouragement of several Arab countries, the UNRWA turned escaping civilians into lifelong refugees who gave birth to refugee children, who have in turn had refugee children of their own.

During its half-century of operation, the UNRWA has thus perpetuated a Palestinian refugee nation, preserving its resentments in as fresh a condition as they were in 1948 and keeping the first bloom of revanchist emotion intact. By its very existence, the UNRWA dissuades integration into local society and inhibits emigration. The concentration of Palestinians in the camps, moreover, has facilitated the voluntary or forced enlistment of refugee youths by armed organizations that fight both Israel and each other. The UNRWA has contributed to a half-century of Arab-Israeli violence and still retards the advent of peace.

If each European war had been attended by its own postwar UNRWA, today's Europe would be filled with giant camps for millions of descendants of uprooted Gallo-Romans, abandoned Vandals, defeated Burgundians, and misplaced Visigoths—not to speak of more recent refugee nations such as post-1945 Sudeten Germans (three million of whom were expelled from Czechoslovakia in 1945). Such a Europe would have remained a mosaic of warring tribes, undigested and unreconciled in their separate feeding camps. It might have assuaged consciences to help each one at each remove, but it would have led to permanent instability and violence.

The UNRWA has counterparts elsewhere, such as the Cambodian camps along the Thai border, which incidentally provided safe havens for the mass-murdering Khmer Rouge. But because the United Nations is limited by stingy national contributions, these camps' sabotage of peace is at least localized.

That is not true of the proliferating, feverishly competitive nongovernmental organizations (NGOs) that now aid war refugees. Like any other institution, these NGOs are interested in perpetuating themselves, which means that their first priority is to attract charitable contributions by being seen to be active in high-visibility situations. Only the most dramatic natural disasters attract any significant mass-media attention, and then only briefly; soon after an earthquake or flood, the cameras depart. War refugees, by contrast, can win sustained press coverage if kept concentrated in reasonably accessible camps. Regular warfare among well-developed countries is rare and offers few opportunities for such NGOs, so they focus their efforts on aiding refugees in the poorest parts of the world. This ensures that the food, shelter, and health care offered—although abysmal by Western standards—exceeds what is locally available to non-refugees. The consequences are entirely predictable. Among many examples, the huge refugee camps along the Democratic Republic of Congo's border with Rwanda stand out. They sustain a Hutu nation that would otherwise have been dispersed, making the consolidation of Rwanda impossible and providing a base for radicals to launch more Tutsi-killing raids across the border. Humanitarian intervention has worsened the chances of a stable, long-term resolution of the tensions in Rwanda.

To keep refugee nations intact and preserve their resentments forever is bad enough, but inserting material aid into ongoing conflicts is even worse. Many NGOs routinely supply active combatants. Defenseless, they cannot exclude armed warriors from their feeding stations, clinics, and shelters. Since refugees are presumptively on the losing side, the warriors among them are usually in retreat. By intervening to help, NGOs systematically impede the progress of their enemies toward a decisive victory that could end the war. Sometimes NGOs, impartial to a fault, even help both sides, thus preventing mutual exhaustion and a resulting settlement. And in some extreme cases, such as Somalia, NGOs even pay protection money to local war bands, which use those funds to buy arms. Those NGOs are therefore helping prolong the warfare whose consequences they ostensibly seek to mitigate.

Make War to Make Peace

Too many wars nowadays become endemic conflicts that never end because the transformative effects of both decisive victory and exhaustion are blocked by outside intervention. Unlike the ancient problem of war, however, the compounding of its evils by disinterested interventions is a new malpractice that could be curtailed. Policy elites should actively resist the emotional impulse to intervene in other peoples' wars—not because they are indifferent to human suffering but precisely because they care about it and want to facilitate the advent of peace. The United States should dissuade multilateral interventions instead of leading them. New rules should be established for UN refugee relief activities to ensure that immediate succor is swiftly followed by repatriation, local absorption, or emigration, ruling out the establishment of permanent refugee camps. And although it may not be possible to constrain interventionist NGOs, they should at least be neither officially encouraged nor funded. Underlying these seemingly perverse measures would be a true appreciation of war's paradoxical logic and a commitment to let it serve its sole useful function: to bring peace.

2

Why We Need an Incoherent Foreign Policy

A solidly practical, one-thing-at-a-time pragmatism is the Anglo-Saxon virtue in the realm of foreign affairs, as in most things. The attempt to interpret systematically all sorts of diverse phenomena is the Teutonic vice of the likes of Clausewitz. But sometimes vice must prevail.

Consider the standard criticism of American foreign policy since the end of the Cold War, and more especially since the advent of the Clinton administration. With rare unanimity, the most varied voices, from the ambassadors of traditional allies at Washington dinner parties to truculent government spokesmen in Beijing, not to mention a multitude of academic and journalistic commentators, insistently criticize the lack of any coherent scheme in the overall conduct of American foreign policy. Worse still, they denounce the mixed signals and contradictory actions that abound even in American dealings with single countries.

There are many examples of such incoherence, but one is perhaps the most extreme, and the country in question is certainly very important, arguably the most important, at least in the long run. Chinese officials, and the Hong Kong tycoons who now habitually relay their views, bitterly complain that U.S.-Chinese relations have become fragile because of the bewildering variety of contradictory pressures emanating from the United States.

On the one hand, they point out, China is regularly called upon to act as a responsible great power at the U.N. Security Council, over the disposition of Iraq for example, and confidently expected to cooperate with the United States in stabilizing the Korean peninsula, almost as if it were a strategic ally. Yet, they complain, the United States now refuses to sell any military equipment whatsoever to China, hampering its efforts to acquire some of the capabilities that befit a great power: a few squadrons of modern fighters, a few competent warships, last-generation battle tanks, and so on. Adding insult to injury, when China exercises the prosaic right of any independent power, great or otherwise, to sell its own weapons to friendly countries and other paying customers, the United States feels free to investigate, embarrassingly publicize, and stridently denounce such transactions, while striving to stop them by intimidating the prospective recipients.

Likewise, the United States explicitly endorses the Chinese claim of sovereignty over Taiwan, and consistently rejects the attempts of the Republic of China to regain diplomatic recognition. Yet when the Chinese armed forces conducted military exercises in the Straits of Taiwan, strictly within the norms of international law, and for the declared purpose of dissuading Taiwanese demands for independence that the United States also opposes, the American reaction was an anachronistic exercise in gunboat diplomacy.

Moreover, while thus negating their verbal acceptance of China's sovereignty over one province, Americans challenge it outright in the case of another, through Congressional statements and actions in support of Tibetan claims, which sometimes include demands for outright independence. Much worse, the executive branch has now joined in these challenges to Chinese sovereignty, by creating the new position of "Tibet coordinator" within the State Department, implying that Tibetan matters no longer belong to the sphere of Washington-Beijing relations on the same footing as for the rest of Chinese territory. One can well imagine how Americans would react if a foreign government were to appoint a "Texas coordinator"—in effect an explicit declaration of the intent to interfere in the domestic affairs of the United States.

Even more contradictory are the commercial pressures. On the one hand, the U.S. secretary of commerce visits China with a large number of accompanying corporate salesmen, explicitly to gain privileged access to its rapidly growing market, because regular access is already available to all. At the same time, the office of the U.S. Trade Representative seems bent on dissolving whatever goodwill is thus achieved, by bluntly threatening sanctions from the very outset of negotiations over any dispute at hand. In this matter too there is an aggravating factor: while acting so harshly with China, the United States seems much more respectful in its economic diplomacy with its subordinate ally Japan, and even with its dependent client South Korea, tolerating any number of transparent evasions of negotiated agreements with only the feeblest protests.

And then there is the vexed question of the dissidents. In many different ways, from formal human rights interventions by the State Department and government-sponsored radio broadcasts, to the varied forms of support offered by academic and eleemosynary institutions, Americans are systematically encouraging Chinese citizens to subvert the very same Chinese government with which the United States is so eager to cooperate on a wide range of issues.

The contradictions are certainly sharp, when executive, legislative and purely private doings are thus conflated. If one accepts Beijing's perspective, overlooking such things as the unbending rigidity of its political repression, not least in Tibet, the well-documented sale of nuclear materials and ballistic-missile technology to Pakistan, and the use of prison labor on a huge scale in manufacturing, the overall argument may even seem persuasive.

What is certainly true is that the effective leverage of the United States over China at any one moment in time would be far greater if a single, unified, policy were pursued by all relevant parties. That would of course require a prior set of fundamental choices: is China to be treated as an adversary or as a global-security partner? Is China to be courted as a market for U.S. exports, or is it more important to protect the U.S. market from the flood of Chinese imports?

Once such choices were made, the United States would be ready to adopt an unambiguous "line" towards China, as not only the Soviet Union once did for each country and each issue, but France for example does still now. The diplomats of the Quai d'Orsay are rarely troubled by the doubts and tensions that afflict their American counterparts, as they implement the logically consistent policies invariably favored by French governments. Nor is there any ambiguity about the scope of their responsibilities: the execution of foreign policy is the realm of professional diplomacy, with no parliamentary intrusions tolerated, and still less those of mere private groupings pursuing idealistic agendas. Naturally, so much consistency and clarity evokes the deference of all respectable mass media, as of most other French institutions, academic, commercial, industrial or financial—all of which very helpfully have strong government ties.

American society is much different. The U.S. Congress lacks the inhibitions of the French National Assembly, American mass media are little given to deference, and few private institutions strive to adhere as closely as possible to government policies, unless they happen to coincide with their own goals. Nevertheless, if the executive branch at least made its own clear-cut choices to set a "line" for each country and issue, it would finally have a consistent set of priorities for each.

Not every new dilemma that came along would thereby be automatically resolved. But the chronic problems at least would each have their preordained solutions, to determine, for example, if human rights complaints are to be vigorously pressed, or merely recorded in obscure documents to ritualistically comply with legislated requirements. As to commerce, the administration would either seek privileged access to the Chinese market for U.S. exporters, tolerating with equanimity the commensurate Chinese penetrations of the American market, or else insist on the strict application of each and every multilateral or bilateral rule, freely using the threat of sanctions to enforce compliance.

With far broader consequences, if the choice were made to turn China into a global strategic partner, outstanding issues would be resolved by systematic negotiations within the framework of standing bilateral arrangements, instead of the present admixture of quiet deals, failed understandings, and angry polemics. Most notably, the administration might agree to resume the sale of selected weapons and military technologies to China, in exchange for satisfactory restraints on Chinese military exports to third countries, and the outright termination of all nuclear and long-range missile exports.

In addition to the important case of Korea, there would likewise be consultations on any other regional issues in which China had a significant stake, from Myanmar to the different West Asia conflicts. As in the case of American dealings with other friendly powers, the aim would be to minimize the effects of divergent interests and to eliminate unnecessary frictions, even if no close cooperation can ensue.

A strategic partnership, even if rather loose, would require each side to defer to the recognized core interests of the other. Accordingly, Beijing would presumably have to stop providing any form of verbal or substantive support to countries actively hostile to the United States, most importantly Iran. The United States, for its part, would have to refrain from interfering in the Chinese disposition of Hong Kong, specifically denying even verbal support for local dissidents. More broadly, the executive branch would have to stop all forms of interference in the domestic affairs of China, except insofar as inflexibly mandated by law. Similarly, Taipei and Beijing would have to resolve their differences as best they could, within the context of their own bilateral balance of power, with no further American intrusions.

Consistently with that choice, the administration in office would adopt the most minimalist interpretation possible of the security and military-supply commitments legally prescribed by the Taiwan Relations Act. China would tacitly be expected to refrain from any use of force against Taiwan, which would not be necessary anyway once the island were left isolated and unprotected.

Conversely, if it were decided that China is inevitably destined to be the Soviet Union's successor as the principal adversary of the United States, most of the foregoing policy prescriptions would have to be reversed.

The denial of any form of military supply would have to be made permanent, and much stronger efforts than hitherto would have to be made to persuade other countries to stop supplying weapons or relevant technology to China. As for Chinese weapon and nuclear exports, they would have to be countered yet more vigorously, dissuading potential recipients with threats or inducements.

It would also become a fixed American practice to press human rights complaints as insistently as possible, and to enhance mass-media and other informational activities aimed at China and Hong Kong. Chinese conduct in the latter would be attentively monitored, and promptly denounced as appropriate.

More substantively, to force China onto the defensive, it would be advantageous to affirm the broadest possible interpretation of the Taiwan Relations Act, and to support Tibetan demands for cultural autonomy, generously defined.

The choice to oppose China systematically would imply much more than that for U.S. foreign policy world wide. In the first place, most obviously, it would dictate a reordering of priorities in American dealings with a good number of other Asian countries, to seek their active participation in the containment of China. That would in turn require the offer of enhanced security guarantees by the United States, as well as a much more forthcoming attitude in supplying weapons, and possibly also an increased presence of U.S. military forces, which might well have implications for the overall defense budget. It is evident that any unrelated disputes with Asian countries would have to be resolved under the new order of priorities, if they were otherwise willing to cooperate in the containment of China.

The redirection of U.S. foreign policy would have to extend far beyond East Asia, beginning with Russia. In what would inevitably amount to a major and prolonged diplomatic campaign, the maximum aim would be to secure an active Russian participation in the containment of China; the minimum aim would be to reduce as much as possible any form of Russian security cooperation with Beijing, notably including arms sales. Just as inevitably, nothing is likely to be achieved without the offer of suitable inducements to Moscow, including the reversal of policies that Russia opposes, beginning with NATO enlargement. Indeed NATO would have to be effectively abolished, or drastically redefined to meet Russian objections. As it is, some supporters of expansion envisage Russian membership in a new NATO that would function as an alliance of democratic states. In a new foreign policy recast to serve the central aim of containing China, Russia would be elevated as the leading partner of the United States in that sort of NATO. Many other changes would logically have to follow in American policy towards its present European allies, and indeed towards Europe and its institutions as a whole, to achieve consistency with the new priority of containing China with Russian cooperation.

Once declared the main adversary, China is bound to react. To be sure, it only has a modest capacity to hurt American interests economically or in any other way, while China's military weakness would no doubt rule out any dangerous direct confrontations. But Beijing could do much to harm the United States indirectly, by supporting whatever countries and non-state groups are still willing to actively oppose it, by violent means too. Chinese military supplies and technology transfers, as well as diplomatic backing from Beijing's UN Security Council veto, would greatly strengthen surviving anti-American elements worldwide, which are now bereft of any great power support. Naturally, the United States would have to anticipate such Chinese reactions, not only by defensive preparations and precautions, but also by urgent efforts to repair American relations with the prospective beneficiaries of Beijing's support, including Iran and North Korea. In other words, to better confront the main adversary, lesser adversaries would have to be conciliated. Again, that could not be accomplished without concessions, this time to so-called "rogue" states.

Upon examining both alternatives for a truly coherent and consistent policy towards China, one can only conclude that there is much to be said for incoherence and inconsistency. Different as they are, each alternative has disturbing, indeed alarming, implications. As compared to their costs and risks, whatever dissatisfactions arise from the current mixture of incoherent policies seem almost inconsequential.

Indeed, in spite of their disorder, the diverse policies now jointly pursued provide what both of the coherent alternatives do not: a muddled but prudent moderation. Given the multiplicity of concurrent American dealings with China in a great variety of different contexts, from human rights to arms sales, from commerce to Taiwan's security, no single mid-point of moderation can be defined for all of them at once. In practice, today's contradictory policies achieve a moderate balance in their combined effect.

True, the full leverage that the United States could potentially exercise over China is thereby sacrificed. Instead of being concerted to achieve the highest-priority purposes at any one moment in time, threats, promises, punishments and inducements are often allowed to chaotically negate one another in ways large and small. That dismal performance, moreover, is by no means confined to the conduct of American relations with China. The potential leverage of the United States is likewise being dissipated in many other directions as well, beginning with Russia, whose government is concurrently assisted economically and undermined politically by the eastward enlargement of NATO.

But consider the global implications of the power-maximizing alternatives, as they would unfold in sequence, stage by stage. To begin with, either one of the two alternatives that would bring coherence to all American dealings with China would also, as noted, require coherence in other directions as well. American policies towards other Asian countries would have to change fairly drastically in either case, while the containment of China would require major revisions in regard to Russia and therefore NATO and so Europe, as well as Iran, and more. Nor could matters stop there, because each policy revision would logically require further adjustments and sometimes drastic changes. For example, an accommodation with Iran would have immediate implications for the entire American stance in Arabia and the Gulf. A partnership with China would require very different but equally sweeping policy changes in other directions as well.

Nor could such a quest for coherence proceed very far before its starting purpose would itself be scrutinized for coherence. Instead of arriving at a China-focused global policy, the entire effort might well end up with a different focus altogether, once all U.S. foreign policies were re-centered to achieve the most perfect power-maximizing coherence.

Whatever its ultimate policy focus, the United States would have what it had during the Cold War, when the imperative of opposing the Soviet Union in all ways, everywhere, yielded highly consistent responses to almost every situation, almost automatically. Once again, as in the Cold War, there would be a clear sense of priorities between different goals in American dealings with each country, regional grouping or issue. Once again, therefore, it would be possible to combine promises, threats, punishments and inducements to maximize American leverage.

That is the result that the critics of the present incoherence are presumably hoping for. The effective power of the United States on the global scene would certainly be increased, exploiting the potential of its current economic, technological, military and informational primacy to a far greater degree than is now the case. The United States in other words, would become the ultimate great power of all history, with far more control over global events than any predecessor could have dreamed.

That state of affairs, however, would not last for very long. During the Cold War, when the United States had a coherent strategy to maximize its own power, the Soviet Union was also present on the scene to absorb and counter much of that power with its own initiatives and responses. The result was some sort of equilibrium.

Moreover, in spite of the relative magnitude of two greatest powers as compared to all others, Cold War conditions created patterns of mutual dependence. The United States was needed by its allies for their protection, but itself constantly needed the active cooperation of its allies. As for the Soviet Union, it was forever eager to court any friendly state that it could not control outright. While that species of pretended neutrality that was called non-alignment meant very little, even firmly aligned countries could exercise a great deal of independence.

It was out of the reciprocal power of the United States and the Soviet Union that third parties extracted their own independence and their own leverage. The Soviet Union's few allies could bargain for its aid because they were of use in the struggle against American power. The much greater number of American allies feared the Soviet Union, yet it was because of Soviet power that the United States had to rely on their cooperation.

But now that the Soviet Union is no more, there is no equilibrium at all. There is only a multi-dimensional American supremacy that is quite unprecedented in all of human history, and which awaits only the determined pursuit of a power-maximizing global strategy to become fully effective for the United States, and intolerably oppressive for everyone else.

Defensive responses and hostile reactions of widening scope and mounting consequence would inevitably follow. If the passive reality of American supremacy, mostly a source of positive reassurance at present, gave way to an active striving for global hegemony, it could only evoke the response that such attempts have always evoked: subterranean resistance by the weak, overt opposition by the less weak. To safeguard their independence, not only China and Russia, but also many erstwhile American allies, would be forced into a global coalition against a newly "strategic" United States. As of now, the absence of a global anti-American coalition proves that the United States is only potentially the sole global superpower that it could be.

How far or how quickly matters would evolve towards overt forms of confrontation, it is impossible to say. But a distinct eagerness to employ at least low-cost, low-risk means to undermine American power and prestige in any available venue, would begin to characterize the behavior of former allies, as it already does in the case of France. Even mere diplomatic skirmishing could generate enough ill-will over time to hollow out the Western alliances and the cooperative security arrangements inherited from the Cold War. They might still persist institutionally, if only for bureaucratic reasons, but they would cease to function substantively. As for the Western-sponsored institutions that have long since become international regulatory or developmental bodies, such as the World Trade Organization, the World Bank, and affiliates, they could not remain unaffected. As was once true of the UN General Assembly, their usefulness to the United States as to everyone else would drastically decline, once a standing coalition emerged to oppose any and every American proposal merely because it was American.

In other words, the entire super-structure of Western and world institutions that the United States largely designed in its own image, and which it sustained at great cost for half a century, would serve American purposes less and less. That penalty alone might outweigh whatever enhancements of power could be achieved in the first instance by a coherent strategy and consistent policies.

Coalition-building against the United States need never acquire a military dimension to be painfully effective. Anti-American diplomatic compacts of variable membership for varied purposes, measures of commercial denial very selective or otherwise, intensified techno-industrial efforts on the lines of the Airbus-Boeing competition, and whatever forms of cultural exclusion still remain technically feasible, could all seriously and cumulatively damage American interests without any suggestion of a military threat, let alone any use of force.

In the past, all these instruments of power would have been regarded as feeble, even inconsequential, as compared to the diplomacy of armed suasion and war itself. But we now live in a post-heroic era, in which the advanced countries of the world—notably including the United States—are most reluctant to accept the casualties of war, and hence to employ it as an instrument of policy. Concurrently, territory (and the military power needed to seize and hold it) counts for much less than before.

Only this great novelty, along with the sense that the United States has no purposeful global strategy in any case, can explain the extraordinary serenity with which the unprecedented military superiority of the United States is now viewed by almost every government in the world. But even if the diminished importance of military power persists in the new situation, the present serenity would rapidly dissipate upon the appearance on the scene of a coherently purposeful United States, no longer content to dissipate its military strength in "social work" interventions. Hence it is possible that coalition-building against the United States would acquire a military dimension after all, even if only tentative to the point of ambiguity, and of purely defensive intent.

With or without a military dimension, the advent of effective coalition measures to resist, absorb and deflect the power of the United States would mark the completion of the sequence. Whatever added leverage could have been obtained by purposeful coherence in the first stage, thereby evoking coalition-building in the second, would be lost in the third and final stage, in which some sort of global equilibrium would be restored once the original enhancement of American power was negated. Even if incidental disasters were avoided along the way, the United States would not merely lose its temporary winnings, but much more than that, because of the damage inflicted by intra-Western quarrels on multilateral institutions and long-established cooperative practices. Their congruence with all manner of American interests and their role in helping to shape a favorable international environment is a most valuable possession, which owes as much to American restraint as to American power.

All this does not mean that the present foreign policies of the United States are the best possible foreign policies, implemented in the best possible manner. It does mean, however, that in the wake of the Soviet collapse there is such a thing as a *culminating point of success* in maximizing the leverage of the United States on the world scene. To overshoot that point, to exceed the limit of what others can accept with sufficient equanimity, will bring no further spoil to a coherent, strategic United States, but only a natural and inevitable decline.

3

Free Will and Predestination in U.S.-China Strategic Relations

Strategy is stronger than politics, just as politics is stronger than commerce. When shared perceptions of the Soviet military threat thrust them together Mao's China had nothing in common politically with Nixon's United States. In the grip of an almost nihilist radicalism, Mao's regime denied even totalitarian freedoms. Nor were there any trade or investment flows between the two countries to sustain economic interests in mutual relations. Yet a very tentative opening dialogue quickly evolved into a de facto alliance against the Soviet Union, complete with tangible forms of intelligence cooperation. A long list of potential contentions, starting with the status of Taiwan—still then recognized by the United States as the Republic of China—was accommodated by both sides without much difficulty.

Today, Sino-American commerce is thriving, motivating powerful interests in its continued growth. Politically, China has evolved from a comprehensively totalitarian system to an altogether more permissive party authoritarianism, allowing much room for personal self-expression as well as exuberant private enterprise. Politically, the United States and China are today less divergent on the whole than the United States and its good ally Saudi Arabia, not least in regard to human rights. In a variety of diplomatic endeavors, including the construction of a global free-trade regime under the aegis of the World Trade Organization, the United States and China are vigorously cooperating.

Yet it is all to no avail. With no strategic threat to bind them together, in the absence of any other rising power of like dimensions, given the proclivities of a democratizing Russia, the United States and China now face each other in a flattened geopolitical landscape where each is the only possible antagonist of the other. That should not be consequential but it is, for in both countries, though far more in China, there are powerful bureaucracies and political interests that actively seek a main enemy to focus against—and they have been finding each other. Mere accidents now become incidents, and incidents are contrived rather than avoided. Although there are other protagonists as well, the armed forces of each side can now enhance themselves by sharpening the confrontation, so they act accordingly. The logic of an incipient strategic confrontation has begun to prevail in Sino-American relations.

In different circumstances, the bombing of the Chinese Embassy in Belgrade during the 1999 Kosovo war would have had no greater consequence than an earnest U.S. apology gracefully accepted. As it was, it became the occasion for outbursts of anti-American hostility, some visibly stage-managed by the authorities, others encouraged by them, still others possibly spontaneous. Again, in different circumstances, the April 1, 2001 collision between Wang Wei's F-8 interceptor and the U.S. Navy's EP-3 reconnaissance aircraft off Hainan Island would have triggered cooperative search and rescue efforts, followed by prompt negotiations to clarify the operating procedures of each side. As it was, the Chinese military authorities immediately refused U.S. help to look for Wang Wei, proof positive that they were already predisposed to exploit the collision politically. It duly became the occasion for a full-bore propaganda campaign against the United States, which in turn unleashed a wave of anti-American hostility by individual Chinese, some of whom started private cyberwars on the Internet. In the aftermath, protracted negotiations over the return of the damaged EP-3 provided further opportunities for expressions of hostility, and they were not passed up. By June 2001, Secretary of Defense Donald Rumsfeld decreed that any and all military visits be canceled.

The commercial interest in continued amity, the many personal and institutional bonds that link Americans and Chinese will not long resist the impulses that are driving the United States and China towards a strategic confrontation.

The motivation to seek a conflict is undoubtedly stronger on the Chinese side. When countries undergo a rapid process of industrialization, their economic advancement is inevitably accompanied by massive social dislocation. In countries as varied as Belgium, Russia, and Japan, as well as Britain, France, Germany, and the United States, the turmoil of industrialization generated internal violence to the point of civil war, unless it was vented in natural or contrived foreign quarrels or conquests. From the viewpoint of ruling elites, even costly foreign wars are preferable to civil wars. In today's China, prospering cities and towns are filled with migrants uprooted from ancestral villages, while their own traditional courtyard-and-alley neighborhoods have been replaced by rows of sterile apartment houses. Either way, the emotional sustenance of extended families and familiar neighbors is lost, with repercussions that range from the social isolation of migrant laborers to the competitive anxieties of the upwardly mobile thrust into a world of strangers. Novel material satisfactions soothe the alienation of many Chinese, but most are still relatively deprived as their own middling advance is overtaken by the visible success of China's new rich. In every village, peasants envy the new houses of fellow villagers who have progressed more than they have, in every urban thoroughfare the mass on bicycles is literally overtaken by the more fortunate riding in cars. Chinese inequalities are not especially extreme, but they have emerged so abruptly after decades of egalitarian indoctrination that they induce intense resentment. Few can be nostalgic for the utter poverty of the past, but equality in misery is emotionally less trying than enormous inequality—and that is the condition of today's China, which has yet to reach the stage of generic affluence where visible differences at least are no longer acute.

The inner feelings of hundreds of millions of Chinese cannot be expressed and thus vented politically by an egalitarian socialist party, or populist practitioners of the politics of envy. Nor can alienation and resentment be assuaged by the conviviality of trade union halls or the spiritual bonding of sectarian movements. All of the above being prohibited, the alienation and resentment remain compressed within individuals, until they explode in the purely personal manifestations of free-floating anger, or in violent village uprisings. County-scale and larger disorders are not that uncommon—in Jiangxi, the 2001 tax revolt encompassed some 20,000 peasants, who sacked and burned both state and party offices. In China, evidently, the totalitarian isolation and preemption of opposition has ended, without giving way to the apathy characteristic of modern democracies.

The potential for immense convulsions is obvious, not least to the rulers of China, whose reaction to the Falun Gong movement betokens naked fear. For some years now, the usual remedy has been to encourage in every way nationalist sentiments to forge unity against the foreign enemy: first Japan, but now primarily the United States. In some segments of the population, a veritable nationalist fever is ranging. A good number of Chinese were outraged when the "24 pigs" were returned to the United States even while Wang Wei's body had yet to be found.

At this point, the Chinese authorities may still be steering the emotions they have unleashed—or vented—against the United States. But while nationalism can serve them, it can also constrain them to pursue an earlier and harsher confrontation with the United States than they might want. China's economic growth is still a fragile phenomenon, greatly dependent on exports and foreign investment. A serious contention with the United States, even well short of war, could inflict catastrophic damage. But such details never deter nationalist fervors. Madness, rare among individuals, is common in large crowds and China, 1.3 billion-strong, is the largest crowd there is.

4

Reagan the Astute

The popular notion of Ronald Reagan as a lazy bungler have long been questioned; but only now, with the publication of his diaries, do we encounter a shrewd and watchful president determined to have his own way. Ronald Reagan's diaries prove his determination to destroy Communism and his enjoyment of office, but the editing falls far below the writing. For years, otherwise reasonable people, including not a few genuine Washington insiders, firmly believed that the late-to-rise and early-to-bed Ronald Reagan was not all that important in the Reagan administration. Word had it that he was stupendously ignorant as well as lazy, frequently confusing historical events within living memory with Hollywood depictions of the same, supposedly mixing up the countries and rulers he had to deal with to the great embarrassment of accompanying State Department officials and his Druze protocol official Selwa Roosevelt, and so averse to reading that his daily intelligence briefing had to be reduced to bite-sized video clips. That being so, it could even be reassuring to believe that Reagan was a mere cipher perpetually manipulated by a shifting cast of hard-faced men, starting with his first political mentors from the ultra-anti-Communist John Birch Society and ending with the administration officials supposedly selected for him by his California kitchen cabinet of businessmen who had funded all his campaigns.

That two of his most important Cabinet appointments, George Schultz at the State Department and Caspar Weinberger at the Pentagon, both came from the globally active but very privately held Californian engineering giant Bechtel was just one of many little facts that added plausibility to the portrait, starting with a range of cultural interests that included Cow Girls of Montana, no books to speak of, and the theatre only if "Chuck" Heston or another of Reagan's A-film heroes was on stage (many were often welcomed at the White House), and involving a working day that was certainly shorter than that of his recent predecessors. So persuasive was this depiction of an affable if often perplexed old actor dutifully reading his scripts, a nice man but with cotton wool between his ears, that it was accepted by pundits worldwide for quite a while, and even by some of the foreign officials who met him at summits. Until I sat with him and a few others serving on the transition team to discuss the El Salvador war in detail and depth, I too half-believed the stories that floated from one Washington dinner party to the next, with the usual embellishments that were elaborated further in diplomatic reporting to foreign capitals. As we now know, Soviet reporting was even more incompetent, for it depicted an impossible Reagan, both childishly inane and a would-be mass murderer plotting a surprise nuclear attack against the Soviet Union—KGB watchers were actually sent to monitor American bases worldwide, to detect any signs of incipient nuclear attacks.

Not coincidentally, many Europeans were also frequently demonstrating against Reagan the cowboy with nuclear weapons, some of them no doubt just the usual physiological anti-Americans, others believers in peace at any price who logically enough wanted their own side to desist because aggressors will not, and others still useful innocents manipulated by KGB "active measures," furiously denied at the time but now gleefully recalled as highly successful by their executors. Nobody could then know of course that Reagan was America's post-nuclear president: early on he told his utterly shocked military chiefs what he could tell nobody else without destroying deterrence, that he would never authorize the use of nuclear weapons, even if the United States were attacked with them.

Memoirs, biographies, and policy studies gradually replaced the bungling bumbling caricature with more realistic depictions, but it is only now, with the publication of his diaries, that we encounter a shrewd and watchful Reagan determined to have his way not only with political opponents and evil or mis-guided foreigners, but also with his own officials and bureaucracies—the greater challenge in many cases, for diversions can be very subtle, and obstructionism is so easily disguised.

Reagan's policy towards the Soviet Union of replacing coexistence with de-legitimization had been proclaimed right through the 1980 campaign in which he defeated President Carter's re-election attempt, but it was so shock-ingly revolutionary that many in Washington and around the world took it for granted that it was mere talk, destined to be quietly set aside once the new administration took office. When State Department officials came to brief his transition officials on policy towards the Soviet Union, they did it by listing the inter-agency issues that would have to be resolved to prepare for the next "ministerial with Gromyko." They focused on process, incidentally noting that there would be close consultations with Anatoly Dobrynin as usual, because in their eyes the only possible policy was to pursue coexistence. That Andrei Gromyko had held his office as foreign minister since 1957 and Dobrynin his Washington post as ambassador since 1962 underlined the stolid continuity of the Soviet Union, which those senior State Department officials assumed would simply continue, as did most people around the world. It followed that any attempt to de-legitimize the Soviet Union was utterly unrealistic in their view, and very dangerous of course, for the recent invasion of Afghanistan had showed that Soviet leaders were willing to use their vast military forces very boldly. (These days it is widely assumed that the decrepitude of the late Soviet Union extended to its armed forces, but that is simply not true. For example, by the time U.S. intelligence detected and assessed that the Soviet invasion of Afghanistan had started, five army divisions and four assault regiments had already secured Kabul and seized key locations throughout the country.) Nor could the State Department satisfy Reagan by calibrating the normal coexistence policies in a hard-line direction, because the Carter administration had already done that in response to the invasion of Afghanistan, imposing a grain embargo among other things. It was only with considerable difficulty that Reagan's first national security adviser, Richard Allen, managed to explain to the State Department diplomats who met the transition team that policy towards the Soviet Union would have to be defined in an entirely new way, with aims very different from the preparation of the next meeting with Gromyko, which was duly "de-scheduled." The only concrete result of that session was the revocation of Dobrynin's unique privilege of entering the State Department directly from the garage. When his car swept into the garage entrance as usual, it was stopped and sent back to park in the street, forcing Dobrynin to enter on foot like all other diplomats. More substantively, Dobrynin lost his famed access to the White House under the new Reagan policy of minimizing instead of maximizing communications as well as inter-state relations with the Soviet Union, which overturned decades of conventional wisdom because its aim was not to domesticate the Soviet leadership but rather to undermine and indeed overthrow the entire regime.

On Wednesday, February 4 1980, during his fifteenth day in the White House, in the context of a cabinet discussion of the grain embargo, Reagan wrote in his diary: "Trade was supposed to make Soviets moderate, instead it has allowed them to build armaments instead of consumer products. Their socialism is an ec(onomic) failure. Wouldn't we be doing more for their people if we let their system fail instead of constantly bailing it out?"

This was no mere outburst, because policies of economic denial and de-legitimization were quickly implemented, beginning with the previously sacrosanct sphere of arms-control negotiations. The new policy alarmed European leaders to the point of panic in some cases, and evoked furious reactions from détente enthusiasts, but it was not much resisted by the State Department because Alexander Haig was the secretary, and he had just enough personal contact with Reagan himself to realize that nothing would change his mind. It was an opposite problem that emerged, because Haig loyally set out to achieve Reagan's purposes strategically, and therefore wanted to turn the new entente with China into a veritable alliance—there was even talk of combining infinite Chinese manpower with U.S. military technology across the board, and not just the long-range radars already secretly installed in Xinjiang. There was a price, however: the abandonment of Taiwan, starting with the denial of arms sales.

But Reagan's outlook was ideological, not strategic. He was not just anti-Soviet power but anti-Communist, and therefore would not abandon Taiwan. He also firmly believed in firmness.

Tuesday October 29 1981 . . .

Met with (Chinese foreign minister) Huang Hua. There is a real push going on.

China is virtually delivering an ultimatum re. arms to Taiwan. I don't like ultimatums. We have a moral obligation & until a peaceful settlement is reached between the mainland & Taiwan we're going to meet that obligation.

Huang Hua had evidently spoken as he did because he had been told of the State Department's position, which he was trying to strengthen. Just as evidently, Reagan was alert to the attempt to derail his policy.

Friday January 10 1982 . . .

I have learned there is a China lobby and it has its moles in the State Dept.

The (Washington) Post had a story on why we should cling to the P.R.C. & never mind Taiwan. A cartoon carried the same theme. The timing is amazing because no word has been spoken about plans (to sell F5E and F104 fighters to Taiwan) & I have told no one (outside the Executive Branch) what my decision will be.

The little inside joke is that "China Lobby" had always been used to describe the right-wing Republicans who had supported Chiang Kai-shek's Kuomintang regime in China and later Taiwan. As for the "moles" they were in reality top officials, not disloyal underlings, as Reagan well knew. He could spot their tricks easily enough:

Monday January 11 1982 . . .

Press running wild with talk that I reversed myself on Taiwan because we're only selling them F5Es & F104s. I think the China Lobby in State Dept is selling this line to appease the P.R.C. which doesn't want us to sell them anything. The planes we are offering are better than anything the P.R.C. has.

Later on if more sophistication is needed we'll upgrade & sell them F5Gs.

That last phrase, incidentally, is one of a myriad fragments of evidence in the diary that Reagan's stance of casual bonhomie—in sharp contrast to the Carter and Clinton displays of relentless diligence—concealed much very detailed knowledge accumulated by reading the documents that kept landing on his desk.

Unlike the F-4 Phantom or F-104 Starfighter, the F 5G was not a fighter in operational service that would often be depicted and reported in the normal course of events, but rather a project of the Northrop Corporation, whose existence was only known to specialists.

Reagan wrote of the "China Lobby" and the State Department and even of moles, but it was the Secretary of State himself who wanted Taiwan to wither away, to better implement the Reagan strategy. Reagan disagreed. "Friday March 26 1982 . . . Al and I are on opposite sides I'm afraid about China. He wants to make concessions which in my view betray our pledge to Taiwan." Earlier in that day's entry Reagan mentioned that he had called George Schultz, who would be Haig's successor, to ask him to go on a mission to Europe and Japan, commenting "What a nice man—busy as he is (at Bechtel) he agreed." But at that point Reagan was not yet thinking of replacing Haig, and he ended the remark on his disagreement with him over Taiwan with "We'll have to work it out." When Al Haig persisted, Reagan resisted. Far from being easily manipulated, as the legend had it, he did not even manipulate back—he just said no.

> Monday March 29 1982 . . . . Meeting with Al Haig about China and Taiwan. State wanted to send a paper to the P.R.C. and letters from me because we are about to send mil.(itary) equipment and spare parts to Taiwan. I objected to some of the terms they wanted in these papers -the note of almost apology to the P.R.C. I'm convinced the Chinese will respect us more if we politely tell them we have an obligation to the people of Taiwan and no one is going to keep us from meeting it. We didn't send the papers.

There was no disagreement about the strategy of squeezing the Soviet Union—at that point the Soviet army was maintaining some forty-two divisions on the Chinese border, most of them in remote locations at ruinous cost for transport alone. But there was a disagreement about diplomatic tactics—as always Reagan believed in firmness—and a much greater disagreement about the magnitude of the task. Reagan was convinced that there was no need to sacrifice Taiwan, because the Soviet Union was on its last legs: "March 26, 1982 Briefing on Soviet Ec. They are in very bad shape and if we can cut off their credit they'll have to yell uncle or starve."

Haig obviously disagreed, and kept pressing for his more active Chinese alliance.

"Tuesday May 4 1982 . . . . Turned State dept down on a message they wanted me to send our Ambassador in China urging him to have informal talks with Chinese preceding George Bush's arrival. The talks were to soften the Taiwan issue some more. We can't do that -the Taiwanese have proven their friendship." In the event, Taiwan barely came up during Reagan's visit to China in April 1984, when he made it clear that he was not seeking an active alliance, the entente already established ever since Kissinger's first visit being quite enough to keep the Soviet Union expensively off balance.

That was of course the essential Reagan strategy, to peacefully dismantle the Soviet Union by overstretching its economy in every possible way, from the simple—the acceleration of the military-technological competition through the Strategic Defense Initiative, aka "Star Wars," and of the plain military competition by building up every branch of the U.S. armed forces—to the more subtle effect of de-legitimization: it induced Soviet leaders to strive to supply more and better food and consumer products to compensate for the loss of ideological credibility, fervor having long gone. That stressed rigid Soviet planning even more without increasing output anywhere enough, until Gorbachev's perestroika reforms came along to make the economy more flexible and more efficient by removing bureaucratic compulsion. But in the absence of all the varied material and social incentives that propel capitalist economies which could not just be synthesized, there was nothing else to keep the system operating. It duly collapsed, as some did nothing while others stole all they could. Before the final breakdown, by January 1988, Reagan could follow the unravelling:

> Thursday January 5 . . . NSC Time—Colin (Powell) brought in our expert on Soviet U. He sees a split developing between Gorbachev & Ligachev (the Intelligence community's designated "hardliner" of the moment). We'll soon see an Ec. Plan to make Soviet enterprises self supporting. In June the once in every 4 yrs. Soviet (Party) Cong(ress) will meet. There should be some hint as to division in Soviet U. Under the Glasnost plans.

In the diaries there is very much more on politics of every sort—Reagan was not at all above manoeuvres high and low—and on all the large subjects of government, beginning with the economy and the tax-cutting supply-side fiscal policy. Reagan was harshly criticized at the time by most professional economists and conventional-wisdom pundits until the results by way of growth, employment and reduced inflation became too positive to be denied (the same happened with George W. Bush and his 2001 tax cuts, except that his critics still refuse to recognize that he was right, in spite of record-low unemployment). On the environment as on all else, Reagan favored the market, with limits, of course, that tended to be more restrictive over time.

On foreign policy, relations with Europe and Japan naturally loom large in the diaries, along with much on the various military episodes, both successful, as in Grenada, or not as in Beirut; there is also much detail on the Iran-Contra episode. Reagan was fully aware of the Iran end of that arms-for-hostages affair (legal but wildly imprudent), though he did not know of the Contra end, which violated the Congressional law that cut off funding to the rebels.

Reagan's studied pose of amiable vagueness that exposed him to accusations of incapacity and inattention greatly helped to shield him from the scandal, because many believed that the poor old dear did not know of the secret goings on, which he actually monitored closely and indeed commanded. It is most unfortunate that the scandal, the inquiries, the trials and the press and academic commentaries did not pause to first consider the utter incapacity of the CIA to operate covertly to any effect, which had driven the president's men to do it themselves in the first place. An opportunity was missed, as it was after 2001, so the United States must still do without, or send out incompetents who fail.

The diary is also full of fun. Reagan did not merely take time off to have fun as all presidents must do to survive (Jimmy Carter failed in that too, visibly declining in office), he also enjoyed himself presidentially. Of course, he relished every opportunity of kicking the Soviet Union in the shins: "Friday July 24. . . . Then off to Ukrainian Church for lunch & ceremony recognizing Captive Nations Week. Extremely well received. The Soviets will be unhappy."

There are many other such entries.

During his 1984 China visit, the old movie actor enjoyed the opportunity of being bugged and debugged exactly as depicted in Hollywood spy movies –one just hopes that there was a real security expert around and not just CIA incompetents, because hidden microphones so easily found are only there for misdirection, to cover the real ones: "Friday April 27 A breakfast meeting with my gang at our Villa (in the Beijing leadership compound). We kept a noisy tape going all through the meal to nullify any hidden microphones. We later learned there were such. Indeed Dave Fisher unscrewed the plate on his light switch & removed one for a souvenir. Later 5 were found in our quarters." Back in 1981, Reagan enjoyed a lark:

> Monday March 16 . . . S(enator) Paul Laxalt came by . . . he had a letter from an Irishman in Nev.(ada) who complained because he didn't think I knew the R. W. Service poem " The Shooting of Dan McGrew". We put in a call to Nevada and after I convinced him I really was who I said I was I recited the poem to him. He's a Dem(ocrat) who I think may now turn Repub.

There are some complaints in the diaries but no real bitterness, not even against those who accused him of being a racist, as several black politicians did. Having lived most of his life in the only American community where anti-Semitism was a career killer and racism was unacceptable, Reagan was if anything an anti-racist. Not coincidentally, he was the first American president who appointed officials who happened to be black because they were the best officials he could get, and not because they were black, including the "Colin" mentioned on many pages, for it was under Reagan that Colin Powell started his career in high office. In that too, George W. Bush is his successor. When he did encounter outright racism, Reagan knew what to do:

> Monday May 3 1982 . . . Read this morning of a black family—husband and wife both work in govt. printing office. They live in a nice house near U of Maryland. They have been harassed and even had a cross burned on their lawn . . . . We cleared the last part of the afternoon schedule and Nancy & I went calling. They were a very nice couple with a 4 year old daughter . . . the whole neighborhood was lining the street . . . I hope we did some good. There is no place in this land for the hate-mongers and bigots.

Regrettably, there is still a place for shoddy, thoroughly unworthy editors.

Douglas Brinkley, to whom this precious historical document was unaccountably consigned, has not done any of the things that should have been required of the editor of such material. Any authentic diary as this one certainly is, must be full of incomplete, abbreviated or downright cryptic references which need to be elucidated by amplifications and insertions, explanatory footnotes and more extended notes too. Brinkley's work in that regard is not subject to detailed criticism because, in an extraordinary and damaging omission, he does not provide any explanatory material at all—the square brackets in the above quotations are my own. The index is unacceptably cursory and full of mistakes, so that Selwa "Lucky" Roosevelt and Lucky Roosevelt both appear, while the one Kirkpatrick listing covers two of them. Worse still, the diaries are incomplete, with many entries fully or partially abridged, not to conceal crimes or misdemeanors but just to shorten the text. The approach of this editor is best illustrated by his own explanation of how that came about: "Because the complete Reagan diaries would fill two or three fat volumes, I had to be selective in deciding what to choose to include in this abridged version"—the only one available so far. Anybody who thinks that three volumes, however "fat," would be too many to publish a document of such importance, is bereft of historical sense and should never have been allowed near Ronald Reagan's diary.

Part 2

Post-Cold War Hot Wars

5

To Intervene or Not to Intervene

If the Bosnian Muslims had been bottle-nosed dolphins, would the world have allowed Croats and Serbs to slaughter them by the tens of thousands? If Sarajevo had been an Amazonian rain forest or merely some American woods containing spotted owls, would the Serbs have been allowed to blast it and burn it with their artillery fire? If the rustbucket ships that recently came from China had brought panda bears instead of humans, would the United States have procured their swift Mexican deportation?

The answers are too obvious, the questions merely rhetorical. And therein lies a very great irony. At long last a genuine transnational humanism has arisen, fulfilling the highest hopes of the rare pioneering globalists of the nineteenth century and before. No longer does disinterested benevolence abruptly stop at the boundaries of state, nation or culture. Instead it now encompasses all life both animal and vegetable across the entire globe, with only one exception: homo sapiens.

The reason is not mysterious. Anything that is thought to be over-abundant is scorned and, by definition, unwanted. When tigers are allowed to kill villagers, but the villagers are not allowed to kill tigers, the World Wildlife Fund, and much of the world with it, applauds India's "Project Tiger." For, of course, there are only a few Bengal tigers left, while there is a great surplus of Indian peasants. When the Bolivian government protects Amazonian lowlands by stopping the influx of starving colonists from the overpopulated Andean high plateau, even cold-hearted bankers are so filled with transnational gratitude that they forgive billions of dollars of Bolivia's debt. But the world was harsh with Brazil when it allowed its own hungry colonists from the arid northeast to cut out subsistence farms in the Amazon.

The young people brimming with environmental awareness, the academics and popular singers who guide them, and the parents who most generously fund them, have so far overcome any narrow-minded provincialism. They have succeeded in caring very deeply for the Amazon basin that they are unlikely ever to visit. Ideally, they would like to see all the colonists expelled, all dams slighted, all mines shut in, all ranches abandoned. In their place, they advocate "sustainable use" planning, whereby only the native tribes and a few thousand acculturated nut gatherers and rubber tappers would be allowed to earn their living within that considerable portion of the earth. But neither the environmental enthusiasts nor their professional lobbyists have any alternative plans for the destitute peasants now converging on the Amazon, the sort of people who must regularly choose between feeding all their children or buying medicine for just one.

There is, of course, the eagerly believed futility argument: thin, acidic rainforest soils cannot feed the hungry anyway. Nicely contrived to evade the dilemma, it is even true of commercial, one-crop, repetitive farming. But if the argument were valid for the settlers who get by with small patches of maize and beans and a few chickens, it would also be self-validating. Deeply conservative peasants would not be abandoning their ancestral villages to attempt the perilous journey, if those who went before them were already streaming back in failure. Bolivian, Ecuadorian, Peruvian, and Brazilian peasants who burn the forest to clear their own patch of land do know what they are doing. They can see with their own eyes how well-fed are the settlers who occasionally return from the Amazon to visit the old village. Keeping the Amazon intact and keeping the hungry hungry are therefore one and the same. But for the cognizant outside world there is no dilemma: the trees of the Amazon win hands down.

It would be superfluous to consider any further examples. For the prevailing view of today's enlightened—the "environmentally sensitive"—is obvious enough: humanity is the planet's skin disease, now disastrously spreading into what remains of wilderness, threatening the survival of all wild animals and many rare plants too. That leaves only the less enlightened to care for humans more than for animals or trees, but of course their benevolence does not transcend the boundaries of country, village or tribe, or even of family alone. No wonder therefore that there are urgent plans to save the Amazon, and no plans to feed the would-be settlers; that there is a tiger emergency campaign, as well as gorilla, lemur, and rhino emergencies, but no campaigns for the African and Asian peasants whose very lives are one long emergency.

Only the logical conclusion is resisted: the environmentally enlightened still remain unwilling to applaud nature's own remedy for the planetary skin disease: a vigorous rate of infant mortality. Because the new nature worship must still coexist with residues of monotheism, including the notion that each human life matters in itself, mutually contradictory purposes are inevitable. Thus many of the enlightened send money both to save unspoiled nature in the Third World and also to assist Third World children, though it is precisely the latter who will destroy the former. But the nearly universal acquiescence in China's "one-child policy" shows that infanticide is definitely becoming more acceptable. For it is no secret that the virtually compulsory abortions are routinely performed even at very, very late stages of pregnancy, when it is unambiguously babies that are being killed, and not fetuses by anyone's definition. Yet, illogically enough, the many who strongly approve of China's policy would be horrified if duly delivered babies were killed after birth in a Chinese version of Treblinka. The distinction, of course, is merely aesthetic.

In the present state of ethical confusion, even the otherwise discriminating are apt to follow whatever plausible moral lead is given to them, whether by environmental activists, the likes of Mother Teresa, or even U.S. presidents. True, the last one viewed the pursuit of any moral purpose in U.S. foreign policy with extreme distaste, as a deviation from what he fondly imagined to be a "tough-minded" *realpolitik*, truly a grown-up game for an eternal adolescent. (No one ever explained to Bush that its rules apply only to acutely insecure countries, which are compelled to disregard all other purposes and all moral considerations merely to survive.) As for Bill Clinton, his moral antennae are switched off by deep-seated fears of being thought a sissy. But so far he continues to reserve his solicitude for the victim categories officially recognized by the Democratic Party of the United States, beginning with blacks and ending with such sub-groups as "physically challenged" lesbian Native Americans, but excluding, for example, Bosnian Muslims. Still, the ethical confusion of our times does greatly expand the potential scope of the moral leadership that the presidency of the United States could exercise, for example by persuading the American public that Bosnian Muslims should be actively protected, just as if they were spotted owls or bottle-nosed dolphins.

We have already seen what is the state of affairs in the absence of such presidential leadership: there is enough political support in the United States and beyond for global action to stop aggression, but only if it is aimed at animals and plants rather than human beings—even the sort of aggression that features armed killers on the one side, and unarmed victims on the other. Of that Bosnia is the more than sufficient proof, in a way that previous horrors were not.

Every form of attack on unarmed civilians, from sniping to artillery barrages and starve-them-out road blockades has been shown over and over again on television, and also the aftermath of massacres and gang rapes, as well as of cruel prison-camp detentions. In place of a barrier of ignorance, there has been the "real time" transmission of every species of horror; only Treblinka-type death factories have been absent, no doubt because in Bosnia the killers have a pre-industrial mentality.

Two new things can therefore be learned from the Bosnian experience in particular. To begin with the smallest lesson, the claim of television and its celebrants that the "global media revolution" has changed the nature of world affairs by exposing public evildoing as never before, has itself been exposed as self-congratulatory rubbish by the Bosnian events: media coverage only inhibits reasonably law-abiding and passably humane governments that are otherwise inhibited anyway. In this case, the media has neither shamed Milosevic, nor brought public opinion in favor of the only solution—military intervention—that could possibly end the horror.

The second lesson of Bosnia is more important, but much harder to accept in its hideous amplitude. We now know enough, though the many Holocaust documentaries and museums may not, to end the myth that the world was indifferent to the Nazi persecution and genocide because of widespread and deeply rooted anti-Semitism. For the Bosnian killings continue unimpeded, though there was never such a thing as anti-Bosnianism.

The truth is much simpler: the only way to stop determined killers is to kill the killers, and there is no general willingness to kill killers because killers can kill right back. Just ask chairman of the Joint Chiefs of Staff General Colin Powell, whom nobody has ever accused of anti-Bosnianism, but who has steadfastly opposed any use of U.S. force whatever to protect the Bosnians. The Serbians, he has explained over and over again to both the Bush and Clinton administrations, would shoot back. Nazi Germany could of course shoot back a hundred times more powerfully, so that Powell's objection was a hundred times more valid for Nazi Germany. That is why indeed nobody intervened against them, but only fought the Nazis when the Nazis (or, in the American case, the Japanese) attacked them.

That surviving Holocaust survivors still feel an acute need to endow their sufferings with retroactive significance is humanly more than understandable; that the raw material of Hitler's death industry should want to play protagonist after the fact, is just as understandable; and the determination of professional Holocaust-rememberers from Elie Wiesel down, to keep marketing their products is only slightly more questionable. But after the Bosnian events, who can now doubt that it was, and is, all for naught? That much was made blindingly obvious at the inauguration of Washington, DC's own Holocaust Museum, when President Clinton courageously criticized the policies of a dead Adolf Hitler, while studiously refraining from committing to any action whatsoever against the living killers of Bosnia. "Never again" is indeed a credible promise for the Jews themselves, but that is only so because not all Jews expend their efforts and resources to memorialize the consequences of past impotence, preferring instead to nurture a respectable capacity for counter-force derived from all possible sources. To others, it not only can happen but is happening on a daily basis, given the general failure to stop killers far less formidable than the Nazis—unless their victims are spotted owls or bottle-nosed dolphins.

This, therefore, is the unvarnished face of the world in which we live, the world in which the Holocaust is as compelling a historical fact as the War of the Roses, the world in which the government of the United States of America must decide if, when, where and how to intervene against today's aggressors and killers. That is not a choice that can be made without agonizing between contradictory responsibilities, and it never was, but it has now been greatly complicated both by a severe bureaucratic deformation within the U.S. armed forces, and by a colossal over-estimation of the capacities of that lowest-common denominator of governments that is the United Nations.

Little need be said about the military deformation, by now perfectly evident to all. For various reasons, ranging from the delayed recognition that the military professionals were abused by their political masters during the Vietnam War, and shabbily treated by Americans at large in the aftermath, to the unintended consequences of the 1987 Defense Reorganization Act, from Caspar Weinberger's deliberate downgrading of civilian control over military planning to the unique role of that most war-averse and politically astute of generals, Colin Powell, the proper equilibrium between the civilian and military leadership of the United States has been badly skewed, in two separate ways.

On the one hand, there has been an impermissible erosion of civilian authority, manifest in the effective veto power illegitimately acquired by the military leadership over intervention decisions. Yet constitutionally it is the civilian authorities alone that should decide whether, when, where and how to intervene against today's aggressors and killers, albeit with such military advice as they care to solicit. There has been no *coup d'état* and the Constitution has not been rewritten to place the chairman of the Joint Chiefs of Staff above the president and his secretary of defense, but in real-life American politics a situation has now been created in which those two civilians feel that they must defer to military preferences, because of the very real risk that they would otherwise be undermined politically by their nominal military servants. There has been so much practice of the Art of the Leak in place of the Art of War, that if Operation Desert Storm had been a disaster, a complete dossier would have been ready to be rushed into print to place all the blame on President Bush—for purely military decisions, as well.

Within the Pentagon's day-to-day administration, the erosion of civilian authority is palpable at all levels. Most notably, the Under-Secretariat for Policy, once the key instrument of civilian supervision over military planning and military operations, and once occupied by the likes of Robert "Blowtorch" Komer who ate admirals and generals for breakfast, has been sadly reduced as compared to the imperious Joint Staff. Thus, in smaller decisions as in largest ones, military preferences prevail over civilian ones, contrary to both Constitutional theory and the past practice of government.

And what are those military preferences? No doubt there are still one or two hopelessly outdated peaceniks around who imagine that the Pentagon is full of bellicose generals and admirals nervously juggling steel balls while eagerly searching world maps for possible wars to fight. The rest of us know that our senior military commanders have enthusiastically embraced the so-called Weinberger "doctrine" authorized by no legislation and endorsed by no president, which presumes nevertheless to rule out any U.S. military action whatsoever unless a long list of conditions are met, including a victory fully guaranteed in advance by overwhelming force, irrevocable public support for whatever operations are undertaken skillfully or otherwise, and a precisely defined objective that may not, repeat not, be changed in accordance with shifting circumstances. Under parallel conditions, hospital emergency rooms would refuse to accept any patients whose recovery was not certain, who would not agree to renounce a malpractice suit in advance, and who might develop other ailments while under treatment; and teachers would simply refuse to admit children in their classrooms unless all their previous grades were straight As, and all their previous conduct was exemplary.

Certainly the guarantees now routinely demanded by the Joint Chiefs of Staff before sanctioning U.S. military action are not of this world. Victory can never be guaranteed in advance, even a nation most patriotic by current Western standards is apt to criticize glaring military errors, and objectives alone cannot remain reliably fixed in a world in flux. The result—fully intended—is in practice to rule out military operations almost always and almost everywhere against enemies who might shoot back.

So established and so widely accepted is this doctrine of inaction that civilian State Department and White House officials, who would want to interpose formidable and supremely well-protected U.S. military forces between cruel aggressors and unarmed victims, are branded as irresponsible warmongers who would "toy with American lives" and very effectively silenced. Instead of a proper equilibrium between diplomats who should professionally favor diplomatic solutions, and military leaders who should professionally offer military options, we therefore suffer from a paralyzing reversal of roles, in which the military simply refuse to offer military options when asked for them and are not disciplined to do so. Abnormally enough, nowadays the normal response of the Joint Staff to civilian requests for usable military options are long-winded memos explaining all the political, cultural, and psychological reasons why nothing can be done by force.

Inter-service bureaucratic calculations play their nefarious part as well. Today's precision airpower would be the instrument of choice in most cases, the one least likely to result in U.S. casualties. But, in order to sustain the policy of cutting equally from all services, any independent use of airpower is vehemently resisted—not least in the case of Bosnia. Reporters looking for answers to the common-sense question of why U.S. airpower cannot be used in Bosnia have found the Joint Staff replete with officers eager to lecture them about the general futility of airpower and its particular uselessness against elusive militias, ignoring the abundance of stable, well-defined targets such as main battle tanks and field artillery pieces used to shell Sarajevo.

The same voices have eagerly endorsed the disingenuous Anglo-French claim that airpower cannot be used anyway, because it would endanger UN troops on the ground. Instead of breaking village sieges, the British battalion pathetically begs Serb militiamen to let through a few food trucks now and then; instead of silencing Serb fire, the French battalion had even allowed Serb militiamen to shoot a top Muslim leader riding in its own convoy—without firing back. Such troops might as well have stayed home. Thus the highly effective instrument of U.S. airpower is renounced for the sake of symbolic troop contingents that seem to spend all their time performing for the TV cameras, while doing almost nothing to actually protect the Muslims left defenseless by the UN's own arms embargo.

The ultimate implication of the Weinberger-Powell doctrine is that U.S. military forces should be reserved for self-defense alone, on the lines of the Swiss armed forces. If that strategy is indeed to be adopted, then surely we should drastically reduce U.S. military forces (and their higher command even more) to the dimensions of a militia writ large, because there are no plausible aggressors of U.S. territory. But of course today's military leadership—there is hope at least of forthcoming change—wants both super-power resources at its command, and a small-power strategy that would exclude the use of force to protect American values in the larger scheme of things, including the defense of the defenseless against mass murder.

To put it bluntly, now that the age of deterrence is past, soldiers are useful insofar as they are willing to fight. Membership in the military profession is not compatible with a refusal of its combative essence. In the American case moreover, the willingness to fight and if needs be die to defend one's own country is not enough because it is American values on the global scene that are being violated, but not American soil. If and when proper civil-military equilibrium is restored, our civilian leaders will once again have to exercise immense caution before exposing fellow-citizens in uniform to the vicissitudes of combat. In the meantime, it is the excessively self-protective caution of our military leadership that is the issue at hand.

The second great complication that now attends the always agonizingly difficult decision of whether, when, where and how to intervene against today's aggressors and killers, is the "multi-lateralist" delusion. Of the consequences of waiting upon the resolve of our traditional European allies, nothing at all need be said after their shameful failure of Yugoslavia, except to note parenthetically the supreme innocence of leaders who fondly imagine themselves to be hard-bitten cynics: they truly believe—they really do—that their countries will evade the foreseeable and unforeseeable consequences, that the bill for their inexcusable inaction will not be tendered, with penalty, and compound interest. But of course no delusions persist on that score in the United States.

What does persist, especially within the ranks of the Clinton administration is a gross overestimation of the capacities and potential of the United Nations as an instrument of peace. That in turn is shaped by a well-established, indeed conventional view about the past and possible future of the United Nations that still lingers, even though the Bosnian events should already have exposed it as exactly wrong.

The tale begins amidst the bright hopes of 1945, when the United Nations was established by the victorious allies to keep the peace thereafter. Upon being notified of a war imminent or already underway, the Great Powers meeting as the UN Security Council were to investigate and deliberate, to then variously warn, demand, threaten, or fight conjointly as the case might be, so as to prevent or stop the war, secure a prompt withdrawal of the invaders if any, and/or obtain compensation for damage inflicted by the aggressors, if any. Thus the UN's "collective security," which was to advantageously replace its traditional national counterparts, both in the form of unilateral Great Power interventions (that often ended up by starting wider wars), and of self-defense by the lesser fry themselves (normally hard to distinguish from aggression). And, of course the Great Powers themselves would not fight one another—they were still "The Allies" after all—but instead resolve their differences diplomatically in the Security Council chamber.

Because Great Power wars were ruled out, while any fighting among lesser powers would be stopped before it had properly began, the UN and the workings of its Security Council would make warfare itself virtually useless as an instrument of state power. It followed that the accumulation of the means of war would be eventually recognized as equally useless. The UN's collective security would therefore ensure both peace now and disarmament in due course.

But then, the conventional version continues, the gears of the splendid machine of collective security were fatally blocked by the advent of the Cold War. Because each of the Great Powers could veto any action by the UN Security Council at any time, the emergence of globally hostile rival camps meant that the Council could not confront threats to peace which originated in either camp—and of course that is where most of them did originate. As it happens, the United States did succeed in securing the endorsement of the UN Security Council for military action in Korea, but that resulted from what was essentially a mere technicality: because Stalin miscalculated, the Soviet Union simply failed to exercise its veto. Nothing of substance ensued anyway: the North Korean and later the Chinese invasions were not stopped and then reversed by the mechanism of collective security, but had to be fought step by step by the forces of the United States and its own strategic allies, exactly as in the bad old days before the UN The only difference was that the U.S. commander-in-chief was labeled the UN commander, the United States and allied forces were called UN forces, and UN flags were flown in place of U.S. or other national flags.

After Korea, there were no more fortuitous exceptions: each time the Security Council convened, the Soviet Union would veto U.S.-sponsored actions to keep the peace, and vice versa. During the 1950s, 1960s, 1970s and into the 1980s, everyone therefore knew better than to expect the UN to assure peace by collective security. It was very clear then that whatever international outrages the United States would not confront, with or without its own allies, would remain uncontested. Then came the gradual abandonment of Soviet grand strategy by

Gorbachev, the crisis in the Gulf, the collapse of the Soviet Union, and the final end of the Cold War.

Repeated in a hundred editorials and after-dinner speeches, the conventional wisdom offered up for the new era held that the UN could and would at long last fulfill the hopes that had attended its birth. No longer automatically blocked by reciprocal super-power hostility, the machine of collective security would from now on function as intended, to confront threats and defeat them if matters reached that extremity. The successful conduct of the Gulf crisis and Gulf war within a UN framework, with Security Council authorizations at each step of the way, was presented as firm evidence of the dawn of a new age, in which aggressors would be dissuaded first of all, and if needs be confronted by the Security Council, and if needs be defeated by a broad array of UN-sponsored coalition forces.

The role of the United States could not exactly be ignored in this rendition of the Gulf crisis and Gulf war, but neither was it fully admitted that what had happened was not more than a U.S. action in UN garb, in effect a Korea II, rather than a UN action with the United States acting as its chief executive agent. Certainly, if the United States would have accepted the Iraqi conquest of Kuwait, it would have been accepted all round. And if the United States would not have engaged Iraq, nobody would have engaged Iraq. Because that is the crucial point—the willingness to engage. We do not live in a pre-1914 world of rival Great Powers eager to become involved in any crisis that comes along, governed by ambitious elites that see every local conflict as full of promising opportunities, and in command of military forces that can freely be sent into action whenever and wherever combat could pay off in added territory, added diplomatic influence or both.

In today's world, it goes without saying that the ruling elites of developed states have no interest whatever in territorial aggrandizement or diplomatic influence gained by force; that they regard crises and local conflicts not as opportunities but as traps to be avoided at all costs; and that only a very few developed states are still capable of war under any circumstances except, perhaps, for self-defense strictly defined. Given the general unwillingness to engage, it is not surprising that if we subtract whatever the United States did in the Gulf conflict from all that was done within the framework of the UN, the result we obtain is zero.

The implication is not that UN Security Council was useless as a venue during the Gulf crisis—on the contrary it was very useful indeed for the pseudo-multilateral diplomacy of the Bush administration. But it does mean that the chamber, furniture, fittings and procedures of the UN Security Council should not be construed into a sentient being itself capable of acting in place of the United States, thus being able to assume responsibilities that the United States refuses to accept. In theory, nobody of barely-normal intelligence or above could possibly believe otherwise. In practice "let us leave it to the UN Security Council" is the commonplace slogan of the new post-Cold War isolationism.

Matters would stand quite otherwise if in the political life of the world's developed states at least, there were a widespread moral compulsion to protect homo sapiens per se, as bottle-nosed dolphins and many other species are now protected, of course by politicians who cannot risk the accusation of being indifferent to their survival. Such a moral compulsion to protect homo sapiens too automatically turned into a political compulsion, would be reflected in *necessarily* activist policies in the face of unambiguous international aggressions, featuring for example mass expulsions and killings of unarmed civilians. Such activist policies would in turn be most effectively implemented not by single states, perhaps quite small, perhaps remote from the scene, but jointly, to provide not their perhaps feeble security for the insecure, but collective security, much more powerfully. And finally, such collective security could of course be best organized within the framework of the UN. But of course there is no such moral compulsion; thus there is no obligatory activism in the face of aggression; hence there is no national political basis for international collective security. It hardly matters therefore if the gears of the UN machine are blocked or not: the essential raw material—the willingness to engage aggression—is not to be had anyway, except from the handful of countries still marginally capable of waging war.

The agony of Bosnia—only made worse by the lowest-common denominator diplomacy of UN officials, by ineffectual forces under the UN flag, and by the UN arms embargo on the Bosnian Muslims that was the wholly disproportionate price for both—has now fully contradicted the conventional view of the UN's past, and thus of its future potential. We may now look back to recognize that the Cold War did not in fact incapacitate the UN, for what has no capacity cannot be incapacitated. On the contrary, the Cold War actually inflated the UN's apparent importance, because when the super-powers did choose to settle local conflicts, it was usually convenient for both to have their bilateral arrangements rubber-stamped in the UN Security Council, and sometimes to have UN-flagged units on the scene to observe the resulting cease-fire or armistice lines, monitor troop and weapon movements if constrained, and try to intercept third-party infiltrators if possible.[1] But in Bosnia, as in other locales of aggression, there are no Great Powers eagerly intervening by proxy, which might eventually reach an impasse that UN-stamped arrangements could then conveniently freeze.

In today's post-Cold War world, the UN can therefore offer only its endless procedural delays, its always very costly and often corrupt administration of subordinate agencies, and of course the lowest-common denominator diplomacy of its secretary-general. It should not therefore be invoked to also offer an alibi for American inaction in the face of barbarous aggression. The world's only Great Power, infinitely more powerful militarily than Croats, or Serbs, or both, has stood by to passively watch horrors not seen on European soil since the

Holocaust. Let us at least confront what we have not done, and what we have become: a nation supremely well-armed that has allowed the marginally armed to terrorize and kill the unarmed. But was that what Americans would have wanted to do, if properly lead? And is that what Americans want to be? If the answer is yes, our children are destined to live in a nightmare world of unresisted aggressions. If the answer is no, we should cure our military deformation forthwith, and liberate ourselves from the multilateralist and UN delusions.

Note

1. Because of China's role as the sometime conditional protector of the Khmer Rouge, the UN operation in Cambodia has assumed Cold War lineaments, and has functioned accordingly, that is, sufficiently well, so far.

6

NATO Started Bombing to Help Milosevic

"We will keep bombing until Milosevic steps down," Tony Blair insisted last week. He was instantly corrected by Jamie Shea, NATO's U.S. spokesman: "We will keep bombing," he stressed, until Milosevic *backs* down." The tumble over terminology identifies a fundamental fissure in NATO—a fissure running through not just the war's planning, but its very purpose.

When the war began, NATO's aims were clear and limited. The aim of the war was not an independent Kosovo, or the overthrow of President Milosevic, the man now routinely referred to as the Butcher of the Balkans, the new Hitler, and a genocidal war criminal. It was, in fact, to reinforce Milosevic's position within Serbia.

The United States, led by Secretary of State Madeleine Albright, persuasively argued that only Milosevic could deliver an agreement on Kosovo. The Serbian opposition was and is much more determined to hold onto Kosovo, at whatever cost, than he is. If Milosevic were to sign the Rambouillet agreement, which the Kosovar Albanians had ratified, he would have to have the excuse that he had no alternative. The bombing would, it was thought, be enough to show the Serbs that their president had "no alternative."

The limited aim of an autonomous, but not independent, Kosovo—with its own law-courts, but without its own army or Foreign Ministry—had a series of very clear and specific implications for the means by which NATO was to fight the war. First, the Kosovo Liberation Army (KLA) was not to be armed or trained. Second, the force used against Serbia was to be deployed in a very measured way. Its point was not to destroy Milosevic, but to persuade him back to the negotiating table. Far from being regarded as an enemy of humanity, he was believed to be an indispensable figure to NATO: for he was the only Serb leader capable of resolving the Kosovo question on NATO's lines.

There was, therefore, no question of attacking Milosevic's apparatus of power or his political infrastructure, still less his person. So the plan of attack was extremely gentle. There were less than fifty targets for the original bombing offensive. Most of them were minor, remote air defense targets. If it seemed strange that so many bombing missions were canceled due to rain in the first two weeks, the reason is simple: the aim was not to hurt Milosevic, but to give him an excuse for capitulating on Kosovo. That aim suited Western politicians perfectly for another reason: none of them wanted to see any of their pilots get hurt. A campaign which did no real damage to Serbia would also be one which did not risk any lives.

"War lite" was therefore to everyone's taste. Unfortunately, Milosevic refused to walk down the path made for him. Instead of rushing into NATO's open arms, he sent his police units into Kosovo and proceeded to evict as many Kosovar Albanians as possible, as quickly as possible. Milosevic's failure to behave according to plan has caused a rapid reappraisal of NATO's war aims. It has also dramatically altered the means which must be used to achieve them.

What is the aim of the war now the original justification for it, and the strategy behind it, have both been shredded? NATO has started bombing Milosevic's power base. It has targeted his home, his TV station, and his party's headquarters. But let us be clear: the change of tactics has not come about because politicians like Clinton and Blair have suddenly "discovered" that Milosevic is guilty of genocide. Everyone with any involvement in policy towards the Balkans has known for years that Milosevic was guilty of mass murder. His behavior in Kosovo, though hideous, is so far relatively mild compared to the genocide he perpetrated in Bosnia. There is evidence that he over-ruled ultra-nationalists who recommended the "Bosnian solution" to the Kosovo problem: massacring all Kosovar Albanians, rather than just expelling them, which has been Milosevic's policy.

No, the targeting of Milosevic is simply a reflection of frustration at his failure to act as he was supposed to. It is a familiar pattern: a dictator is demonized as a monster only when Western foreign policy fails, and he ceases to respond in a predictable way to threats and offers. It happened with Saddam, with whom the United States and Great Britain were happy to "do business" when he behaved as predicted, despite his hideous cruelty and use of chemical weapons against his own people. Only when statecraft failed, and he did something quite unpredicted—invaded Kuwait—was he turned into "the new Hitler."

The motives behind targeting Milosevic are no more "moral" than they were in the case of Saddam. NATO's aims are in disarray as a consequence. Everyone recognizes that Milosevic remains the least horrible Serbian leader amongst a very horrible bunch. Removing him would make the situation worse, by ensuring he was replaced by a harder line nationalist. So what is the aim of the war?

There are two competing answers to that question. One is the creation of an independent Kosovo. This could not be done without a full-scale invasion by NATO, which does not seem very likely. A supposedly formidable military alliance which is unwilling to fly planes below 15,000 ft. because of the risk to its pilots' lives is not going to risk the deaths of thousands of ground troops. The aim of an independent Kosovo is opposed by some NATO members, and does not yet have U.S. backing. Without the U.S., it will remain a gleam in Tony Blair's eye.

The other alternative is much more likely. The goal is to persuade Milosevic to agree to some compromise. The hope is that the bombing, if it is intense enough, will force Milosevic to turn to the Russians, empowering them to negotiate a settlement with NATO. Any deal would inevitably involve the partition of Kosovo, with the Serbians hanging on to the resource-rich north, whilst the south would be an international "protectorate" run by a coalition of NATO, Russia, and non-aligned countries.

That would, of course, be a victory for Milosevic. But that does not stop many NATO leaders from fervently praying for it. It would allow NATO to exit the war with some dignity intact. It might even be played up to suggest that NATO had achieved a homeland for the Kosovars and peace in the Balkans.

A great power congress to solve Kosovo would be like the great nineteenth-century congress of Berlin, which redrew the map of Europe. It would not have much to do with ethics. But then no foreign policy ever does. It is the greatest of the Blair government's illusions, or its most chilling cynicism, to pretend that its foreign policy is, or could be, any different.

7

Pablo Escobar and the War on Drugs

Pablo Emilio Escobar Gaviria (1950-1993), most talented and richest of Colombian drug bosses, lived his contradictions. A gold-framed portrait of the Virgin Mary surmounted the bed in which he slept with teenage prostitutes. Of course, he was devoted to his wife and family in the unconditional Latino manner. "Whether his concern for his parents or his children would overcome his stringent security consciousness is not clear" reads an excessively cautious CIA profile quoted by Mark Bowden.

Escobar was a hunted man, pursued by what might even be called a "bi-national, multi-agency task force" if the various Colombian and U.S. forces had been better coordinated. With the many millions of dollars at his disposal, he could easily have left his city of Medellin, and Colombia altogether, for much safer abodes—in South America there are still many places where one can live without papers, have first-class plastic surgery, and buy genuine identity cards and passports to fit the new face. But Pablo would not abandon his wife and children, whose lives were then being very deliberately threatened by special Colombian police units. Pablo remained nearby to protect them with his remaining network of gunslingers, lawyers, publicists and money-men, until he was found after fifteen months by the most elaborate and costly manhunt ever mounted against a mere criminal. He was immediately killed, for his American and Colombian pursuers would trust no court to convict him, no prison to hold him, nor indeed the politicians who would administer the process. In 1991, he had surrendered voluntarily after successfully negotiating with the government the passage of an anti-extradition law and his right to be held in a new prison, built to his own design, whose guards immediately became his servants, procurers, runners, and agents.

Medellin, in the *departemento* of Antioquia in western Colombia, also lives its contradictions. Imagined by some as a landscape of slums and shacks in

Review of Mark Bowden, *Killing Pablo: The Hunt for the Richest, Most Powerful Criminal in History*, Atlantic Books, 2001.

which *pistoleros* shoot it out over bags of cocaine, Medellin is one of the most attractive cities in Latin America. Its wonderful "eternal springtime" tropical mountain climate and profusion of flowers embellish slums, charming old streets and handsome new quarters alike. Even the downtown commercial center of skyscrapers and office towers has its imaginative architectural elements. As Colombia's second largest city and commercial center of the region's industry, mining, ranching, and agriculture, Medellin has rather more than its share of banks and even a local stock exchange, as well as an abundance of restaurants, night clubs, and hotels. An efficient airport offers some thirty non-stop and direct flights a day to Miami alone, a good indicator of the high level of economic activity even at a time of acute depression, and even now that Medellin is no longer the capital of the world's drug trade as it was in the 1980s, when Pablo Escobar was the boss of the eponymous "Cartel."

Money alone is enough to have office blocks and hotels and air traffic, whether it is flower money or drug money, but there is much more to Medellin than its money. This year's edition of the international poetry festival organized by the local literary magazine *Prometeo,* which once again attracted large and enthusiastic audiences, was no isolated feat amidst the carnage but a fair reflection of Antioquia's remarkably active cultural life. Medellin's thirty or so museums are not all well kept, but neither are they inert depositories. Along with the several universities, and all sorts of other institutions, they serve as venues for a great many cultural associations. Many a city of two million elsewhere in the world can envy Medellin's cultural dynamism. That indeed is the point. The people of Medellin and Antioquia are far removed from the siesta-Latino stereotype, being equally dynamic in work, crime, and culture alike.

Mark Bowden's own contraction is central to this book, a sufficiently substantial work which need not have been fattened further by its inordinately large type. While inviting us to read about "the richest, most powerful criminal in history," Bowden keeps harping on the mediocrity of Pablo Escobar, dismissing him as "just a thug." That reflects his sources, not Colombian documents or texts but rather interviews with gringo DEA operatives, soldiers and other expressions of U.S. officialdom, whose views he uncritically relays. Bowden is one journalist who has tremendous respect for the salaried servants of the U.S. government sent to grapple with sinister foreigners in strange places.

That is his method, which ensured vast sales for *Black Hawk Down,* his highly readable account of the October 1993 Mogadishu raid by U.S. Rangers and Delta commandos, which ended with eighteen dead soldiers, many more wounded, and hundreds of dead Somalis, without even getting near to its goal. By focusing on the sentiments of the protagonists, mostly young men in their first trial of combat excited to be in action with the veteran Deltas, by vividly relaying their collated thoughts, statements and deeds as reported to him in interviews, Bowden converts the record of a foolish operation, badly planned, badly lead and poorly executed into a dramatic tale of heroism. He is evidently unaware of how a competent commando force might have acted, indeed under the illusion that he was writing about just such a force, as opposed to U.S. Special Operations troops as they actually are, endowed with the fanciest equipment, very expensively trained, certainly brave, but deprived of vital operational experience by the obsessive fear of casualties of their superiors, and of suitable officers by the otherwise war-winning West Point tradition of management first, leadership second, tactics last.

Bowden did not denigrate his Somalis as savages or anything of the kind. He even went to dangerous Mogadishu to find protagonists on the other side to give them their say, and if the Somalis are mostly presented as inexplicably reckless warriors, the products of an incomprehensibly combative culture, that is how they are seen by mostly everyone, including fellow Somalis in a reflective mood. The Colombians come off much worse in this book, being mostly incompetent, or corrupt, or both.

At one level, that is merely accurate reporting. The Colombian armed forces are indeed incompetent, and by deliberate volition in a country full of highly competent people. That is easily done: the generals use up their budgets to buy Mach 2 fighters and other baubles on which they get commissions, instead of the infantry training and exercises that yield real combat power. As for corruption, Colombian politicians are indeed venal more often than not, distinctly more so than in other Latino countries if only because the oligopolistic drug trade can afford much higher bribery overheads than more competitive legitimate businesses.

But as gringos often do, in focusing on Latino public vices Bowden misses the private virtues—ranging from family lives suffused with love to a macho courage that also emboldens the imagination. He therefore entirely misses the point about Pablo Escobar, reporting a great many facts in detail but always through the viewpoint of the gringo operatives he interviewed—salaried and pensioned mediocrities who prudishly disapproved of Pablo's sexual appetites while of course envying his ability to satisfy them at will. They ridiculed the chubby Pablo as a fatso, and utterly failed to comprehend the Napoleonic scope of a man who prevailed over all contenders to become the big boss in his twenties, who took time off from running the Cartel to win a national parliamentary election, who answered truth to power by writing powerful indictments of Colombia's non-justice system, and whose own version of the inevitable drug lord villa transcended the usual with its multiple artificial lakes, a petting zoo with lions, elephants and hippos, and equally imaginative entertainments for his many guests.

Yes, Pablo was more self-indulgent than the average DEA agent, and certainly had more fun that any hundred of them, but he spent very much more to build public housing for Medellin's poor, and was even more Napoleonic in his business. It was Pablo who replaced precarious hops by light aircraft with direct flights to the U.S. by large, multi-engine transports. (The Cartel could afford to lose three for each one that got through, and hardly lost one.) It was Pablo who pressed for more imaginative solutions, such as the use of remote-controlled submarines for boat pickups at the other end, the new Mexican Pacific coast routes, and more grandly, personally negotiated with both the Sandinistas of Nicaragua (successfully) and with Panama's military chief Noriega (unsuccessfully) to obtain forward bases of operation. Pablo's response to the threat of large-scale herbicide attacks on Colombia's coca leaf patches was just as Napoleonic: he sent his men into Peru to provide seeds, tools, horticultural instruction and interim living allowances to landless peasants and Lima slum dwellers willing to try coca farming. The Pablo Escobar agricultural-extension scheme was an enormous success, unlike the World Bank's disastrous projects. Thousands went north to farm coca, and Peru soon outproduced Colombia.

It seems that Bowden's informants had not even asked themselves *how* Pablo Escobar had risen to command the Medellin Cartel. Their notion, continually repeated by Bowden, that Pablo did it all by being very violent, is of course absurd. There were a great many young punks in Medellin willing and able to kill when Pablo entered the cocaine business as a very young man. Not all of them were stupid, though hardly any could have matched Pablo's wits. He killed many, but not in order to fight his way to the top of the Medellin Cartel, for there was no such thing until Pablo himself created it. His contribution to the coca protection racket was not an extra edge of violence, but the very opposite: a reliable insurance system. If you shipped on your own without paying the Cartel fee, Pablo had you killed. If you paid your fee, shipped with the Cartel and the merchandise was intercepted, the Cartel refunded all your costs, allowing you to try again. Anybody could have a go at extorting money from the visibly rich coca traffickers who enlivened Medellin's night life, but only Pablo could credibly insure their business, while Cartel membership alone was also very valuable because it provided incidental protection from Medellin's many unaffiliated punks and gunslingers. His system was very different from normal protection rackets, whose membership is wholly enforced because it offers no rewards.

The same combination of threats and incentives kept Pablo safe from the Colombian courts and police until the Americans got into the act: *plomo o plata*, ("lead or silver"). Bribery was hardly Pablo's invention, and nor was the intimidation and murder of judges or policemen, then as now a common occurrence in Colombia. But Pablo offered both, leaving the choice to his victims and always keeping his word either way. Almost all preferred to live with a bit of extra change in their pockets. It was simple, but it was new, and it worked.

It was, however, another Napoleonic venture that the U.S. government now has excellent reasons to recollect wistfully. Under pressure from the FARC guerrillas, who were moving into the Cartel's coca-growing areas to tax them for themselves, Pablo hired world-class combat instructors to train his own armed units, which defeated the flyblown guerrillas in one clash after another, until they retreated into the jungle once again. Denied coca revenues, the FARC remained a marginal threat, less important in those days than the ELF in the northeast, which attacked oil pipelines to extract payoffs, as it still does. Once again, Pablo showed that, unlike most people who have a lot of money, he knew how to spend it well. In need of military strength, he did not waste his money by buying fancy equipment, as the United States is now doing for the Colombians, but rather went for the real thing: serious, British-style infantry training, the very thing the Colombian army still lacks.

Having now moved into the coca-growing areas to tax both crops and shipments, the same FARC that Pablo repelled with ease has become Colombia's most intractable threat, entangling the United States in one more counter-insurgency campaign. "The Colombian Labyrinth" is the title of the inevitable RAND study documenting the explosive growth of the FARC. Having started with just 3,600 men in 1986 when Pablo was at the height of his power and they had no coca money, they now have some 15-20,000. Naturally they have all the weapons they can use, and also the money to buy influence in the capital.

The U.S. government is living its own contradictions. Having killed Pablo Escobar with the notable assistance of the volunteer-vigilante terrorists, Los Pepes, it destroyed the Medellin Cartel only to find that it had merely shifted its business to the Cali Cartel, which not coincidentally was behind Los Pepes. So the futile war started once again, this time against the Cali Cartel, which was duly dismantled after years of vast effort, only to give way to much less visible networks of many small operators, who ship as much cocaine as before. But there is one difference: under Pablo Escobar the Medellin Cartel was willing and able to keep the FARC guerrillas in remote jungle hideouts, while the post-Escobar networks of independents pay their dues to the FARC, leaving the job of fighting them to the ill-prepared Colombian army today, and perhaps U.S. forces tomorrow.

The greater contradiction, however, is the notion that it is even worth trying to prevent the inflow of exotic drugs extracted from plants. In 1999, the combined efforts of federal, state and local anti-drug police discovered 2,700 methamphetamine laboratories in California, another 600 in the state of Washington, 400 in Arizona and so on down the list of all fifty states. On August 15, 2001 the DEA announced the triumphant conclusion of Operation Silent Thunder, in which some 100 federal agents and local detectives found "more than a dozen *large* methamphetamine laboratories" in and around Los Angeles. But the expected total for the year—in California alone—is again expected to exceed 2,000 laboratories.

Methamphetamine may perhaps be especially in demand of late—one can never know such things with any certainty—but it is only one of many compounds that have been declared illegal over the years. Recently-announced "huge" seizures featured Ecstasy capsules imported from Amsterdam and even venerable LSD, which still has its fans. Such molecules were born illegal but others become so. In slack times, local drug cops can always keep themselves busy by investigating the nearest hospital, to uncover the inevitable diversions of prescription mind-bending medicines to paying customers or just friends. All this merely proves that there is no need of traditional drugs extracted from exotic plants to keep hop heads happy and the DEA in business.

But of course, the top priority of the DEA and other drug hunters are still very much the traditional drugs, not least because they are trafficked by swarthy Latinos, wily Levantines or sinister Orientals—at least in the popular imagination. Such are the media depictions, which the DEA has no reason to challenge because they add greatly to public support for enforcement. Seizures of marijuana, cocaine, and heroin shipments, the arrest of dealers large and small continue to be announced on a daily basis, along with discovery of marijuana plantations in cropped fields, national forests, southland hothouses, and illuminated basements all over the United States. Many Americans (there are no exact statistics) are in prison for simple possession unalloyed with any other crime, but possession arrests are rarely the subject of press releases. Unless local police are having fun by suborning student-agents to stage yet another "campus-wide crackdown," or more fun still by frequenting discos and night clubs in zero-risk undercover operations to catch drug use in the act in a "vice-city clean-up," possession arrests are mere routine—a matter of stopping and searching cars driven too fast, or too slowly by younger drivers at party time, especially if they are black.

The sheer monotony of it all should long ago have extinguished media interest even in the DEA's more elaborate operations, but its well-staffed press offices (they are, after all, the Agency's budget-enhancing profit centers) still succeed in attracting media coverage by reusing the same standard trick to inflate their success and by supply well-produced action photographs and video clips. The drug cops learn new tricks from the TV cop series they obsessively watch, just as TV cop-series scriptwriters hang out with drug cops to hear their stories.

Drug-war entertainment may be bad, indifferent or even good, but the drug-war reportage is a continuing scandal of systematic misrepresentation. Simply by conceding column inches and scarce TV news minutes to these stories, media editors implicitly affirm their significance, even though they know perfectly well that enforcement is not merely ineffective, inefficient, insufficient or incomplete but entirely futile. The thoroughly documented long-term decline in the prices of all illegal drugs—even cocaine, once the luxury white powder of the rich and fashionable can now be consumed by the poorest of the poor in crack form—evidently reflects a continuing expansion in their supply from sources both foreign and domestic.

For now, it is only marijuana that is being grown increasingly within the United States, reducing the interception of imported marijuana to mere protectionism. With no need of any swarthy Latinos, wily Levantines or sinister Orientals, all manner of ordinary Americans grow the stuff as best they can.

Easily circumventing all supposed climactic and soil requirements, these fine American growers produce resins that beat the best stuff that ever came out of Mexico or Morocco. They could certainly produce coca leaf and opium poppies as well, but it is the failure of interception in spite of all claims of success that precludes domestic production, for it could not possibly compete with ever cheaper imports.

While domestic enforcement is a fraud perpetrated against the taxpayers who pay for unmerited salaries and fringe benefits, interception at the borders by the U.S. Customs Service and Coast Guard is worse than useless because it has perverse effects. Without it, the economies to scale of smuggling would not favor so strongly the bigger outfits that can afford the loss of any one aircraft or ship. That was the rationale of Pablo's cartel, of its Cali imitators, and of the Mexican cartels that started off as Pablo's subsidiaries. All big drug bosses are different from the little guy with a bit of merchandise, because they can and do corrupt policemen, judges and politicians.

Mr. Bowden likes his DEA, CIA, and U.S. military sources. He therefore validates their futile striving in the service of policies that cannot succeed in stopping the flow of drugs, but which do inflict enormous collateral damage, by way of mass imprisonment within the United States, and criminalization abroad, starting right across the Mexican border in Tijuana and Ciudad Juarez. It is a general principle of strategy that effective tactical conduct in the service of a mistaken goal is actually counter-productive. Japan's brilliant feat at Pearl Harbor was ultimately disastrous, because it lacked any strategy to win the war. Japan would have been much better off if the operation had been a total fiasco of missed bombs and errant torpedoes, thus evoking American ridicule rather than vengeful hatred. It was the same for the effective tactics that killed Pablo Escobar. Because they were not part of some winning strategy, there being indeed no such strategy, the United States and Colombia would now be far better off if Bowden's heroes had been lazy, incompetent and corrupt, and the coca that still comes in unimpeded was paying for Pablo's expensive contradictions, rather than the guerrillas and counter-guerrillas who are destroying lives and hopes in Colombia.

8

The Global Rise of Separatism:
It's Not Just Nationalism

The collapse of the Soviet Union has caused a further change that is even more momentous and has an even broader impact: the entire importance of military and diplomatic strength on the world scene has been drastically reduced. In the Balkans, the Middle East, the Indian subcontinent, and other unfortunate lands, bitter territorial and ethnic struggles persist as they did throughout history. Military strength therefore remains as important as ever in those parts of the world, and so does diplomacy in its classic form, still serving, as it always did, to convert potential armed strength into actual leverage and influence—to intimidate adversaries, or reassure weaker allies. Thus geopolitics, which was until yesterday the chief concern and core activity of all major states, has suddenly been reduced to a provincial phenomenon, a symptom of backwardness.

By contrast, within the central arena of world affairs, where North Americans, Europeans, Japanese, and other advancing nations both collaborate and compete, military-diplomatic strength has suddenly lost its historic importance. In spite of budget cuts, physical military capabilities are still everywhere present in huge abundance. But they no longer play an important role within central arena of world affairs, because North Americans, Europeans, East Asians, etc. no longer threaten or reassure one another as they used to. Not all is brotherly love between them—indeed economic quarrels may well become even more bitter. But for the first time in history the use of force has become almost unthinkable between the first-rank nations of the world.

That the Soviet Union no longer exists to threaten directly, or to support aggressive smaller states such as Cuba, Vietnam, Syria, etc., is the too-obvious reason for this truly fundamental transformation of world politics. Actually the cultural, social, and psychological demilitarization of the more advanced democratic-capitalist societies has been underway for decades, indeed ever since the First World War.

It is a long time since the public opinion of any advanced country has willingly supported the deliberate and offensive use of military force to achieve territorial conquest. And there has been increasing cultural and social resistance even to the negative use of military strength, for deterrence and defense. As for the use of force to help other countries against aggression, the 1991 Gulf War defined the limits of what was acceptable as far as the American public was concerned: first, unambiguous aggression, and second, almost insignificant casualties.

Most Europeans and Japanese are even less "warlike." But it is only now that the collapse of the Soviet Union allows these long-term cultural, social and psychological trends to fully express themselves, by removing the imperative necessity of defense and deterrence against a global military threat. It only now, therefore, that the essentially post-military nature of advanced modern societies stands revealed. They are not demilitarized, but they are certainly most unwilling to use force, and would not start wars against one another under any circumstance.

To be sure, the advanced states in the central arena of world affairs must still contend with potentially aggressive peripheral states, especially those which have acquired both long-range missiles and chemical weapons, and are now trying to acquire nuclear weapons. Moreover, the condition of both Russia and China is not sufficiently stable to guarantee the continuation of their new "post-military" national policies.

But even with these exceptions and reservations, it cannot be denied that military strength and classic diplomacy have suddenly lost much of their traditional importance in world affairs. A most unexpected side effect is the worldwide emergence of ethnic and regional separatisms.

The larger and more centralized state was obviously favored when security against attack and invasion was still a most pressing need. Insofar as they had a choice at all, people were frequently willing to accept all the disadvantages of living in a larger state more remotely governed, because such a state could provide greater physical security for their families and themselves.

In a "post-military" context, on the other hand, the priority of security falls away, and the operative priority is to have a responsive government, which reflects local cultural, social and economic desires. Moreover, the emergence of post-military conditions is of course organically connected with the breakdown of the Soviet empire—the second largest empire in all of human history, only to the Mongols. Long-felt national identities until then submerged could therefore express themselves for the first time. Additionally, some national identities were actually formed under Soviet rule, which compacted tribes into nations by promoting education and modernization.

In any case, a responsive government which reflects local cultural, social and economic desires requires independence or autonomy within commensurate boundaries. Often the desired boundary lines are ethnic, but to focus on this misses the point: the global separatist trend released by the decline of military power in world affairs needs no ethnic impulse.

In fact, where there are no convenient ethnic boundaries, separatism very easily takes a regional form, as in Italy with the "northern leagues" and in purely Russian-Russia, primarily St. Petersburg and Sakhalin. In some cases, as in Spain, even the multiple separatisms of Catalonia, Galicia and the Basque region have been accommodated peacefully by decentralization, while Czechoslovakia has divided without war, and Canada's confederation is simply becoming looser and looser. Elsewhere, state structures have been sufficiently federal all along (as in America) to provide responsive local government. But in many other cases, of which Yugoslavia is by far the most tragic, the outcome is paradoxical: the very separatism made possible by the global decline of military power causes armed conflicts which make military power more important than ever, but only within peripheral areas outside the central arena of world affairs. Of the bitter ironies of history there is no end.

Among the winder implications of separatism's rise, the first is that conventional risk assessments must be revised to include the possible direct or indirect impact of separations. Most notably, the stability of Italy, the world's fifth largest industrial economy, is now seriously at risk for the first time since the Communist Party upsurge of 1945-48. In the shortest term, the "northern leagues" will probably continue to win pluralities in local elections almost everywhere in the north. A southern boycott of northern-made products may result. Even outbreaks of violence cannot be excluded. But the longer-term effects are more substantial and not so hypothetical, for they are already underway: the country's entire political system is in dissolution, because it was based on the primacy of the southern-dominated Christian Democrats.

Second, there is a definite tendency for separatism to induce further separatism. For example, Ossetians, Abkhaz and Adhjars all lived in their nominally autonomous republics under the Georgian Republic, whose own sovereignty was of course purely nominal while the Soviet Union lasted. But when Georgian independence became real, the Ossetians and Abkhaz started fighting for their individual independence. There has been a similar process within Moldavia, with the Gagauz and the Russians-Ukrainians fighting for separation from Moldova's Romanian identity. There is a much greater potential for such conflicts in ex-Soviet Central Asia and within the Russian Federation itself. In the milder circumstances of Western Europe, the proliferation of separatisms is so far mainly linguistic. In Spain, for example, the Valencia region successfully demanded the use of Valencian rather than standard Spanish, only to find that its Alicante sub-region does not accept Valencian and instead wants its own slightly different spelling. Likewise, the assertion of stronger regional identities in northern Italy has already inspired the rise of a separatist linguistic movement in the Alpine regions: their language, much closer to Latin, is different from the Italian that even northerners speak.

Finally, the disruptive extension of separatism to trade relations cannot be excluded. If the worldwide trade liberalization trend of the past was still progressing at full strength, this would not be such a live concern. But as GATT's recent troubles have shown, the liberalizing momentum has gone. That facilitates the degeneration of cultural-political quarrels into trade quarrels. The outlook is currently mixed. For example, there has been no interference with free trade within Spain. Likewise, the Czech Republic and Slovakia are retaining open borders. At the other extreme, trade relations between the ex-Soviet republics have mostly broken down, albeit because of export restrictions rather than import prohibitions. As a middle case, Croatia and Slovenia had agreed to continue free trade after their separate separations from Yugoslavia. But as of November 1992, the industrially inferior Croats had started to collect some import duties on some Slovenian products.

Thus, the global rise of separatism does not only threaten violence in traditional hot spots and political aggravation even in developed Western Europe. It would be excessively optimistic to believe that the free-trade norm will always prevail in a world where there are more and more political boundaries.

9

Bandenkrieg

Three weeks ago, my good friend Robert Callen McKenzie, ex-U.S. Army, ex-Rhodesian SAS and lately a training officer on private contract, yet a sweet-natured if excessively audacious idealist all the while, was killed in Sierra Leone while leading an attack on a bandit camp for Sierra Leone's bandits-in-power. The chaotic violence that now engulfs that country cannot be described as a civil war, inasmuch as the contending forces—notably including the "govern-ment"— represent nobody but themselves. It cannot be described as a guer-rilla conflict, because no side seriously pretends to be fighting for a cause or, more technically, because there is no tactically inferior force that must elude a government army or an occupier in nature or the night. It is not anyone else's war fought by local surrogates in the familiar Cold War manner, for no greater power from without seems to care a fig for what happens in Sierra Leone.

Only the German term *Bandenkrieg*, conventionally translated as "guerrilla" but literally and more usefully "warband war," properly describes what is hap-pening in Sierra Leone, as also in Liberia, Somalia and some two-dozen other places that were once countries, including Afghanistan, Georgia, and the former Yugoslavia. In all these places, certainly, the warring bands do their trafficking and plundering in symbiosis with larger and somewhat more organized forces motivated by the much more elevated purposes of tribal, ethnic and religious hatred, or even territorial aggrandizement. But these bands' sort of combat is entirely different from politically motivated civil or guerrilla warfare.

The distinction between the two kinds of forces is clear or consequential. It is true that warring bands, like political factions, will tend to be homogeneous according to the prevailing ethnic or religious classifications, and that they too will rape, torture and kill gratuitously and gratis any vulnerable member of their enemy. But warring bands will also readily do business with one another across whatever dividing lines apply, and even more, they will fight or not fight,

---

Review of the Report of the Commission on Global Governance, *Our Global Neigh-bourhood*, Oxford University Press 1995.

seize positions or abandon them, specifically to do business. When there is enough *Bandenkrieg* in the mixture, wars tend to be made by lulls of fighting in between long bouts of commerce. Certainly that has been the case in the former Yugoslavia, in the interstices of both international wars and above all under the cover of the four unending civil wars. In all those cases, predators can not only raise a thirst but also acquire Mercedes-Benz automobiles, even buying them on occasion.

Fashionably entrepreneurial, self-reliantly financed by trafficking or economic predation (diamonds in Sierra Leone, opium in Afghanistan, and smuggled goods in Yugoslavia) and capable of lasting for ever, the *Bandenkrieg* is becoming today's most prevalent expression of armed violence. It was just the same in other historical moments of great power paralysis, most broadly, as far as the West is concerned, in the wake of the Roman downfall until warband leaders evolved into territorial chieftains, then imperceptibly turning into the nobility of the sword. So it was, more recently, in the exhausted aftermath of the First World War, especially in the Baltic borderlands, Versailles-Poland, Ukraine and the Caucasus, as well as nascent Turkey—whose *Bandenkrieg* was soon absorbed and displaced by Ataturk's properly organized warfare cum ethnic cleansing.

Now also, there is neither a plausible danger of great power wars, nor the tranquility once imposed by each power within its own sphere of influence, which were at no time more rigidly enforced than during the Cold War, when each superpower efficiently suppressed divisive animosities within its own camp.

After the long decades of the American-Soviet struggle, themselves preceded by a century of especially intense great power rivalries that twice exploded in world wars, not to mention all the earlier centuries of conflict, the absence of anything resembling a great power confrontation in these post-Cold War days of ours is certainly an enormous novelty. That much has been duly recognized and rightly celebrated, and so has the obvious corollary: the waning of the many local and regional conflicts that had been instigated or at least encouraged and materially supported by the Soviet Union, the United States and China during the Cold War years.

What has yet to be recognized, however, is that the absence of great power tensions reflects a yet more momentous absence—of anything that can rightly be called a great power among today's leading countries, notably including the United States. It is this absence of functioning great powers that is the cause of today's unprecedented predicament: the world's inability to cope with the violent disorders that persist even in the absence of external instigation, encouragement or material support, from small power aggressions and wars, to the *Bandenkrieg* that killed my friend Robert McKenzie.

The product of a self-appointed commission of the usual international worthies, originally formed at Willy Brandt's initiative from the preexisting

Independent Commission on Disarmament and Security better known as the Palme Commission; the World Commission on Environment and Development, better known as the Brundtland Commission; and Julius Nyerere's South Commission, *Our Global Neighbourhood* has chapters on poverty and development, international trade and dependence, international finance, migration, environmental protection, UN reform, and the strengthening of international law. But the multiple authors and editors of this surprising well-compiled compilation of pretty-conventional diagnoses and pretty-conventional therapies, evidently recognized the primacy of security before all other ameliorative endeavors.

It is simply too obvious that there is no investment or development without rather high levels of perceived security (the outbreak of the very attenuated, remarkably bloodless Chiapas insurgency was enough to end investment in Mexico literally overnight), that wars cause forced migrations, that the fragile bits of the environment are not merely despoiled but often destroyed by warring parties, and that respect for international law can hardly coexist with active warfare.

Unfortunately, this commission of commissions was prevented by the nature of its membership from recognizing the source of the problem, to wit the absence of functioning great powers. Instead there is a fair amount of irrelevant and counter-productive material on arms control.

One proposal of great merit, on the other hand, is that a 10,000-man UN force be established under Security Council control, albeit under the Secretary-General's command, as per current UN forces. Evidently with the shameful goings-on of Bosnia and Somalia freshly in mind, the authors of *Our Global Neighbourhood* use all sorts of adjectives to indicate that *this* UN force cannot be like many of the member-state armed forces in UN service. Primarily, and in stark contrast to the existing forces cobbled together under UN supervision, the force would have to be competent and willing to fight. Certainly there are plenty of adventurous souls who would volunteer for a quality-controlled UN force analogous to the Foreign Legion, if (and only if) it were billed as an eager-to-fight force. Equally certain, the permanent members of the Security Council could put together a competent command structure.

One obvious difficulty is the cost: real armed forces, unlike those in UN service who daily disgrace their respective uniforms world-wide, are expensive. Another is that 10,000 soldiers are too few to control Bosnia-scale violence yet numerous enough to be seen as very threatening by a good many dictators. Yet the number is a sensible compromise, even though the report's stitch-in-time theory, that a prompt but small intervention can avert the need for a much larger one later on, is obviously wrong. Such a small intervention can only work if the enemy has reason to fear even larger counter-measures for continuing the violence, which in this case would not be forthcoming.

Of course, these and many more objections easily come to mind. But at this point in human history it is not clever objections that are needed but rather a willingness to experiment with some practical remedy, however constrained, for the *Bandenkriegen* and assorted disorders of our great-powerless days.

Part 3

America at War

10

The Warning

Whether it is Pearl Harbor, the fall of the Shah, or any other sudden calamity, it is only in retrospect that minor incidents are recognized as warnings that should have been heeded. In their own time, they were submerged by the flux of everyday events and easily overlooked. Intelligence experts speak of warning "signals" and obscuring "noise," forever hoping to discover some magic technique that will extract the right signals from the mass of irrelevant or misleading noise. Needless to say, no such technique exists, and we keep being surprised by surprise.

When an enormous 4,000-pound bomb shears down a concrete apartment tower killing nineteen Americans and grievously wounding many more, the incident is not minor and cannot simply be overlooked. Yet the warning it contains can still be ignored, and so far that is exactly what is happening in the case of the Dhahran bombing.

No, it is not terrorism that we need to be warned about. In the absence of the central tension and supreme dangers of the Cold War, the sporadic attacks of the IRA, GIA, FIS, Hamas, Hizballah, and of all their variants around the globe receive plenty of attention, and often evoke exaggerated security responses. That President Clinton has now embarked on his own crusade against terrorism as Reagan and Bush did before him, is no doubt politically advantageous during an election year, and may even lead to one or two additional countermeasures. But to treat the Dhahran attack as a warning that terrorism can be very lethal, is totally redundant and in fact misleading.

Even the media stories which remind us that Saudi Arabia is ruled by a family dictatorship which prohibits any expression of public opinion, do not proceed to examine, or even mention, the logical implication of that fact, i.e., that the supply of Saudi oil could be interrupted at any time, with disastrous consequences for the entire industrial world. The Federal Reserve in the United States as central banks everywhere nowadays, have been ruthlessly sacrificing employment and growth to keep inflation within their preferred, very low, limits. Yet if what happened in Iran seven years ago were to be repeated in Saudi

69

Arabia, none of their interventions and protestations could stop an inflationary tide that would swiftly nullify years of painful sacrifice.

History hardly ever repeats itself, the Saudi kingdom is not Iran, thousands of princes are more resilient than a solitary, mortally ill Shah, but the very little that the two situations have in common is amply sufficient to justify enormous concern.

First, rulers who prohibit all political expression also deprive themselves—and their allies—of any accurate estimate of the nature, extent and depth of the opposition ranged against them. At present, absolutely nobody can know, not the Saudis, not the U.S. government, not even the terrorists themselves, if the only violent enemies of the regime are the two men who drove the truck-bomb and the third man who drove the getaway car, or virtually the entire population of the country presumably minus the 6,000-odd princes, but including unknown numbers of disaffected policemen, soldiers, security men, and princely body-guards (all rather poorly paid, amidst the luxuriant profligacy of their rulers, their myriad children and assorted courtiers).

Second, given that dictatorships do not last for ever, the first point necessarily means that their disintegration proceeds quite invisibly until it is far advanced—indeed usually so advanced that only an outside intervention by uncontaminated foreign troops can save the regime, by shooting down protesting crowds if necessary. That is how the Soviet Union restored Communist Party rule over Hungary in 1956, and over Czechoslovakia in 1968; and that is how the British and French have repeatedly helped friendly dictators in trouble. But the United States did not send a praetorian guard to keep the Shah in power in 1979, and absent an overt, bona fide foreign threat, will not protect the Saudi rulers from their own people.

Finally, when oil-producing dictatorships fall so does their oil production; catastrophically at first during the transitional upheavals, less catastrophically thereafter but then permanently. Iran has yet to match the Shah's peak production of six million barrels a day, in spite of significant discoveries of new oil reserves.

In that perspective, the critical difference between Saudi Arabia now and Iran in 1979, is not any one or all of the many and great social, ethnic, historical, political, religious, or cultural differences, but rather the single fact that while Iran's oil exports were an important influence on world prices, Saudi Arabia's are quite simply decisive. At full tilt, with eight or more million barrels a day coming out of Saudi Arabia oil prices decline, slowing down inflation world-wide other things being equal. At zero exports, or even at the level of one or two million barrels a day, oil prices would immediately double if not triple, seriously disrupting the world economy and leaving each country with an unhappy choice between rampant inflation or truly drastic cuts in government services and spending.

It follows that it is not terrorism or the exotic particulars of Saudi absolutism that should detain our attention in the wake of the Dhahran bombing, but rather the world's extraordinary, and extraordinarily imprudent dependence on Saudi oil exports. Even Americans who care not a fig about Middle Eastern politics could find themselves paying heavily for its consequences, when commuting in their fashionable 13 mpg muscle cars and toy trucks at $4 or $5 per gallon. As for the Europeans who have rejected nuclear energy while providing no substitute for it (all of them but for the French ... and the Ukraine), they risk a sharp further increase in unemployment, already disastrously high in many regions of Europe.

To ignore the Dhahran warning on the grounds that the only useful remedy—a stiff oil tax—is a political impossibility, is an evasion of responsibility by all those who know the numbers, including many politicians not a few reporters, and absolutely every energy expert. What is or is not politically feasible is not fixed and frozen for all time. It depends on the climate of public opinion. If the public was warned of the dangers of its addiction to cheap oil as insistently as it is warned about the dangers of smoking cigarettes, it would accept high oil-import taxes to encourage other energy sources. That the present climate of opinion is of exactly contrary effect proves nothing at all. The last time there was any public debate about the insecurity of imported oil was more than fifteen years ago, when Iran's revolution cut supplies, driving up prices and causing widespread shortages. Since then, hardly any political or opinion leader has even tried to raise the subject, leaving the public bereft of information and guidance.

Nor is it true that this silence was amply justified by fifteen years of increasing supplies and falling prices. Had oil demand been dissuaded by a large enough tax, many more people would now be employed in conservation activities and in producing other forms of energy, while the West would be emancipated from the necessity of coddling a repulsive regime, and having to fear for its safety.

It is of course useless to speculate on the future of Saudi rule given the lack of the most basic political information. It might last a century, a year, or a week. What is important for the United States, as for other oil-importing countries, is to heed the warning of Dhahran. Once the added security measures have been implemented, once Iran's standing encouragement of Saudi terrorists is dissuaded by economic counter-threats, no time should be wasted before squarely confronting the altogether broader issue of energy security.

As for the tiny fragments of information that have come out from the great silence of Saudi Arabia, they are not reassuring. First, the attack showed some real tactical competence. It was not just a crude, self-triggered, suicide bomb that went off as in the Israeli bus bombings, nor was the bomb detonated at random into an available market crowd, as often happens in Algeria. The Dhahran terrorists chose a very high-value target indeed. As such, it was of course protected but they still found an effective way of attacking, even though the security perimeter *functioned exactly as it was supposed to function* (they could not drive the truck inside). The implication is that these terrorists, unlike Hamas or Algeria's GIA, are not confined to soft targets. They might next attack an important princely residence, a major oil facility, or—more likely—another concentration of U.S. citizens, civilian if not military.

Next, this is not one more instance of mindless terrorism, bereft of a coherent strategy. The weakest aspect of Saudi Arabia's supposedly super-Islamic regime, is of course its paradoxical dependence on the protection of the United States of America, the chief "Christian" power in Muslim eyes. The Dhahran bombing effectively dramatized that shameful dependence, while killing no "innocent Muslims." It is a far cry from the Hamas bombs-on-buses in Israel, which were actually counter-productive, weakening Hamas itself as well as the entire Palestinian movement.

Moreover, the capture of four men supposedly implicated in the November 1995 car-bomb attack in Riyadh and since executed, evidently did not lead to the penetration of the terrorists' network. In other words, they are sufficiently well-organized to be securely compartmented. Or, worse still, the two groups were unconnected to begin with, each being merely parallel expressions of a violent opposition movement of unknown dimensions, with an unknown number of further, self-motivated and self-sufficient terrorist teams.

Finally, press interviews with resident Westerners in the Dhahran area have revealed an upsurge of anti-Western feeling. Even shopkeepers who benefit by their custom have become overtly rude of late. Whether that behavior is spontaneous or coerced by peer pressures, the implication is that the terrorists have the priceless advantage of operating in a supportive atmosphere, as far as local opinion is concerned. How far these sentiments are shared by other Saudis elsewhere is again completely unknown.

To be sure, the eastern El Haza province where Dhahran is located is also the home of the country's Shi'i minority, presumably the most favorably disposed to Iran's brand of fundamentalism. That is often cited as a reassuring factor in itself, even though El Haza contains the country's most important oil facilities. The suggestion is that while the 160,000 Shi'is of El Haza might be disloyal, the millions of other Saudis are not. But when the Riyadh terrorists were captured it turned out that they were neither foreigners (as had been suggested) nor Shi'is from El Haza. They were perfectly orthodox Sunnis from unsuspected parts of the country—in fact three out of four came from the same north-central Nedj province that is the power base of the Saudi ruling family. That is where the tribes are supposedly most loyal, on that account being preferentially recruited for the National Guard which is kept as a counter-coup counterweight to the army. In other words, the reassuring factor is not reassuring at all. The true political situation in the all-important Nedj being itself quite unknown, it is hardly worth mentioning that the large western Hejaz province seized by the Saudis seventy years ago but still unabsorbed, is also said to be restive. The only truth is that in a closed society nobody can know the truth—for all we or anyone else can know, the spirit of revolt has spread across the entire country, waiting only for the spark that will trigger the massacre of the princes, the downfall of the regime, and a world-wide energy crisis.

But one thing we do know with absolute certainty. Current Western energy policies perpetuate an absurd and growing dependence on the oil of a single country ruled in a manner that virtually guarantees a violent upheaval some day. Must the crisis erupt with hyper-inflation and unemployment before anything is done?

11

Terrorism by Subcontractor

The great "millennium bug" scare will probably be one of the world's great non-events, but there is a genuine reason for the acute fear of U.S. intelligence that the new year might be inaugurated by spectacular bombings in several American cities. The first indication that Islamist terrorists had marked up the date in their calendars came from Jordan, where a ring of local extremists was rounded up earlier this month.

In Jordan as elsewhere, the larger community of Islamic fundamentalists includes both very large social and political groups that do not themselves engage in any form of terrorism while defending and funding it, and violent Islamists that do nothing else.

In Jordan as elsewhere, their targets are mostly local rather than foreign: women who defy their village version of Islamic norms, the rare intellectual who dares to examine Islam critically as Christians do every day, and—above all—governments that are insufficiently Islamic, as all of them except for Afghanistan's Taliban apparently are, including ultra-strict Saudi Arabia.

In Jordan as elsewhere, local security outfits try to keep track of what the Islamists are doing and saying —and one great problem is precisely that the two hardly correlate: agents and intercepts keep picking up word of a myriad of supposedly imminent attacks that never materialize, making it very hard to detect the real threats. Overheated young men with nothing much else to do talk a lot and do little –even with a multitude of Israeli targets within walking distance, the various Hamas groups in Jordan, Gaza, and the West Bank only pull off the occasional minor bombing or murder, never beginning to compete with Israel's road accidents when it comes to the total casualties they inflict.

Evidently there was some specifically persuasive talk that triggered the arrests in Jordan, very likely intercepted telephone or e-mail dialogues in which American targets were mentioned.

That is a very significant indicator because Jordan's Islamists have acted—if at all—against local and Israeli targets with no previous attacks against American ones. The implication was that a "general contractor" somewhere outside

75

Jordan, Osama Bin Laden or his equivalent, was seeking to enlist Jordanian activists to serve as his sub-contractors, so to speak. It followed logically that there would be other sub-contractors elsewhere, *in fact many of them* because Jordan's Islamists are quite low in the rankings as compared to the Shi'ite Hizballah of Lebanon and Paraguay, Pakistan's Taliban admirers, Egypt's Brotherhood offshoots, the Gaza-based Hamas, Iran's "official" terrorists operated by Pasdaran headquarters, and Algeria's Groupe Islamique Armée. At that point, the threat to *American* targets was already assessed as very serious, but it was still believed that this did *not* mean targets in the United States itself, and the State Department warning that went out in fact focused on the threat to Americans abroad.

As the leading "Christian" nation and the prime source of seductive Western culture, the United States is of course the great enemy of Islamists everywhere, quite aside from its Israel connection.

Yet there have been very few Islamist attacks in the United States, simply because it is far away for most of them, and its border controls are known to be quite strict for travelers arriving by air or sea. That the U.S.-Mexican border can be crossed easily in many places is well-known, but Mexico is a difficult and exotic country for Islamists, for its border controls are strict and—more important—it does not contain any welcoming community of Islamic immigrants of any size. Terrorists arriving into Mexico City would have to connect by themselves with the people-smugglers—and moreover, the standard operating procedures used to cross the U.S.-Mexican border illegally is to walk across—making it difficult to carry serious quantities of bomb-making materials. None of these obstacles apply to Canada, as the world now knows: there are several different Islamic immigrant communities that contain their activist circles at least inclined to be sympathetic to terrorists, while security controls are famously lax simply because "politically correct" Canadians do not differentiate between seventy-six-year-old Madame Dupont coming to visit her grandchildren and bearded young men from Islamic countries.

As soon as Ahmed Ressam was arrested at the Port Angeles ferry crossing in Washington State on December 14, the theory formulated after the arrests in Jordan was both confirmed and re-defined. Yes, a "general contractor" was trying to mount a concerted terrorist offensive on a very large scale by enlisting (and financing) allies world-wide but no, his targets were not merely American but *in* America. Further, it seemed likely that several different cities were targeted, because Ressam would not have planned to travel by air with his explosives, suggesting that Seattle was his assigned target. Next there was the arrest of Buabide Chamchi at Beecher Falls Vermont on December 19, by when it was known that Ressam had at least two other associates, who may or may not be in the United States already. All of these, however, originate from just one sub-contractor, the Montreal affiliates of Algeria's GIA, by far the most violent Islamist group worldwide these days, though—very significantly—it too has no prior record of attacking American targets. There is still no word of the others whose men might already be in the United States. At this point, the very visible intensification of border controls is being accompanied by much less public efforts by the FBI and local police to detect active Islamist terrorists within the immigrant communities in the United States itself; but lacking as they do the required cultural or language skills, their chances of finding the terrorists, if any, are small.

12

Iraq: How to Regain the Initiative

It has long been obvious that the number of U.S. and other coalition troops in Iraq is insufficient. Once headquarters and logistic support elements are deducted, the number left over to guard sensitive places, manning checkpoints, and conducting patrols is less than 60,000. It is enough to compare that number with the 37,000 of the New York City Police Department or the 29,000 of the London Metropolitan Police to recognize it as absurdly small, given the size and population of Iraq, the raiding culture of many of its inhabitants, the abundance of weapons and ammunition, and of course the increasing number of Sunni insurgents, violently hostile Shi'a, and imported Islamic militants.

One early result was to antagonize the population at large, which was left exposed to widespread armed robbery and worse, while public services from electricity to the water supply, as well as oil field installations, were devastated by pervasive looting. Later, the coalition forces themselves started to come under attack, while reconstruction was hampered by insecurity.

Things are much worse now. Iraqi oil exports cannot increase because of persistent sabotage and the looting of expensive new equipment for its scrap value. In spite of very high oil prices, revenues are used up by food and other current imports with nothing left over for reconstruction. The U.S. Congress was very generous in funding it, but persistent attacks against contractors of all nationalities have stopped almost every project: of the more than $4 billion allocated by the United States for water and sanitation works, only $16 million has been spent; of $786 million for public health, just $2 million has been spent; of $367 million for roads, a mere $ 7 million has been spent. Even those miserable sums—less than half a percent of the available funds—overstate the results achieved, because much of the money was spent for the bodyguards.

The failure of reconstruction is much less dramatic than the car bombs, shootings, ambushes and hostage-takings that dominate the headlines, but is even more important in undermining confidence in the interim Iraqi government of prime minister Ayad Allawi. That fragile coalition, of Kurds and Arabs, Sunni and Shi'a, returned exiles and those who never left, is dismissed by its enemies as the tool of the Christian invaders. But it might still have been popular if it could have brought prosperity and security, instead of persisting mass unemployment and increasingly deadly violence.

There are different estimates of how many troops would be needed to reach a tolerable level of security. Some hold that tripling the number of combat soldiers and military police to 180,000 or so would be enough. Others insist that many more would be needed, not less than 240,000 or so, as well as their attendant logistical support.

But with the U.S. Army, National Guard, and Marine Corps already badly over-stretched, as also the British Army, while allies such as Italy already contribute all they can, it hardly matters what troop level is held to be sufficient because no large increase could be achieved anyway. The Bush administration has cited the very magnitude of the real need in steadfastly refusing to increase the number of troops in Iraq, on the argument that any small increase would be useless anyway, while still adding to the strain on the Army and Marine Corps that are already suffering from excessively long tours of overseas duty. Its answer instead has been to accelerate the recruitment and training of the Iraqi police, border guard, and National Guard, Allawi's new name for the former Civil Defense. In the latest increase, another $ 1.8 billion dollars are to be spent to train and equip 45,000 more Iraqi police, 16,000 border guards and twenty more National Guard battalions. The money is to come from unspent reconstruction funds. Not much has been heard of the new Iraqi army that was to have some twenty-five battalions, after many in the first battalion deserted, while the second battalion flatly refused to fight when sent into action at Falluja in April.

It makes perfect sense to build up the Iraqi police and other security forces to repress crime, but they have conspicuously failed to be of any help in dealing with the Sunni insurgents that keep attacking U.S. forces, or the Mahdi militiamen of the Shi'i rabble rouser Moqtada Sadr that have attacked British, Italian, and other coalition troops. Instead, the police at best remain neutral when Iraqis of any description are attacking foreign troops. Sometimes they have joined in the attacks, or given their uniforms and vehicles to the attackers, sometimes allowing them to surprise coalition troops with deadly results. Iraqi police have even failed to pursue with any real energy the insurgents who have made the Iraqi police itself their prime target, with frequent and deadly car-bombings and assaults on police stations. That is inevitable: Iraqi policemen and their families live among the population at large, at the mercy of the very insurgents and militiamen they are supposed to control. Nothing much can be expected from them.

So what can be done? With very few troops and no prospect of any more, with the growth of new Iraqi security forces almost irrelevant, there is only one remedy. The present rushing about from one town to the other, to fight first one lot of insurgents and then another, must come to an end. In each of these cases, casualties are taken as well as inflicted, the local population at large also suffers deaths and destruction, and then the troops leave and the insurgents regain control—if they ever really lost it. Nothing enduring is achieved, except to increase the already intense Iraqi hatred of foreigners and all their works.

Instead, the available troops should be stationed where they can do the most good, and kept there. That means mostly in central Baghdad, in over-watch positions along the major highways, and in the oil fields of course, essential to provide revenues for the interim Iraqi government. To abandon much of Iraq may seem cruel, but at present, in the attempt to protect all with grossly inadequate means, no place is now adequately protected. Doctors do the same when overwhelmed with casualties: to save those who can survive, others must be left to their fate. Politically, moreover, a calculated disengagement is the only way of imposing responsibility upon the clerics, tribal chiefs and notables who pass their days in criticizing the occupation and the new Iraqi interim government over endless cups of coffee, while doing nothing whatever to maintain law and order, or improve local circumstances in any other way.

From a military point of view, a garrison policy would not only avoid the troop casualties and collateral damage to civilians of hit-and-run operations, but would also gain a much bigger advantage. Once each unit remains in one place on a sustained basis, its soldiers will be able to spot the elusive enemy in the only possible way: by acquiring an intuitive understanding their immediate environment. At present, with all their rushing about, soldiers and junior leaders cannot observe local patterns of movement, habits and manners for long enough to spot what is out of place, to detect the differences that presage an imminent attack and give away insurgents exposing them to capture or destruction. Only prolonged observation of normal, every day life will reveal the meaning of the premature shattering down of shops normally open, of hurried movements by the normally leisurely, of the taxi parked where none was seen before, even of people wearing a slightly different pattern of clothing, or moving about as locals would not. When detected in good time, insurgents are easily defeated—and it has now become urgent to achieve tactical victories, to break the spiral of successful attacks that attract more volunteers for the insurgency, and further undermine the prospects of a democratic Iraq.

13

Iraq: The Logic of Disengagement

Withdraw Now

Given all that has happened in Iraq to date, the best strategy for the United States is disengagement. This would call for the careful planning and scheduling of the withdrawal of U.S. forces from much of the country—while making due provisions for sharp punitive strikes against any attempt to harass the withdrawing forces. But it would primarily require an intense diplomatic effort, to prepare and conduct parallel negotiations with several parties inside Iraq and out. All have much to lose or gain depending on exactly how the U.S. withdrawal is carried out, and this would give Washington a great deal of leverage that could be used to advance U.S. interests.

The United States cannot threaten to unleash anarchy in Iraq in order to obtain concessions from others, nor can it make transparently conflicting promises about the country's future to different parties. But once it has declared its firm commitment to withdraw—or perhaps, given the widespread conviction that the United States entered Iraq to exploit its resources, once visible physical preparations for an evacuation have begun—the calculus of other parties will change. In a reversal of the usual sequence, the U.S. hand will be strengthened by withdrawal, and Washington may well be able to lay the groundwork for a reasonably stable Iraq. Nevertheless, if key Iraqi factions or Iraq's neighbors are too shortsighted or blinded by resentment to cooperate in their own best interests, the withdrawal should still proceed, with the United States making such favorable or unfavorable arrangements for each party as will most enhance the future credibility of U.S. diplomacy.

The United States has now abridged its vastly ambitious project of creating a veritable Iraqi democracy to pursue the much more realistic aim of conducting some sort of general election. In the meantime, however, it has persisted in futile combat against factions that should be confronting one another instead. A strategy of disengagement would require bold, risk-taking statecraft of a high order, and much diplomatic competence in its execution. But it would be soundly based on the most fundamental of realities: geography that alone ensures all other parties are far more exposed to the dangers of an anarchical Iraq than is the United States itself.

Spain, Naples, and Iraq

If Iraq could indeed be transformed into a successful democracy by a more prolonged occupation, as Germany and Japan were after 1945, then of course any disengagement would be a great mistake. In both of those countries, however, by the time U.S. occupation forces arrived the local populations were already thoroughly disenthralled from violent ideologies, and so they eagerly collaborated with their occupiers to construct democratic institutions. Unfortunately, because of the hostile sentiments of the Iraqi population, the relevant precedents for Iraq are far different.

The very word "guerrilla" acquired its present meaning from the ferocious insurgency of the illiterate Spanish poor against their would-be liberators under the leadership of their traditional oppressors. On July 6, 1808, King Joseph of Spain presented a draft constitution that for the first time in Spain's history offered an independent judiciary, freedom of the press, and the abolition of the remaining feudal privileges of the aristocracy and the church. Ecclesiastical overlords still owned 3,148 towns and villages, which were inhabited by some of Europe's most wretched tenants. Yet the Spanish peasantry did not rise to demand the immediate implementation of the new constitution. Instead, they obeyed the priests, who summoned them to fight against the ungodly innovations of the foreign invader—for Joseph was the brother of Napoleon Bonaparte and had been placed on the Spanish throne by French troops a month earlier. That was all that mattered for most Spaniards—not what was proposed, but who proposed it.

By then the French should have known better. In 1799 the same thing had happened in Naples, whose liberals, supported by the French, were massacred by the very peasants and plebeians they wanted to emancipate, mustered into a militia of the "Holy Faith" by Cardinal Fabrizio Ruffo (the scion, coincidentally, of Calabria's most powerful landowning family). Ruffo easily persuaded his followers that all promises of merely material betterment were irrelevant, because the real aim of the French and the liberals was to destroy the Catholic religion in the service of Satan. Spain's clergy repeated Ruffo's ploy, and their illiterate followers could not know that the very first clause of Joseph's draft constitution had declared the Roman Apostolic Catholic church the only one allowed in Spain.

The same dynamic is playing itself out in Iraq now, down to the ineffectual enshrinement of Islam in the draft constitution and the emergence of truculent clerical warlords. Since the U.S. invasion in 2003, both Shiite and Sunni clerics have been repeating over and over again that the Americans and their mostly "Christian" allies are in Iraq to destroy Islam in its cultural heartland, as well as to steal the country's oil. The clerics dismiss all talk of democracy and human rights by the invaders as mere hypocrisy—except for women's rights, which are promoted in earnest, the clerics say, to induce Iraqi daughters and wives to dishonor their families by aping the shameless disobedience of Western women.

The vast majority of Iraqis, assiduous mosque-goers and semi-literate at best, naturally believe their religious leaders. The alternative would be to believe what for them is entirely incomprehensible: that foreigners have been unselfishly expending their own blood and treasure to help them. As opinion polls and countless incidents demonstrate, Americans and their allies are widely hated as the worst of invaders, out to rob Muslim Iraqis not only of their territory and oil, but also of their religion and family honor.

The most direct and visible effects of these sentiments are the deadly attacks against the occupiers and their Iraqi auxiliaries, the aiding and abetting of such attacks, and their gleeful celebration by impromptu crowds of spectators. When the victims are members of the Iraqi police or National Guard, as is often the case these days, bystanders, family members, and local clerics routinely accuse the Americans of being the attackers—usually by missile strikes that cleverly simulate car bombs. As to why the Americans would want to kill Iraqis whom they are themselves recruiting, training, and paying, no explanation is offered, because no obligation is felt to unravel each and every subplot of the dark Christian conspiracy against Iraq, the Arab world, and Islam.

It is the indirect effects of the insurgency, though, that have ended whatever hopes of genuine democratization may still linger. The mass instruction of Germans and Japanese about the norms and modes of democratic governance, already much facilitated by pre-existing if imperfect democratic institutions, was advanced by mass media of all kinds as well as by countless educational efforts. The work was done by local teachers, preachers, journalists, and publicists who adopted as their own the democratic values proclaimed by the occupiers. But the locals were recruited, instructed, motivated, and guided by occupation political officers, whose own cultural understanding was enhanced by much communing with ordinary Germans and Japanese. In Iraq, by contrast, none of this has occurred. An already difficult task has been made altogether impossible by the refusal of Iraqi teachers, journalists, and publicists—let alone preachers—to be instructed and to instruct others in democratic ways. In any case, unlike Germany or Japan after 1945, Iraq after 2003 never became secure enough for occupation personnel to operate effectively, let alone to carry out mass political education in every city and town, as was done in Germany and Japan.

No Democrats, No Democracy

Of course, many Iraqis would deny the need for any such instruction, viewing democracy as a simple affair that any child can understand. That is certainly the opinion of the spokesmen of Grand Ayatollah Ali Sistani, for example. They have insistently advocated early elections in Iraq, brushing aside the need for procedural and substantive preparations as basic as the compilation of voter rolls, and seeing no need to allow time for the gathering of consensus by structured political parties. However moderate he may be, the pronouncements attributed to Sistani reveal a confusion between democracy and the dictatorial rule of the majority, for they imply that whoever wins 50.01 percent of the vote should have all of the governing power. That much became clear when Sistani's spokesmen vehemently rejected Kurdish demands for constitutional guarantees of minority rights. Shiite majority rule could thus end up being as undemocratic as the traditional Sunni-Arab ascendancy was.

The plain fact is that there are not enough aspiring democrats in Iraq to sustain democratic institutions. The Shiite majority includes cosmopolitan figures, but by far its greater part has expressed in every possible way a strong preference for clerical leadership. The clerics, in turn, reject any elected assembly that would be free to legislate without their supervision—and could thus legalize, for example, the drinking of alcohol or the freedom to change one's religion. The Sunni-Arab minority, for its part, has dominated Iraq from the time it was formed into a state, and its leaders have consistently rejected democracy in principle because they refuse to accept a subordinate status. As for the Kurds, they have administered their separate de facto autonomies with considerable success, but it is significant that they have not even attempted to hold elections for themselves, preferring clan and tribal loyalties to the individualism of representative democracy.

Accordingly, although elections of some kind can still be held on schedule, they are unlikely to be followed by the emergence of a functioning representative assembly, let alone an effective cohesive government of democratic temper. It follows that the United States has been depleting its military strength, diplomatic leverage, and treasure to pursue a worthy but unrealistic aim.

Yet Iraq cannot simply be evacuated, its fledgling government abandoned to face emboldened Baath loyalists and Sunni-Arab revanchists with their many armed groups, local and foreign Islamists with their terrorist skills, and whatever Shiite militias are left out of the government. In such a contest, the government, with its newly raised security forces of doubtful loyalty, is unlikely to prevail. Nor are the victors likely to divide the country peacefully among themselves; civil war of one kind or another would almost certainly follow. An anarchical Iraq would both threaten the stability of neighboring countries and offer opportunities for their interference—which might even escalate to the point of outright invasions by Iran, or Turkey, or both, initiating new cycles of resistance, repression, and violence.

How to Avoid a Rout

The probable consequences of abandoning Iraq are so bleak, in fact, that few are willing to contemplate them. That is a mistake. It is precisely because unpredictable mayhem is so predictable that the United States might be able to disengage from Iraq at little cost, or perhaps even advantageously.

To see how disengagement from Iraq might be achieved with few adverse effects or even turned into something of a success, it is useful to approach its undoubted complications by first considering the much simpler case of a plain military retreat. A retreat is notoriously the most difficult of military operations to pull off successfully. At worst, it can degenerate into a disastrous rout. But a well-calculated retreat not only can extricate a force from a difficult situation, but in doing so can actually turn the tide of battle by luring the enemy beyond the limits of its strength until it is overstretched, unbalanced, and ripe for defeat. In Iraq, the United States faces no single enemy army it can exhaust in this way, but rather a number of different enemies whose mutual hostility now lies dormant but could be catalyzed by a well-crafted disengagement.

Because Iraq is under foreign occupation, Islamic, nationalist, and pan-Arab sentiments currently prevail over denominational identities, inducing Sunni and Shiite Arabs to unite against the invaders. So long as Iraqis of all kinds believe that the United States has no intention of withdrawing, they can attack American forces to express their nationalism or Islamism without calculating the consequences for themselves of a post-American Iraq. That is why Muqtada al-Sadr's Shiite militia felt free to attack the U.S. troops that elsewhere were fighting Sunnis bent on restoring their ancestral supremacy, and why its actions were applauded by the clerics and the Shiite population at large. Yet if faced with the prospect of an imminent U.S. withdrawal, Shiite clerics and their followers would have to confront the equally imminent threat of the Baath loyalist and Sunni fighters—the only Iraqis with recent combat experience, and the least likely to accept Shiite clerical rule.

That is why by moving to withdraw the United States could secure what the occupation has never had: the active support of its greatest beneficiaries, the Shiites. What Washington needs from them is a total cessation of violence against the coalition throughout Iraq, full cooperation with the interim government in the conduct of elections, and the suspension of all forms of support for other resisters. Given that there is already some acquiescence and even cooperation, this would not require a full reversal in Shiite attitudes.

With Friends Like These

Iran, for its part, has much to fear from anarchy in Iraq, which would present it with more dangers than opportunities. At present, because the Iranians think the United States is determined to remain in Iraq no matter what, the hard-liners in Iran's government feel free to pursue their anti-American vendetta by political subversion, by arming and training al-Sadr's militia, and by encouraging the Syrians to favor the infiltration of Islamist terrorists into Iraq.

Anarchy in Iraq would threaten not merely Iran's stability, but also its territorial integrity. Minorities account for more than half the population, yet the government of Iran is not pluralist at all. It functions as an exclusively Persian empire that suppresses all other ethnic identities and imposes the exclusive use of Farsi in public education, thus condemning all others to illiteracy in their mother tongues. Moreover, not only the Baha'i but also more combative heterodox Muslims are now persecuted. Except for some Kurds and Azeris, no minority is actively rebellious as yet, but chaos in Iraq could energize communal loyalties in Iran (especially among the Kurds and the Arabs). An anarchical Iraq would offer bases for Iranian dissidents and exiles, at a time when the theocratic regime is certainly weaker than it once was: its political support has measurably waned, its revolutionary and religious authority is now a distant memory, and its continued hold on power depends increasingly on naked force—and the regime knows it.

Once the United States commits to a disengagement from Iraq, therefore, a suitably discreet dialogue with Iranian rulers should be quite productive. Washington would not need to demand much from the Iranians: only the end of subversion, arms trafficking, hostile propaganda, and Hezbollah infiltration in Iraq. Ever since the 1979 revolution, the United States has often wished for restraint from the theocratic rulers of Iran but has generally lacked the means to obtain it. Even the simultaneous presence of U.S. combat forces on both the eastern and western frontiers of Iran has had little impact on the actual conduct of the regime, which usually diverges from its more moderate declared policies. But what the entry of troops could not achieve, a withdrawal might, for it would expose the inherent vulnerability to dissidents of an increasingly isolated regime.

As an ally of long standing, Turkey is in a wholly different category. After hindering the initial invasion of Iraq, it has helped the occupation in important ways—but it has still done less than it might have done. The reason is that Turkish policy has focused to an inordinate extent on the enhancement of Iraq's Turkmen minority, driven not by a dubious ethnic solidarity (they are Azeris, not Turks) but by a desire to weaken the Iraqi Kurds. The Iraqi Turkmen are concentrated in and around the city of Kirkuk, possession of which secures control of a good part of Iraq's oil-production capacity. By providing military aid to the Turkmen, the Turkish government is therefore assisting the anti-Kurdish coalition in Kirkuk, which includes Sunnis actively fighting Americans. This amounts to indirect action against the United States. There is no valid justification for such activities, which have increased communal violence and facilitated the sabotage of oil installations.

Like others, the Turkish government must have calculated that with the United States committed to the occupation, the added burden placed on Iraq's stability by their support of the Turkmen would make no difference. With disengagement, however, a negotiation could and should begin to see what favors might be exchanged between Ankara and Washington—in order to ensure that the U.S. withdrawal benefits Turkish interests while Turks stop making trouble in Iraqi Kurdistan.

Even Kuwait, whose very existence depends on American military power, now does very little to help the occupation and the interim Iraqi government. The Kuwaiti Red Crescent Society has sent the odd truckload of food into Iraq, and a gift of some $60 million has been announced, though not necessarily delivered. Given Kuwait's exceptionally high oil revenues, however, not to mention the large revenues of Kuwaiti subcontractors working under Pentagon logistics contracts, this is less than paltry. The serious amounts of aid that Kuwait could well afford would allow the interim government to extend its authority and help the postelection government to resolve differences and withstand the attacks destined to come against it. In procuring such aid, it would not take much reminding that if the United States cannot effect a satisfactory disengagement, the Kuwaitis will be more than 10,000 miles closer to the ensuing anarchy than the Americans themselves.

As for the Saudi regime, its relentlessly ambiguous attitude is exemplified by its July 2003 offer of a contingent of "Islamic" troops to help garrison Iraq. Made with much fanfare, the offer sounded both generous and courageous. Then it turned out that the troops in question were not to be Saudi at all—in other words, the Saudis were promising to send the troops of other, unspecified Muslim countries—and these imaginary troops were to be sent on condition that an equal number of U.S. troops be withdrawn.

In the realm of action rather than empty words, the Saudis have not actually tried to worsen U.S. difficulties in Iraq, but they have not been especially helpful, either. As with Kuwait, their exploding oil revenues could underwrite substantial gifts to the Iraqi government, both before and after the elections. But Riyadh could do even more. All evidence indicates that Saudi volunteers have been infiltrating into Iraq in greater numbers than any other nationality. They join the other Islamists whose attacks kill many Iraqis and some Americans. Saudi Arabia and Iraq share a border along which there are few and rather languid patrols, rare control posts, and no aerial surveillance, even though it could be readily provided. And the Saudis could try harder to limit the flow of money from Saudi jihad enthusiasts and do more to discourage the religious decrees that sanction the killing of Americans in Iraq.

As it is, the Saudi authorities are doing none of this. Yet an anarchical Iraq would endanger the Saudi regime's already fragile security, not least by providing their opponents all the bases they need and offering Iran a tempting playground for expansion. Here too, therefore, hard-headed negotiations about the modalities of a U.S. withdrawal would seem to hold out possibilities for significant improvements.

The Syrian regime, finally, could also be engaged in a dialogue, one in which the United States presents two scenarios. The first is a well-prepared disengagement conducted with much support from inside and outside Iraq that leaves it with a functioning government. The second is the same thing accompanied by punitive action against Syria if it attempts to sabotage that outcome—much easier to do once U.S. forces are no longer tied down in Iraq. For all its anti-American bluster, the Syrian regime is unlikely to risk confrontation, especially when so little is asked of it: a closure of the Syria-Iraq border to extremists and the end of Hezbollah activities in Iraq (funded by Iran but authorized by Syria).

Of all Iraq's neighbors, only Jordan has been straightforwardly cooperative, incidentally without compromising any of its own sovereign interests.

The Ultimate Logic of Disengagement

Even if the negotiations here advocated fail to yield all they might—indeed, even if they do not yield much at all—the disengagement should still occur, and not only to live up to the initial commitment to withdraw. Given the bitter Muslim hostility to the presence of U.S. troops—labeled "Christian Crusaders" by the preachers—their continued deployment in large numbers can only undermine the legitimacy of any U.S.-supported Iraqi government. With Iraq more like Spain in 1808 than like Germany or Japan after 1945, any democracy it sustains is bound to be more veneer than substance. Its chances of survival will be much higher if pan-Arab nationalists, Islamists, and foreign meddlers are neutralized by diplomacy and disengagement. Leaving behind a major garrison would only evoke continuing hostility to both Americans and Iraqi democrats. Once U.S. soldiers have left Iraqi cities, towns, and villages, some could remain a while in remote desert bases to fight off full-scale military attacks against the government—but even this could incite opposition, as happened in Saudi Arabia.

A strategy of disengagement would require much skill in conducting parallel negotiations. But its risks are actually lower than the alternative of an indefinite occupation, and its benefits might surprise us. An anarchical Iraq is a far greater danger to those in or near it than to the United States. It is time to collect on the difference.

14

Who is the Enemy?

Had the September 11 attacks marked the beginning of a veritable if unconventional war, as some immediately declared and some still say, the nature of the struggle, and certainly the identity of the enemy should have emerged with some clarity from the ensuing actions and reactions. As it is, what happened on September 11 remains a unique, receding catastrophe. It is far from clear if the struggle is millennial or ephemeral, central or peripheral, and there is a conspicuous reluctance even to name the enemy. We are all so keenly aware of the mechanisms of prejudice that we instinctively recoil from naming the nationality of individual criminals, and even more their religion, for to do so inevitably implicates the national or religious multitudes in the guilt of just one, or a few, or in this case nineteen hijackers out of two hundred million Arabs, and much more than a billion Muslims. But to ignore the ethnic and religious identity of the nineteen as if they were, say, bank robbers whose common ethnicity and religion were merely coincidental, is disingenuous, and if done in earnest would preclude coherent precautions against further attacks.

That is exactly true of the cumbersome airport security arrangements now in effect in the United States, which must specifically abjure any hint of "ethnic profiling" at the insistent direction of the Secretary of Transportation Norman Mineta, who describes himself in his own official web-site as "one of the 120,000 Japanese-Americans sent to internment camps after Pearl Harbor." Mineta likes to remind everyone that the only post-September 11 attempt to attack a U.S. airliner was perpetrated by an eccentric British-West Indian convert to Islam, not by an Arab-looking man with a Muslim name. Thus, passengers traveling out of Washington's Dulles international airport as late as August 2002 were greatly inconvenienced, but not seriously scrutinized. The overburdened airline staff and minimum-wage security employees, many of them Pakistani immigrants, and some sporting fundamentalists' beards, seemed to be selecting a great many grandmothers for second searches, then solemnly breaking off the tiny blades of their nail clippers. They studiously fail to pay any special attention to anyone who looked like an Arab or Muslim, especially if a bearded young man named

Muhammad—for that happens to be Mineta's specific example of forbidden "ethnic profiling." Under his guidelines, and in justifiable dread of costly anti-discrimination law suits (*agent provocateur* entrapments are admissible in the courts), airline staff instead select passengers for extra scrutiny on the basis of strictly objective criteria other than race, nationality or religion, such as travel on a one-way ticket, or the purchase of any ticket with cash. Both, as it happens, are characteristic of traveling grandmothers, while the September 11 hijackers boarded with far more common two-way tickets purchased with credit cards.

So who is the enemy? It cannot be terrorism as such for it is merely a generic tactic, against which generic precautions may be useful, but which offers no substantive targets that can be engaged in war. The same is true of terrorists, suitable condemnation for all who deliberately attack civilians at large, but not a defined group against which a battle can be fought, let alone a war. The virtually official "war on terror" is therefore nothing but obfuscation, a deliberate elision of the simple truth that the September 11 hijackers were Arab Muslims motivated by hugely amplified renditions of common Arab and Muslim resentments, some very new but others dating back centuries. Osama bin Laden's first and most complete video-taped version started with the loss of Moorish Spain and ended with the continuing desecration of the Arabian Peninsula by armed Christians ever since 1990, with many other resentments listed in between. Receiving mentions were the abolition of the Caliphate in 1924 by the apostate and imaginary pseudo-Jew Kemal Atatürk, the loss of part of Kashmir in 1947, the loss of part of British Palestine to the Jews in 1948, the loss of more of Palestine in 1967, and further losses in Bosnia, Chechnya, Xinjiang ("East Turkestan") and elsewhere. To all this, bin Laden added an even greater resentment: the humiliating subjection of nominally independent Muslim rulers to the materialistic power of the Christians. Finally, there was the original resentment, at the loss of Islamic purity in the lands of impudently lax Muslim rulers, who sanction fornication or its tantamount: the brazen display of female hair and unveiled faces by women allowed to leave their homes unescorted, to work and play alongside unrelated men in unsupervised proximity, to boldly drive automobiles, and in some places even to display their near nudity in bathing suits on public beaches, while the hypocritical Muslim rulers of Saudi Arabia and such who at least forbid those outrages, themselves secretly indulge in forbidden sex and the drinking of alcohol.

Since September 11, Western, Arab and Iranian specialists have educated us with remarkable unanimity in the sources of these vehement beliefs, for as usual mass murderers distill their hatreds at one remove or several from impuissant scribblers and ranters, in this case chiefly the minor Egyptian poet, dismissed educator, unsuccessful journalist, ignored literary critic, spurned lover, and prolific author Sayyid Qutb, who was executed by Nasser's government in 1966 in its repression of the Muslim Brotherhood, whose central thesis was that only violence could restore Muslim purity and Arab honor both defiled by materialistic Western powers (his writings are admirably summarized by Adnan Musallam in his *Sayyd Qutb: The Emergence of the Islamicist 1939-1950*, published by the Palestinian Academic Society for the Study of International Affairs); and Muhammad bin 'Abd al-Wahhab of the Nejd in northeast Arabia, the eighteenth-century founder of a puritanical and rigidly intolerant version of the strictest Hanbali school of Islam that bears his name as a reproach (it is to dub them as a sect that their enemies call them Wahhabis). That is the creed that the Saudi ruling family—long allied with the United States and loyal customer of British artisans in the luxury trades—has been propagating first with the sword in their conquered lands of Arabia where no religion but Islam may be practiced, and then after the explosion of oil revenues, with their characteristic gleaming white Mosques and well-appointed schools, in such places as Afghanistan, Pakistan, Indonesia, Central Asia, Chechnya, Sudan, Bosnia, Kosovo, and Macedonia—all not coincidentally scenes of bloody religious strife—as well as in most other places with Muslim populations, including both the United Kingdom and the United States, where children are indoctrinated in the Wahhabi prohibition of any amity with Christians or Jews just across the Potomac from the White House, in the Saudi Islamic Academy of Alexandria, Virginia, sponsored by Bandar bin Sultan, long-serving Saudi ambassador in Washington, generous host and provider to its elite and convivial guest at the home of Bush *père* and, if only for show, at the ranch of his son. The fateful encounter between Sayyd Qutb's ideal of youngsters "fighting for the cause of Allah by killing and by getting killed" and Muhammad bin 'Abd al-Wahhab's rejection of any tolerance for milder Muslims and all non-Muslims did not occur by chance but by government policy, for when the Saudis established schools and universities with their oil revenues, they imported mostly Egyptians to teach in them, and it was not the urbane and reasonably sensual or successful who were attracted to the puritanical boredom of Arabia, but rather failures in desperate need of employment, and many followers of Qutb who had himself praised the Saudis for whipping "poets who flirt with love poetry" in contrast to Egypt where "they applaud those who guide boys and girls toward immorality, and train them in shamelessness." With much of the curriculum devoted to Wahhabi indoctrination even in officially secular universities not to speak of Islamic ones, and with Qutb's disciples often teaching history, political science and other subjects, the resulting synthesis could hardly be a liberal education. It was not by accident, as *Pravda* would have had it in the old days, that fifteen of the nineteen hijackers were Saudis with some university education.

The same specialists have also taught us that in spite of their Islamic garb and antecedents, the violent doctrines of the Islamists are essentially political in nature, for it is not spiritual solace but power on earth that they all want, from Egypt's Muslim Brotherhood founded in 1929, to today's Al Qaida, other holy warriors ("Jihadists") everywhere. And not in spite of but precisely because of the evident fact that these doctrines constitute an anti-modernist ideology, they are as quintessentially modern as Fascism, Nazism, and Leninism, from all of which the Islamists have certainly derived operating principles if only unconsciously—though not in the case of the founder of the Muslim Brotherhood, Hasan al-Banna, who was an admirer of Mussolini, and emulated his *camicie nere* militia to stomp opponents before preferring to recruit assassins in mufti. But anti-modern political modernists though they are, today's Islamists or rather the Sunni ones, remain tributaries to the antique religious doctrines of Muhammad ibn 'Abd al-Wahhab: they serve the essential purpose of legitimizing their murders by denying any right to exist to Christians, Jews, and Zoroastrians, all unequivocally inferior but all allowed their lives and their ways of worship as "peoples of the book" under the laws of mainstream Islam, both Sunni and Shi'i, which impose death or conversion only on pagans, such as the animists of southern Sudan even now. Wahhabis reject this abject mildness, should kill all who resist conversion, including Shi'is (that is why the Islamist but Shi'i Hizballah of Lebanon, Iran and Paraguay must beg to differ) and most reluctantly tolerate infidel oil engineers, other skilled or unskilled servants and American troops on their soil only as an unavoidable compromise, to which they refuse to add the sin of allowing them their ways of worship. Because orthodox mainstream Muslims are no more allowed to kill innocent Christians, Jews or Zoroastrians than fellow Muslims, without the heterodox sanction of Wahhabism, the modern Islamists of Al Qaeda could not have proclaimed their global war against Christians and Jews as such, even non-imperialist Christians and non-Zionist Jews, under which they have perpetrated their one and only certified post-September 11 operation, the suicide truck bombing of the ancient synagogue on the island of Djerba, home to the last remaining, utterly inoffensive and inherently non-Zionist Jewish community in an Arab state.

The specialists have therefore exposed for us a very widespread misconception, for it is not the religious medievalism of countless media commentaries that we face, but yet another political perversion of modernity. Even without the specialists' detailed understanding of the chains of thematic or textual transmission, it is obvious enough that the e-mail reliant, technology-fixated, world-traveling engineers who commanded from afar or personally lead the September 11 attacks, as also most other Jihadist leaders around the world, are both subjectively religious in extreme degree and substantially secular in their aspirations. It is military or quasi-military strength and political power that they crave above all, and while the rules of personal conduct they seek to impose on women are meant to replicate their nostalgic fantasies of mores in seventh century Arabia in the time of the Muhammad, that only shows that the Islamists are contemporary even in their sexual obsessions, equally manifest in the febrile rutting of Sayd Qutb's denunciations of naked women, as he called bathers, on Alexandria's beaches in the years of *Justine, Balthazar, Mountolive,* and *Clea,* as in the extreme misogyny of the Taliban, who were forever inventing new restrictions to curb the irresistible seductive power of any woman over any man in any situation. Nor it is irrelevant that the September 11 attackers were extremely prudish or virgins presumptive by all accounts—early reports that sensationally held otherwise have turned out to be fabrications—or that Hamas announced its emergence in the Gaza strip in the early 1970s by killing dozens of women and young girls accused of prostitution or merely loose living, before even attempting to attack Israeli occupiers, while its current indoctrination of suicide-bombing candidates strongly emphasizes the sexual joys of an after-life serviced by black-eyed beauties galore.

Yet when the essentially modern, sexually obsessed, doctrinally heterodox and utterly politicized Islamists of Al Qaeda executed their September 11 attacks, they appear to have attracted at least the instantaneous, and then very often wildly enthusiastic approval of many if not most Muslim Arabs who are none of the above, and of many other Muslims around the world who are not Islamists by any means. In Tunisia, the mildest and most Mediterranean of Arab countries, the Western joint venture partners and investors in a newly revived French colonial winery (!) who happened to be visiting on September 11, witnessed and later reported the riotous joy of their Tunisian co-owners, executives, trainee oenologists and laborers at the televised scenes of catastrophe and carnage in New York and Washington—and that in a winery dedicated to the production of forbidden drink. Overall, the evidence of immediate approval—reservations came later for some at least—is overwhelming, and of the widest scope geographically and socially. Evidently the deed resonated with, and at least briefly assuaged, deeply-felt Muslim grievances.

Their burden and sum is that history itself has been deformed by evil conspiracies that are retarding God's own promise of Islam's planetary supremacy, allowing all-powerful Christians and even a handful of Jews as well as Hindus to rampage in Muslim lands, where they should all instead be content to live meekly in the prescribed state of conditional toleration. Each separate grievance derives from a violation of Islam or an injustice perpetrated against Muslims—in Kashmir, Palestine, Chinese Sinjiang and more—which results from an imposition of superior material strength on weaker Muslims. But contrary to an infinity of moralistic complaints cynically aimed at specifically Christian sensibilities, it is not the injustices as such (they after all could be moderated or ended) but rather the imposition of strength in itself that is excruciatingly painful, for others are simply not supposed to have the power to impose their will on Muslims, to whom God himself vouchsafed superior strength as compelling proof of the superiority of their creed over its Jewish and Christian predecessors. Many others also condemn the present world order as unjust in many different ways, but the injustice that propelled the lethal resentment of September 11, and generated such widespread satisfaction in massacre and mayhem, was that Muslim states and the ideal community of all Muslims are much less powerful than they ought to be.

That is not a grievance that can possibly be remedied by the secular powers subsumed in the "Christians and Jews" aforementioned, a.k.a., the "the

British, the French, the Dutch (!), and now the Americans" of Sayyid Qutb's 1946 complaint to which the Hindus and of course the Israelis should now be added. For the weak to appeal to the strong for succor is common enough in these times of United Nations interventionism, for the poor to beg or even demand transfers of wealth from the rich is an everyday occurrence, sometimes on the largest scale in world gatherings, global summits and such. But for the politically, economically, educationally and technologically weak to demand a transfer of power itself from the powerful, on the grounds that God himself so prefers it, cannot possibly evoke a positive response, or indeed any response, let alone remedies, or even the most partial of solutions.

So perhaps obfuscation has it all over accuracy, and we must soldier on in the struggle against a tactic and an adjective. Obfuscation as to the nature of the enemy certainly made it so much easier for Muslim countries to acquiesce in or even actively collaborate in the campaign of Afghanistan, where the power of the Taliban to shelter America's enemies was so swiftly and elegantly demolished by a few on the ground and not many bombardments, notwithstanding the high mountain terrain, the imminent snows, the inhibiting Ramadan season, and reputedly fanatical powers of resistance that were supposed to defeat American hopes of victory as surely as the Soviet once had been, according to many commentators of many kinds.

Obfuscation has also made it easier for the police forces and security agencies of Muslim states to collaborate in the detection and arrest of Al Qaeda activists and supporters, even to a slight and grudging extent in the case of Saudi Arabia, and far more in earnest, in Malaysia, Egypt, Algeria, Tunisia even Libya and eventually Pakistan on the largest scale. These efforts added their important contribution to the very energetic police sweeps that immediately after September 11 rolled up Islamist cells established over many years in the United States, Western Europe and elsewhere, which had long been allowed to operate unmolested in spite of mounting suspicions. As a result, active networks were uncovered and imminent attacks were perhaps prevented in places as diverse as Rome, Singapore and Paraguay's Ciudad del Este.

Alongside even more *sub rosa* Intelligence cooperation, that was the below-stairs counterpart of the post September 11 diplomatic and strategic coalition that the supposedly cowboy-unilateralist Bush Administration swiftly formed with the Russian Federation, the People's Republic of China and India as well as the NATO allies, Japan and many other countries, thus incidentally greatly outnumbering the world's sum of Muslims very numerous as they are—a comparison that was of course quite irrelevant in a war fought against terror with many Muslim states as allies. It was in that context and with that help that the Afghanistan war was fought, with Russian air traffic controllers smoothly directing US military flights over Federation territories, which landed at former Soviet bases in ex-Soviet Uzbekistan, and in Kirgizia in close proximity to an unprotesting and unalarmed China—a war fought with the active combat of troops from as far afield as Australia, some of which such as the Germans had not fired a warlike shot since 1945, or, such as the Norwegians, had never previously fought at all as uniformed soldiers.

Of course the enthusiasm of participation cooled when it came to the long-term security of Afghanistan that most insecure of countries, while the powerful, even brutal, first police reactions were soon moderated or merely dulled by constitutional norms, specific legal rules, police inhibitions in fear of accusations of discriminatory misconduct, and even tacit political calculations in the French case, as well as to a degree the embarrassed apprehension of the post-religious in contending with any manifestation of religiosity however outlandish and suspect. Its most evident result in both much of Europe and the United States is the almost absolute and utterly unrequited tolerance of local Muslim clerics who justify and commend and invite violence in the name of Islam, thereby implicitly favoring the recruitment of their congregants by actively extremist groups. It would be nice to think that Muslim ranters are left unmolested because of deep-held principles but one fears that moral laziness may be the truer explanation, while in countries such as France and Germany where incitement is a crime, the simple refusal of police forces to enforce the law reflects a failure of political will in contending with millions of Muslim citizens in need of educational and cultural as well as economic advancement. Matters are indeed arranged better in the United States, in whose individualizing sink or swim economy fanaticism is soon domesticated except for the hardest cases, which the Western world's most punitive justice apparatus soon immures or even executes.

It is true that the obfuscation of the "war on terror" allows governments around the world that are fighting—or just repressing—opponents to do so with greater impunity or even approval, and in some cases material help, so long as those opponents can be described as terrorists, i.e. practically anyone who uses violence in any form against civilians at large for any reason, or who can be accused as such with passing plausibility. Hence we had this very week the latest and perhaps most exotic addition to the official list of terrorists, who are therefore *ipso facto* enemies of the United States as well, no matter whom or what they oppose: the East Turkestan Islamic Movement as it is called in English, originating in China's Shinjiang-Uighur autonomous region, and not conceivably a veritable enemy of the United States one might think, except for the fact that Uighur recruits trained by Al Qaeda were captured in Afghanistan while fighting for the Taliban. It was only Chinese oppressors they wanted to attack, the Uighurs protested to passing Americans in pleading for their release and probably their lives, but now evidently it is all the same, we are all joined in fighting... terror.

15

Snobs Make Better Spooks

CIA officials used to have all sorts of irritating habits. If offered a perfectly good *Chateauneuf-du-Pape* at a Georgetown dinner party, they would praise it of course—by stressing their dissent from the "universal opinion" that unblended reds are better. If told of an especially good *trattoria* in Rome, they might express much gratitude for the information, deploring their own laziness in always going to the same old Sabatini they had first encountered while vacationing in Italy with their parents. Even more irritating was the propensity of first-generation CIA officials to interject memories of Groton, Yale, or skiing holidays in St. Moritz in any remotely relevant conversation.

There is none of that sort of thing anymore. Today's CIA people are not wine snobs. Many of them prefer beer, while others refrain even from coffee, as befits good Mormons. Nor are they partial to foreign foods in funky *trattorias*; cheeseburgers are more their style. Instead of being Ivy League show-offs, they are quietly proud of their state colleges, however obscure.

Unfortunately, much good has also been lost along the way, including that easy familiarity that comes from an early acquaintance with foreign ways. It is one thing to read up on, say, current French policy for the airliner industry starting from scratch, quite another if the new information is layered over personal experiences with things French going back to teenage visits and junior-year-abroad touring, or even years of residence with expatriate parents.

When it comes to the operational side of the CIA's work—mostly the recruitment of agents in place—it is certainly more difficult to strike just the right tone with a foreign diplomat or functionary without any broader background of experience than can be gained in Salt Lake City or Dayton, Ohio. Of course most people that CIA officials must strive to understand—or recruit—are not suave Europeans but rather Middle Eastern thugs, Russian weapon traffickers, Chinese bureaucrats, Latin American officers and others unsavory characters. But with them too the challenge is to interpret and manipulate motivations, urges, obsessions and priorities that drastically diverge from those prevalent among the middle classes of Middle America—the source of most of today's CIA recruits.

To be sure, there is plenty of talent all over the United States and in every level of society. Yet a narrow provincialism seems to be the hallmark of younger CIA officials. One reason is simply that applicants are much more likely to be approved by the CIA's security investigators if they have lived in one place all their lives, with no prior foreign travel or foreign contacts (each must be reported in detail, no matter how routine the travel, or how casual the contact). Moreover, there seems to be a distinct preference for applicants who resemble the security investigators themselves, exceptionally sober people who have never danced in a London disco, had a Japanese girlfriend or Brazilian boyfriend, nor tried smoking pot even once during their college days.

In other words the CIA is now screening out exactly the sort of person that it used to actively recruit: venturesome young Americans with as much foreign experience as possible.

Because espionage is such a small part of the business of intelligence, as compared to the purely intellectual work of analysis, none of the above would matter very much if the CIA could still attract the smartest graduates of the best universities. But those days are long past. The Ivy League graduates that used to fill its ranks now mostly want to become investment bankers—it is there that the adventure lies, as well as the money of course. Nothing can be done about that.

But the CIA could do much better if it pursued diversity in its recruiting, not the by-the-numbers diversity of so many women or Afro-Americans but rather a diversity of experience. Plenty of young Americans have lived abroad from childhood with their corporate-executive parents, and many others have done so as post-graduate volunteers for third world relief and developmental outfits. As of now, many thousands of young Americans live in Moscow, Prague and other Eastern European capitals, enjoying the excitement of their post-Communist transition, including the abundance of attractive sexual partners eager to connect with Westerners. At present, all such are mostly rejected if they seek to join the CIA. So are non-typical applicants in general; security investigators find that "their background is just too complicated."

One rejected applicant was earnestly asked why on earth he had gone to live in Prague after graduation, surviving on odd jobs instead of starting a career back home. When he jokingly replied "girls," the investigators did not conceal their shocked disapproval. When he dropped the ill-received jocularity to say that after growing up in the Midwest he had wanted to live awhile in one of the world's most beautiful cities, they were openly disbelieving. They had never been to Prague, of course, nor did they seem to know of its architectural splendors.

A more egregious case is that of the adventurous and quite brilliant young woman who had worked for a refugee-relief scheme in the most lawless region of South Asia before finding her way to an even more dangerous part of the world—an area of great importance for U.S. foreign policy. She became so interested in the area's on-going struggle and the local culture that she decided to study it systematically, exiting from her U.S. marriage to go back to work in the area. She made a great many friends, from village women to guerrilla leaders, thus multiplying the number of "foreign contacts" she faithfully reported on the security form. In the process she learned a language known to few CIA officials, if any at all, as well as what makes the locals tick. But this was of little import: her chances of being hired would have been much better had she remained celibate or married in Salt Lake City or some other such place without ever leaving the country.

The non-drinking, non-smoking, non-carousing, mostly-monolingual CIA officials of today do not have the vices of their more adventurous contemporaries, nor those of their flamboyant Ivy League predecessors. But it is rather unfair to expect them to cope with all those foreigners out there.

Part 4

Post-Heroic War

16

When Military Reform Fails

To evoke the intense loyalty without which combat is impossible, armed forces must be clannish and conservative, proud keepers of exclusive traditions and reassuring continuities. That has always been an obstacle to modernization. Procopius recounts a sixth-century debate over the new compound bow, deplored as cowardly by devotees of the sword. Opposition to the new is much stronger when it is not only traditional weapons that are endangered, but also institutions—the very repositories of group loyalty. Famously, the British and French armies grossly misused their tanks in 1940 because they insisted on absorbing them into the infantry and cavalry, instead of creating new tank-centered formations, as the Germans did with their Panzer divisions. While the Germans thus acquired a wholly new ability to penetrate fronts, British and French tanks only added some incremental strength to front-lines that could no longer be defended. It made no difference at all that British and French tanks were jointly superior in both quality and numbers: organizational innovation trumps mere technical innovation used in the same old way—even very superior equipment. That is why the successive "military revolutions" that have changed the course of military history over the centuries were always the product of massive, deliberate—and usually painful—institutional reforms, rather than just the result of incorporating new technology into old formats.

By the time Admiral William A. Owens became the second-highest uniformed officer in the land, as vice chairman of the Joint Chiefs of Staff in 1994, he had become convinced that the U.S. armed forces had the opportunity to achieve spectacular progress across the board. But this advancement would come only if they would truly *adapt* to the electronic age, instead of just adopting new technologies for their traditional forces. As he lucidly explains in his introduction, and in greater detail throughout the book, electronic sensors, telecommunications and computer networks could do much more than increase the

---

Review of William A. Owens with Ed Offley, *Lifting the Fog of War*, Farrar, Straus and Giroux, 2000.

effectiveness of individual aircraft, warships or tanks. They could be the basis of revolutionary advances. If combined into comprehensive "systems of systems," they could provide a wholly new ability to over-watch the entire conflict environment in near real time, day and night and in all weathers. Strategically, that would allow war plans to be calibrated minute by minute if needs be. Operationally, systems of systems would direct precision attacks against specific targets, assess the results, and re-attack them if necessary perhaps with different weapons, all the while monitoring every significant enemy action to intercept and defeat his moves early on.

By thus lifting the fog of war, the United States could achieve huge economies in its use of force. Instead of sending generic forces in the general direction of the enemy, it could employ *all* its forces as commandos are employed in films, with the elegant precision that only an exact foreknowledge of key enemy weaknesses can allow. It would be able to do a Kosovo-like operation in a few days instead of an agonizing, alliance-eroding, eleven weeks, and a Gulf War without the six-month mobilization that mostly piled up unusable mountains of supplies for mostly redundant ground forces.

Military historians know that Owens' systems of systems is not an original American invention: it merely renames the "Reconnaissance-Strike System" brilliantly advocated by Marshal Ogarkov, chief of the Soviet General Staff in the Brezhnev years, evidently as overflowing in its ideas as it was lacking in computers. And not only military experts know that all systems, howsoever combined are only effective against "high contrast" targets—large objects of classic form such as bridges, warships, tanks or tank regiments for that matter. The elusive guerrilla hiding in a jungle or urban landscape, or just in broken terrain with a few bushes and caves, cannot be reliably identified, or monitored, or attacked with precision.

But, even if Owens invented nothing, he was certainly a most notable military innovator—or at least he tried to be. For two years, until his voluntary retirement in February 1996 (he was offered two more but wisely declined), Owens strenuously tried to persuade his colleagues in the Pentagon of three things. First, the end of the Cold War offered the opportunity to recast U.S. military power into new joint forces centered on the electronic technology of the age, replacing the traditional services. Service boundaries had blocked battle cooperation in the 1991 Gulf War and did so again in the 1999 Kosovo war, as Owens explains, but more broadly they block innovation itself—simply because such things as all-force sensor and computer networks are funded by none of them. Second, the attempt to preserve existing Army, Navy, Marine Corps, and Air Force structures was doomed in any case, because of post-Cold War budget cuts. To keep going would result in chronic shortages, hollow forces and interrupted weapon programs. (This prediction is now already a reality.) Third, U.S. armed forces had to be reorganized to provide overseas deployments and peace-keeping units at tolerable cost, and in tolerable conditions for their personnel. At present only one person in uniform out of thirty or more is a combat soldier, Marine, sailor or pilot. All the others serve in quadruplicated overhead and support structures (one for each service), still designed to supply a prolonged world war, still administered as if computers had never been invented. Accordingly, deploying a few thousand soldiers to Bosnia or Kosovo is enough to overstretch the force, imposing long tours and back-to-back assignments that dissuade reenlistment, because the entire load is carried by a fraction of the 1.5 million people in uniform.

Owens documents in detail what ensued. His Army, Navy, Marine, and Air Force colleagues ignored his warnings and resisted his initiatives, fiercely determined to protect both the separate identities of their services, and combat formats dating back to the Second World War. In contrast, none of the major weapons of 1945 had even existed in 1914. Two world wars had changed everything in thirty years. But because no great war intervened to impose change in the fifty years after 1945, weapon and force configurations were simply perpetuated, as they still are, absorbing new technology in a spiral of increasingly baroque complexity, but with little real innovation. That is why today's M.1 tank looks just like a Tiger of 1944, today's fighters are merely improved 1944 jets, and today's aircraft carriers replicate the British angled-deck carriers invented by 1945.

Only submarines are drastically different, true underwater vessels instead of the submersible boats of 1945. This is the result of nuclear propulsion, imposed upon the U.S. Navy by the obsessive energy of Admiral Hyman G. Rickover, himself imposed on an unwilling Navy by a band of powerful Congressmen. Owens served in Rickover's nuclear navy before and after a study period at Oxford. ("It just shows you how low my program has sunk that I'd be willing to have you back" was Rickover's characteristic greeting when he returned from Oxford [p.8]).

Owens should have known that his efforts would be futile, that only an overwhelming *outside* power could impose internal reform on the Pentagon. That his arguments' logic and his budget arithmetic were both compelling was not enough. That Owens was encouraged by Secretary of Defense William Perry, a brilliant innovator in his own right, and by the exceptionally open-minded chairman of the Joint Chiefs, General John Shalikashvili, was not enough. Service loyalties are simply too strong in a society as rootless as ours, where there are neither strong families nor real communities to compete with their tribal solidarity. It was Congress that drastically reformed the top command structure in 1987, ignoring the opposition of almost all senior officers. And only Congress could force the Pentagon to listen to Owens and create new electronics-centered forces, instead of their current, mechanized 1945 forces kitted out with computers.

17

Where are the Great Powers Now?

At Home with the Kids

During the Cold War as before it, local and regional conflicts were often instigated or at least encouraged and materially supported by rival great powers. Now, by contrast, the absence of functioning great powers is the cause of the world's inability to cope with all manner of violent disorders. The result is that not only groups of secessionists and aggressive small powers, such as Serbia, but even mere armed bands can now impose their will or simply rampage, unchecked by any greater force from without. Today there is neither the danger of great power wars nor the protection of great powers capable of war.

By the traditional definition, great powers were states strong enough to successfully wage war without calling on allies. But that distinction is now outdated, because the issue today is not whether war can be made with or without allies, but whether war can be made at all. Historically, great power status required a readiness to use force whenever it was advantageous to do so and an acceptance of the resulting proportional combat casualties.

In the past, those preconditions were too blatantly obvious and too easily satisfied to deserve mention by either practitioners or theoreticians. Great powers normally relied on intimidation rather than combat, but only because a willingness to use force was assumed. Moreover, they used force undeterred by the prospect of the ensuing casualties, within limits of course.

Not-So-Great Behavior

The Somalia debacle, precipitated by the loss of eighteen U.S. soldiers, and the Haiti fiasco, caused by the fear of a handful of casualties, sufficiently exposed the current unreality of the great power concept. In pride or shame, Americans might dispute any wider conclusion from those events. They would like to reserve for themselves the special sensitivity that forces policy to change completely because eighteen professional soldiers were killed (soldiers, one might add, who come from a country in which gun-related deaths were last clocked at one every twenty minutes). But in fact the virtue or malady, as the case may be, is far from exclusively American.

Most recently, Britain and France (not to mention that other putative great power, Germany) flatly refused to risk their ground troops in combat to resist aggression in the former Yugoslavia. Overcoming the fear of reprisals against their own troops, it was only with great reluctance after almost two years of horrific outrages that the two countries finally consented to the carefully circumscribed threat of NATO air strikes issued in February 1994. To be sure, neither Britain nor France nor any other European power has any vital interests at stake in the former Yugoslavia. But that is the very essence of the matter: the great powers of history would have viewed the disintegration of Yugoslavia not as a noxious problem to be avoided but as an opportunity to be exploited. Using the need to protect populations under attack as their propaganda excuse and with the restoration of law and order as their ostensible motive, they would have intervened to establish zones of influence for themselves, just as the genuine great powers did in their time. (Even distant Russia disputed the Austro-Hungarian annexation of Bosnia-Herzegovina in 1908.) Thus the power vacuum would have been filled, to the disappointment of local small power ambitions, and to the great advantage of the local population.

As for why nothing of the kind happened in the former Yugoslavia in the face of atrocities not seen since the Second World War, the reason is not in dispute: no European government was any more willing than the U.S. government to risk its soldiers in combat.

The refusal to tolerate combat casualties is not confined to democracies. The Soviet Union was still an intact totalitarian dictatorship when it engaged in a classic great power venture in Afghanistan, only to find that even its tightly regimented society would not tolerate the resulting casualties. At the time, outside observers were distinctly puzzled by the minimal Soviet theater strategy in Afghanistan. After an abortive effort to establish territorial control, the Soviets decided to defend only the largest towns and the ring road connecting them. They otherwise conceded almost the entire country to guerrillas. Likewise, knowledgeable observers were astonished by the inordinately-prudent tactics of Soviet ground forces. Except for a few commando units, they mostly remained confined inside their fortified garrisons, often failing to sally out even when guerrillas were known to be nearby. At the time, the explanation most commonly offered was the reluctance of Soviet commanders to rely on their poorly trained conscript troops. But there is a better explanation: the Soviet headquarters was under constant and intense pressure from Moscow to avoid casualties at all costs because of the outraged reactions of families and friends.

This example rules out the superficial explanation that television coverage has heightened public sensitivity to casualties. The Soviet Union never allowed its population to see any television images of war like those shown in the United States, yet the reaction of Soviet society to the casualties of the Afghan war was essentially identical to the American reaction to the Vietnam War. Although in both cases cumulative casualties over the span of many years did not reach the casualty figures of one day of battle in past wars, they were nevertheless deeply traumatic.

The War of All Mothers

A better explanation for the disappearance of great powers, which is true regardless of the form of government or extend of free media, is the demographic character of modern, postindustrial societies. The populations of historical great powers were commonly comprised of families of four, five or six children. Families larger than this were more common than those smaller. At the same time, infant mortality rates were also high. When it was normal to lose children to disease, the loss of one more in time of war had a different meaning than it has for today's families, which have two or three children, all of whom are expected to survive, and each of whom represents a larger share of the family's emotional economy.

As any number of historical studies has shown, death itself was a much more normal part of the familial experience when it was not confined mostly to the very old. To lose a young family member for any reason was no doubt always tragic, yet a death in combat was not the extraordinary and fundamentally unacceptable event that it has now become. Parents who commonly approve of their sons' and daughters' decisions to join the armed forces now often react with astonishment and anger when their children are actually sent into potential combat situations. And they are likely to view casualties as an outrageous scandal, rather than an occupational hazard.

The Italians, perhaps more post-industrial than most in this sense, with Europe's lowest birthrate, have a word for these reactions: *mammismo*, which might be translated as "motherism." Today, this attitude has an enormous impact which powerfully constrains the use of force. The Soviet experience in Afghanistan proves that the constraint operates even without a mass media eager to publicize private grief, members of Congress ready to complain at the instance of relatives, or pointed questions being asked in a parliament.

Present attitudes toward combat losses deriving from the new family demography are powerful because they are not confined to the relatives and friends of servicemen on active duty. They are shared throughout society—and were shared even within the Soviet elite, it turns out—generating an extreme reluctance to impose a possible sacrifice, which has become so much greater than it was when national populations were much smaller but families were much larger.

The willingness of combatants in the Gulf War and Falklands War suggest that the opposition to casualties is primarily a matter of the perceived value of the undertaking or the ability of political leaders to justify combat. After all, even during World War II, soldiers greatly resented assignments to what were described as secondary fronts, quickly dubbing any theater that was less than highly publicized as "forgotten." The less immediately compelling the justification, the more likely combat and its casualties are to be opposed. It might therefore seem that the new 2.2-children-per-family demographics and the resulting *mammismo* are irrelevant, that what counts is only what has always counted: the importance of the interests at stake, the political orchestration of the event and plain leadership.

Those contentions undoubtedly have some merit but much less than meets the eye. If lives can only be placed at risk in situations already dramatically prominent on the national scene, on a larger rather than a smaller scale, and only in final extremities, that in itself already rules out the most efficient use of force—early and small-scale to prevent escalation.

Constricted Visions

In the past, there was no question of limiting the use of force to situations in which genuinely vital interests, that is, matters of survival, were at stake. To struggle for mere survival was the unhappy predicament of threatened small powers, which had to fight to defend themselves and could not hope to achieve anything more with their modest strength. Great powers were different; they could only remain great if they were seen as willing and able to use force to acquire and protect even non-vital interests, including distant possessions or minor additions to their spheres of influence. To lose a few hundred soldiers in some minor probing operation or a few thousand in a small war or expeditionary venture were routine events for the great powers of history.

Great powers are in the business of threatening, rather than being threatened. A great power cannot be that unless it asserts all sorts of claims that far exceed the needs of its own immediate security, including the protection of allies and clients as well as other less-than-vital interests. It must therefore risk combat for purposes that may be fairly recondite, perhaps in little-known distant lands, but definitely in situations in which it is not compelled to fight but rather deliberately chooses to do so. And that is the choice now denied by the fear of casualties.

Even now, exceptional strivings by exceptionally determined leaders skilled in the art of political leadership can widen a great power's freedom of action, overcoming in part the effects of the new family demographics. That was obviously the case in the Persian Gulf intervention and the Falklands reconquest; both would have been impossible undertakings had it not been for the exceptional leadership of President George Bush and Prime Minister Margaret Thatcher, respectively. Their leadership was the decisive factor, not the undoubted significance of keeping Iraq from controlling Saudi and Kuwaiti oil, or the equally undoubted insignificance of the Falklands for any practical purpose whatsoever (another illustration of the irrelevance of the "objective" value of whatever is at stake).

Leadership is certainly important, but it cannot be so for great powers, because the routine functioning of a great power cannot depend on the fortuitous presence of exceptional leaders. Even when present, leadership depends on other factors, such as the gross underestimate of Argentine air power or the focus on minimizing casualties that characterized the Falklands and Gulf Wars, respectively. Thus, the freedom of action gained by successful leadership is still very narrow. It is not hard to guess what would have happened to President Bush and his administration if the casualties of the Persian Gulf venture had reached the levels of any one day of serious fighting in either world war.

Nations of Families

If the significance of the new family demographics is accepted, it follows that no advanced low-birth-rate countries can play the role of a classic great power anymore, not the United States or Russia, not Britain, France or, least of all, Germany or Japan. They may still possess the physical attributes of military strength or the economic base to develop such strength even on a great scale, but their societies are so allergic to casualties that they are effectively debellicized, or nearly so.

Aside from self-defense and exceptional cases like the Persian Gulf War, only such conflict as can take place without soldiers is likely to be tolerated. Much can be done by air power, with few lives at risk, especially if bureaucratic resistance to its lone use can be overcome. Sea power too can be useful at times, and robotic weapons will be used increasingly. But Bosnia, Somalia, and Haiti remind us that the typical great power business of restoring order still requires ground forces. In the end, the infantry, albeit mechanized, is still indispensable, although now mostly withheld by the fear of casualties. High-birth-rate countries can still fight wars by choice, and several have in recent years. But even those very few among them that have competent armed forces lack other key great power attributes, including any significant strategic reach.

In the absence of functioning great powers, the entire character of world politics has changed. Under the old *machtpolitik* rules, for example, the United States should have been eager to extend its military influence to the Russian border by granting full NATO membership to Poland and other former Warsaw Pact countries. Instead the United States opposed NATO's expansion. In the central arena of world affairs, only the commercial and industrial policies that I have elsewhere labeled "geo-economic" still have a recognizably conflictual flavor.

Unless the world is content to exist with chronic disorder and widespread violence, a synthetic version of law-and-order interventionism by great powers will have to be invented. The remedies we already have are certainly inadequate. To keep the armed forces of the United States as powerful as possible, the preferred military option, is ineffectual when intimidation will not do it. Yet the United States refuses to fight. The American ability to intimidate will only decline as word spreads.

Improbable Stand-Ins

Two rather improbable schemes are therefore left. Both satisfy the essential requirement of circumventing the intolerance of casualties. Both could be organized quite efficiently, given the will to do so. Yet both would be furiously opposed by the military establishment, and both undeniably have unpleasant moral connotations.

One scheme would be to copy the Ghurka model, recruiting troops in some suitable region abroad, if not in Nepal itself. They would be mercenaries, of course, but they would be of high quality, and a common ethnic origin would assure their basic cohesion. In practice, U.S. Ghurkas would provide the infantry units, with native U.S. forces providing the more technical forms of combat support involving smaller risks and fewer casualties.

The alternative is to copy the foreign legion model, with units that combine U.S. officers and nonnative volunteers who have renounced their national allegiance, perhaps attracted by the offer of U.S. citizenship after a given term of service. Under both schemes, political responsibility for any casualties would be much reduced, if not eliminated. The United States raised ethnic mercenary units in Indochina with rather good results, and it recruited individual foreign volunteers for Europe-based Special Forces, so neither scheme is as outlandish or unprecedented as it may seem. Still, it is unlikely either option will be considered, much less implemented.

If no remedy can be found for the passing of the great powers and the conspicuous inability of the United States itself to play that role, both the United States and the world will soon be familiar with the result. Violent disorders unchecked by effective great power interventions have both immediate and delayed effects, including disrupted export markets, refugees and new sources of international crime and terrorism.

Americans will also have to learn not to see, hear or feel much that would otherwise offend their moral sensitivities. Richer inhabitants of the poorest countries learn from childhood how to step politely over the quadruple-amputee beggar in their path without ever actually looking at him, and how not to see the starving mother and child, the waif and the abandoned elderly who try to beg from them as they walk into a restaurant or bank. Of course, blindness can be practiced, and Americans will need experience to passively ignore avoidable tragedies and horrific atrocities. But we have always been quick learners, and the experience of Bosnia-Herzegovina shows we are already making rapid progress on this subject.

18

Toward Post-Heroic Warfare

The Obsolescence of Total War

Only one thing could possibly link the protracted warfare in the former Yugoslavia, the destruction of Grozny, and the recent border fighting between Ecuador and Peru. Once more, as in centuries past, wars are rather easily started and then fought without perceptible restraint. When belligerents see that no particular penalty is paid for opening fire first or using any and all means of warfare—even the wholesale destruction of cities by aerial or artillery bombardment—self-imposed restraints on the use of force are everywhere eroded. The border fighting between Ecuador and Peru had only just begun when tactical bombing was employed, as if it were no more consequential than one more infantry skirmish.

This new season of war is upon us as one more consequence of the passing of the Cold War. The latter induced or intensified a number of hot wars in the contested zones between each camp as each superpower provided allies and clients with weapons and expertise far beyond their own capacities. Thus the Middle East especially became something of a preferred battleground by proxy.

At the same time, however, the fear that escalation could eventually reach the nuclear level inhibited any direct combat whatsoever by the superpowers themselves in Europe, or anywhere else, even on the smallest scale. Above all, the Cold War suppressed many potential shooting wars in a great part of the world because neither superpower would tolerate them within its own camp. Both, moreover, were notably vigilant in controlling the form and geographic scope of the wars they fought in Korea, Vietnam, and Afghanistan, and also the wars their allies and clients fought, again for fear of an escalation to direct clash and nuclear war.

The concept of war governing those encounters has long been so strongly entrenched that it is not even commonly recognized as a result of particular circumstances, but instead seen as a universal. It only envisages wars fought for great national purposes that can evoke public fervor, by armed forces that

115

represent the aroused nation rather than merely a body of professionals going about their business. Yet that is only one concept of war, as even casual readers of military history well know. Far from an eternal verity, the concept is a rather modern innovation, associated with a particular phase of fairly recent history. Before the French Revolution, most wars were fought for much less than imperative purposes that rarely evoked popular enthusiasm, with prudent strategies and tactics to conserve expensive professional forces. While no great purposes at hand could motivate the entire nation in war, there is much justification for some eighteenth-century warfare of our own, with modest purposes and casualty avoidance as the controlling norm.

The New Culture of War

The Cold War culture of intense but controlled tension, which required disciplined constraints on the use of force, seems to have influenced even nonaligned nations such as India and Pakistan. To use force at all during the Cold War came to be seen almost everywhere as a very grave decision indeed, to be made only after the fullest deliberation, usually after all other means had been exhausted. Further decisions to escalate to regular infantry combat rather than deniable guerrilla operations, armored warfare and artillery support rather than infantry, and aerial bombing rather than ground warfare were deemed worthy of distinct political decisions at the highest levels instead of being left, as in the past, to the discretion of military commanders. The latter complained, sometimes loudly, but they obeyed, thus affirming the new culture of restraint.

Restraint did not prevent 138 wars between 1945 and 1989, by the most expansive count, which killed as many as twenty-three million people. But in the previous forty-four years, which included two world wars, many more were killed. In the absence of any restraint arising from strategic prudence, internal repression killed many more people over the years 1945-89 than all 138 wars combined.

Now that the Cold War no longer suppresses hot wars, the entire culture of disciplined restraint in the use of force is in dissolution. Except for Iraq's wars, the consequences have chiefly been manifest within the territories that had been Soviet, as well as Yugoslav. The protracted warfare, catastrophic destruction, and profuse atrocities of eastern Moldavia, the three Caucasian republics, parts of Central Asia, and lately Chechnya, Croatia, and Bosnia have certainly horrified and moved many Americans. But this diverse violence derives from the same post-imperial devolution of epic, unprecedented scale or from purely localized sources. Hence one could still hope that the new readiness to start unrestrained wars would at least be geographically confined, if only within an area already vast.

The fighting between Ecuador and Peru, the mounting recklessness manifest between Greece and Turkey, and also perhaps Pakistan's increasing boldness over Kashmir suggests the more sinister possibility that a new, much less restrained culture of war is emerging and spreading far and wide. Nothing is now countering a number of perverse precedents. Aggression and willful escalation alike remain unpunished; victors remain in possession of their gains; the defeated are abandoned to their own devices. It was not so during the Cold War, when most antagonists had a superpower patron with its own reasons to control them, victors had their gains whittled down by superpower compacts, and the defeated were often assisted by whichever superpower was not aligned with the victor.

One may wonder what precedents the Ecuador-Peru fighting will set. Without knowing its map-changing results, one cannot assert that other dormant Latin American border disputes will be revived. But it would be most surprising if those disputes were not now undergoing some reappraisal, if only by politicians interested in defining ultranationalist stances for themselves. Moreover, some deceleration, if not an outright reversal, is certain to occur in the downward trend in military spending by many Latin American countries. That most positive development of recent years, which yielded important political and economic benefits, is now endangered. The Ecuador-Peru war could turn out far more costly for Latin America as a whole and indirectly for the United States too than its limited dimensions might suggest.

The Meaning of "War"

Can the United States counter perverse precedents and the new culture of easy and unrestrained violence? Beyond diplomacy is the controversial remedy of armed intervention, with or without a multilateral framework, with or without foreign auxiliaries. But aside from its suitability in any particular setting (in some it is unimaginable), military force collides with the general and repeated refusal of the American public to sanction military interventions.

That political given must be accepted, but it is contingent upon the cost in U.S. casualties of a particular concept of war and particular methods of intervention, the only concepts and methods the U.S. military establishment now offers. If these could be changed drastically to minimize the exposure of U.S. military personnel to the risks of combat, the response of public opinion to proposed military interventions should also change. The United States might then do more to dissuade aggression and escalation.

Much is implicit in American political discourse, the official manuals of the U.S. military services, and the popular understanding of the very word "war" when the United States is a protagonist. Quite naturally, the various Weinberger-Powell-Cheney doctrines, which set out to define several preconditions for any decision to send U.S. military forces into combat, are based squarely, tacitly, and without discussion on the same concept of war. While the three sets of preconditions differ in detail, they all require vital, fervor-arousing U.S. national interests to be clearly threatened, and that the United States employ forces powerful enough to win not only decisively but also quickly, before the fervor abates and the nation is no longer aroused.

War fought for grand purposes is yet another product of the French and American revolutions. With some chronological laxity, however, I here label it "Napoleonic" because grand purposes often imply the decisive employment of large forces in large operations, in true Napoleonic fashion. The concept originally emerged in reaction to the typical warfare of eighteenth-century Europe, ridiculed by Napoleon and systematically criticized by Carl von Clausewitz.

While fully recognizing that the cautious methods of the prior age of warfare were congruent with their times and the habitually modest aims of what were called "cabinet wars," Clausewitz was scathing in his descriptions. Demonstrative maneuvers meant to induce enemy withdrawals without firing a shot were readily called off if serious fighting ensued. Superior forces avoided battle if there was a risk of heavy casualties even in victory. Prolonged sieges were preferred to determined assaults and circumspect pursuits to all-out exploitation in the wake of battle victories. At the strategic level, elaborately prepared offensives had unambitious objectives, promising campaigns were interrupted by early retreats into winter quarters merely to avoid further losses, and offensive performance was routinely sacrificed to the overriding priority of avoiding casualties and conserving forces for another day, with much effort expended to build and garrison linear defenses and fortifications.

Napoleon triumphed over such cautious military practices with bold strategic offensives powered by the mass and momentum of rapidly concentrated forces, and that was the kind of warfare that Clausewitz advocated. Envisaging only wars fought for great national purposes, and with the unification of Germany in mind, Clausewitz exposed the logical error of half-hearted, risk-avoiding methods likely in the long run to be more costly. To be sure, Clausewitz concurrently derived the strongest argument for strategic prudence from his insistence on the primacy of political considerations, but that did not affect his demonstration of the economy of tactical and operational boldness, a formula for efficacy that can easily become detached from its justifying context of correspondingly ambitious goals.

Complete with profound insights into the eternal mechanics and psychology of war, the teachings of Clausewitz remain unsurpassed. Along with parallel examples of the merits of risk-taking drawn from the successes of the great captains of history (a highly selective list that omits prudent victors, favoring Patton and Hannibal, for example, over Bradley or Fabius Cunctator), they pervade the professional discourse of U.S. service academies and war colleges and can easily be recognized in current field manuals and official doctrinal statements. Many such documents are prefaced by restatements of the principles of "war" (concentration, mass, momentum, etc.) that are actually in large part the Clausewitzian principles of Napoleonic war.

These principles were fully appropriate to the circumstances of the two world wars and also of the Cold War, as far as the planning of nonnuclear operations was concerned. Neither fits present circumstances, domestic or international.

There are no threatening great powers on the current world scene, only a hand-ful of quiescent rogue states, and many lesser wars and internal disorders that cannot arouse the nation, for none of them directly threatens the United States or its compelling interests. The preconditions of Napoleonic war-making, or for that matter of military interventions as specified in the Weinberger-Powell-Cheney doctrines, are therefore absent.

Yet its moral economy is damaged as the United States remains the attentive yet passive witness of aggressions replete with atrocities on the largest scale. Moreover, there is no doubt that the diffusion of the new culture of wars easily started and quickly escalated is damaging U.S. material interests. Commercial opportunities, not all of them small, are being lost every day wherever guns are firing, and many more could be lost in the future.

Given the performance of certain modern weapons, if military planning is appropriately modified to fully exploit their technical potential, it may be pos-sible to emulate the casualty-avoiding methods of eighteenth-century warfare and thus conduct armed yet virtually bloodless interventions. To be sure, U.S. aims would have to be correspondingly modest and remain so, resisting all temptations to achieve more than partial, circumscribed, and often slow results as firmly as any good eighteenth-century general.

At present, by contrast, there is a profound contradiction between the prevailing military mentality, formed by the Napoleonic concept of war with its Clausewitzian adjuncts, and current exigencies. The Somalia intervention came to a sudden end after the bloody failure of a daring helicopter raid in true commando style—a normal occupational hazard of high-risk, high-payoff commando operations. But given the context at hand—a highly discretion-ary intervention in a country of the most marginal significance for American interests—any high-risk methods at all were completely inappropriate in prin-ciple. Nor was what happened the result of an error of judgment, still less of malfeasance. In accordance with the prevailing mentality, the senior military planners allowed a role in the Somalia undertaking to U.S. Special Operations Command, which naturally mounted its own kind of operations, which in turn inherently entailed the risk of casualties.

The casualties of war were not a decisive consideration, within reasonable limits, so long as the Napoleonic concept still applied. War fought for great purposes implies a willingness to accept casualties even in large numbers. Moreover, a certain tolerance for casualties was congruent with the demogra-phy of preindustrial and early industrial societies, whereby families had many children and losing some to disease was entirely normal. The loss of a youngster in combat, however tragic, was therefore fundamentally less unacceptable than for today's families, with their one, two, or at most three children. Each child is expected to survive into adulthood and embodies a great part of the family's emotional economy. Even in the past, the United States never had the supply of expendable soldiers that was the fuel of discretionary great power wars fought for colonial aggrandizement or yet more recondite motives. Still less is there such a supply of expendable lives at present, when all other low-birthrate, postindustrial societies refuse to sanction the casualties of any avoidable combat.

It seems impossible that modern armed forces, staffed by professional, salaried, pensioned, and career-minded military personnel who belong to a nation intolerant of casualties, could cope with aggressors inflamed by nationalism or religious fanaticism. Yet to avoid combat and do nothing allows not only aggressive small powers, such as Serbia, but even mere armed bands, as in Somalia, to rampage or impose their victories at will.

Some view the dilemma as unprecedented and irresolvable. Actually, it is neither. If we free ourselves from the Napoleonic concept to recognize the historical normality of eighteenth-century warfare, we can find many situations in which the same dilemma arose and was successfully overcome. As long as two millennia ago, the professional, salaried, pensioned, and career-minded citizen-soldiers of the Roman legions routinely had to fight against warriors eager to die gloriously for tribe or religion. Already then, their superiors were far from indifferent to the casualties of combat, if only because trained troops were costly and citizen manpower scarce. Augustus, famously, went to his grave still bitterly mourning the three legions Varus lost in Germany years before.

The Roman Siege

The Romans relied on several remedies to minimize their troop losses while overcoming enemies from Britain to Mesopotamia. In the first place, it was their standard practice to avoid open-field combat, especially spontaneous engagements, if at all possible, even if their forces were clearly superior. Rather than face the uncertainties of time and place, which could result in an equally unpredictable casualty toll, the Romans routinely allowed their enemies to withdraw to positions of their own choosing, even if well fortified or naturally strong. Having thus turned a fluid situation into a far more controllable set-piece encounter, the Romans would gather forces and assemble equipment and supplies to commence systematic siege operations. Even then, their first priority was not to breach enemy defenses but rather to build elaborate fortifications to protect their besieging units, to minimize whatever casualties enemy sallies could inflict. Overall, the siege was the medium in which the Romans could best exploit both their technological superiority in siege craft and their logistic advantage, which normally enabled them patiently to outlast the food supplies of the besieged. A purposeful, calculated patience was a signal of military virtue.

Trade embargoes and armed blockades, the modern equivalents of the Roman siege, are not tactical but strategic. Unfortunately, so long as the Napoleonic concept prevails, it is impossible to exploit their full capacity to achieve warlike results without the casualties of war. An aroused nation seeks rapid results, whereas the effects of embargoes and blockades are cumulative rather than immediate and may be long delayed. Moreover, the Napoleonic concept only recognizes decisive results, while the effects of embargoes and blockades are usually partial rather than complete, even if very much worth having. For example, since 1990 those means have controlled the military resurgence of Saddam Hussein's Iraq. Its armed forces have not been allowed to recover from the equipment losses of 1991 and have instead been steadily weakened as destroyed or worn-out weapons are not replaced. True, only direct oil exports by tanker or pipeline have been denied, but the lesser quantities Iraq has been able to send out overland have not been enough for rearmament. Nor does the imminent possibility that the United Nations will lift its prohibition on Iraqi oil exports alter the effective containment, without a more active use of force, of a serious threat. Incidentally (in this case), the decisive result that only an all-out war could have achieved would have been even more temporary and indecisive, for the complete destruction of Iraq's military strength would immediately have made containing Iran's threat that much harder.

Likewise, in the former Yugoslavia, amid the utter failure of every other diplomatic or military initiative of the United Nations, European Community, or NATO, only the denial of Serbian and Montenegrin imports and exports—notoriously incomplete though it has been—has had positive effects. In addition to the certain if immeasurable impact on Serbian and Montenegrin war capabilities, the trade embargo has moderated the conduct of Belgrade's most immoderate leadership. The embargo dissuaded at least the more blatant forms of combat and logistic support for the Serb militias of Bosnia-Herzegovina, Slavonia, and Krajina and also induced whatever slight propensity has been shown to negotiate, if only in the hope of securing the lifting of the arms embargo. The prospect of perpetuating the embargo has almost certainly helped to avert an invasion of Macedonia, still now precariously vulnerable to Serb expansion aided and abetted by Greek malevolence.

Even by the most optimistic reckoning, those results are sadly inadequate. Nevertheless, without any cost in blood or treasure, the trade embargo has achieved much more than the expensive and ineffectual UN armed intervention or the tens of thousands of yet more expensive NATO air patrols over Bosnia, flown by heavily armed fighter-bombers that hardly ever fight or bomb, even as the carnage below them continues.

Against those two instances of at least partial success, in the entire record of blockades and embargoes, many outright failures can be cited. But quite a few of them only came to be considered failures because of the premise that results must be rapid to be at all worthwhile. It would take a new (or rather renewed) concept of war that esteems a calculated, purposeful patience to allow the full exploitation of embargoes and blockades, or of any slow and cumulative form of combat. As it is, the Napoleonic and Clausewitzian emphasis on sheer tempo and momentum unconsciously induces an almost compulsive sense of urgency, even when there are no truly imperative reasons to act quickly. British Field Marshal Bernard Law Montgomery was not the first or the last general to achieve success where others had failed simply by insisting on thorough preparations where others had hurriedly improvised.

A compulsive sense of urgency was much in evidence during the first weeks of the 1991 Persian Gulf War, when the systematic air attack of strategic targets in Iraq was viewed with unconcealed impatience by many of the subordinate military commanders on the scene. News accounts duly conveyed their skepticism about the value of strategic bombing and their corresponding eagerness to see the air attack diverted to Iraqi army units and other tactical targets to open the way for a ground offensive as soon as possible.

The most senior officers resisted this upward pressure on the chain of command, which reflected no objective imperatives but only deeply rooted instinct as well as more obvious bureaucratic urges. But the pressure could not be completely denied. Well before strategic bombing was virtually stopped to provide air support for the ground campaign, which began on the thirty-ninth day of the war, many of the aircraft best suited to continue the methodical destruction of Iraqi research, development, production, and storage facilities for conventional and nonconventional weapons were instead diverted to attack some 4,000 individual armored vehicles.

The diversion of the air effort from strategic to tactical targets was to have unhappy consequences. In the aftermath, many important nuclear, biological, and chemical warfare installations remained undestroyed. For in spite of the great abundance of U.S. combat aircraft, less than 200 were fully equipped to attack strategic targets with precision weapons. That number, as it turned out, was simply too small to exhaust in less than thirty-nine days a long list of targets, which included command and control, electrical supply, telecommunication, air defense, and oil refining and storage facilities, as well as air and naval bases, rail and road bridges, and any number of supply depots.

The same compulsive urgency almost certainly played some role in shaping the decision to launch the ground offensive on the thirty-ninth day of the war instead of, say, the forty-ninth. By the former date the air campaign had thoroughly hollowed out Iraq's military strength, not least by cutting off most supplies to frontline units. Hence it cannot be argued that the decision to start the ground offensive sooner rather than later caused any more U.S. and allied casualties than the incidentals of war would in any case have claimed, the total number being so very small. But had the air campaign been prolonged just ten more days, 2,000 more sorties could have been flown against strategic targets. The novel instrument of precision air attack on a strategic scale, so slow in its methodical sequence but so effective in its cumulative results, so costly to acquire but so exceedingly economical in U.S. lives, was simply not allowed enough time to realize its full potential.

The central importance attributed in the immediate aftermath of the war to the swiftly victorious ground offensive was also suggestive of the dominant influence of the Napoleonic concept on civilian opinion. Though little more than a mopping-up operation, it resonated with the prevailing mentality much more than the air campaign because it was both rapidly executed and visibly decisive.

Patient Air Power

The key argument against proposals to employ U.S. offensive air power in Bosnia rested on the implicit assumption that only rapid results are of value. After first noting that anything resembling area bombing would inevitably kill many civilians, the chiefs argued that the potential targets were simply too elusive, or too easily camouflaged in the rugged Bosnian terrain, to allow effective precision attacks. They took it for granted that any air operation would have to be swiftly concluded, or even amount to no more than a one-time attack. Any one precision air strike certainly can easily fail because the assigned targets are concealed by bad weather, are no longer where last spotted, or are successfully camouflaged. There is no doubt that weapons such as the 120-millimeter mortars much used by Serb militias to bombard Sarajevo can be quickly moved and readily camouflaged; even much more elaborate howitzers and field guns can be elusive targets.

But this argument utterly obscured the drastic difference between a one-time strike, or any brief operation for that matter, and a patiently sustained air campaign with sorties flown day after day, week after week. If one sortie fails because of dense clouds, the next one, or the one after that, will have clear visibility. If one sortie misses a howitzer just moved under cover, the next might spot another actually firing. If one sortie is called off because the target is too close to civilians, another can proceed to completion. What was the great hurry to finish an air operation quickly? The fighting in Bosnia continues unabated even now, years later, because military leaders did not think they could stop it in a few days.

But of course the other presumption of the Napoleonic concept of war—that only decisive results are worth having—was even more consequential. As the most senior U.S. military chiefs correctly pointed out, air strikes alone could not end the war in the former Yugoslavia, nor save the Bosnian state from its enemies, nor safeguard civilians from rape, murder, or forcible deportation. Therefore, it was argued by implication, air power alone was useless. Actually, if might have been even worse, with Serb militias retaliating against UN troops, causing their withdrawal and the possibility of an American-led ground deployment.

Given the dubious assumption that UN troops were in fact usefully protecting vulnerable civilians, and the prior assessment that air attacks alone would be useless, the conclusion was inevitable. True, air attacks alone could not possibly have ended the war or saved Bosnia. But a sustained air campaign could most certainly have reduced the use of artillery against cities, a particularly devastating form of warfare. That would have sufficed to ameliorate a tragic situation and demonstrate the active concern of the United States—much less than a total remedy, but much more than nothing.

Casualty-Free Warfare

A further aspect of Roman military practice is relevant for current acquisition policies as well as tactical doctrines. It is enough to recall images of legionary troops to see how far offensive performance was deliberately sacrificed to reduce casualties. The large rectangular shield, sturdy metal helmet, full breastplate, shoulder guard, and foot grieves were so heavy that they greatly restricted agility. Legionnaires were extremely well protected but could hardly chase enemies who ran away, nor even pursue them for long if they merely retreated at a quick pace. Moreover, to offset the great weight of armor, only a short stabbing sword was issued. The Romans evidently thought it much more important to minimize their own casualties than to maximize those of the enemy.

Much better materials than iron and leather are available today, but it is symptomatic of an entirely different order of priorities that till now very little research and development funding has been allocated to advanced body armor. In fact the best such items now available have been privately developed for sale to law enforcement agencies.

The modern equivalent of Roman fortifications is not to build walls or forts with modern techniques, but rather to emulate the underlying Roman priorities. That applies to weapons as much as tactics. Most notably, current cost-effectiveness criteria do not yet reflect the current sensitivity to casualties. In setting overall budget priorities, alternative force categories—ground, maritime, and air—are still evaluated by cost and combat performance, without treating casualty exposure as a coequal consideration. Yet the risk of suffering casualties is routinely the decisive constraint in practice, while the exposure to casualties for different kinds of forces varies quite drastically, from the minimum of offensive air power to the maximum of Army and Marine infantry. Also revealing is the entire debate on stealth aircraft, which are specifically designed to evade radar and infrared detection. When judged very expensive, stealth planes are implicitly compared to non-stealth aircraft of equivalent range and payload, not always including the escorts the latter also require, which increase greatly the number of fliers at risk. Missing from such calculations is any measure of the overall foreign policy value of acquiring a means of casualty-free warfare by unescorted stealth bomber, a weapon of circumscribed application but global reach. Casualty avoidance is not yet valued at current market prices.

Present circumstances call for not simply a new concept of war, but a new mentality that would inject unheroic realism into military planning in order to overcome excessive timidity in military practice. A new post-Napoleonic and post-Clausewitzian concept of war would require not only a patient disposition, but also a modest one. It would bid us accept partial results when doing more would endanger our soldiers and doing less would endanger our self-respect.

19

Post-Heroic Military Policy

The New Season of Bellicosity

The strategic culture of the Cold War combined great eagerness to accumulate weapons with great caution in their use. Fearing that any act of war might start a progression of moves and countermoves leading to catastrophe, the nuclear powers strenuously avoided any direct combat with each other. There were many wars, but the remarkably deliberate and controlled behavior that became a new norm for nations around the world deterred the thoughtless escalation of confrontation and the eruption of war through sheer miscalculation. With the end of the Cold War, the armed forces, military expenditures, fear of nuclear attack, and learned habits of restraint are all much diminished. Today, disputes over minor diplomatic aims or mere posturing for domestic constituencies are enough to provoke reckless displays of bellicosity or imprudence. Thus China advanced its claim of sovereignty over Taiwan in March with military exercises that were clearly meant to be as alarming as possible. For their part, Taiwan's leaders, in their futile pursuit of UN membership, had earlier seen fit to score largely symbolic diplomatic points in defiance of emphatic Chinese warnings—as if there were no danger of war, and the balance of power were nothing more than an academic construct.

Likewise, a long-standing territorial dispute between Greece and Turkey over an islet in the Aegean Sea, inhabited only by about a dozen goats, quickly escalated into a confrontation. Naval forces were deployed in dangerous proximity to each other, accompanied by much nationalist bombast from politicians on both sides and frenzied media coverage. A group of Turkish journalists deliberately exacerbated tensions by planting a flag on the ten acres of rock. When a mutual withdrawal of forces was eventually negotiated with U.S. help, Greek editorialists accused newly installed Prime Minister Costas Simitis of treason. The episode was reminiscent of the war-mongering press campaigns of the last fin-de-siècle, being not merely pre-nuclear but pre-1914 in its raw truculence.

The Republic of Korea also asserted a claim earlier this year over small uninhabited islands in the Sea of Japan. President Kim Young Sam, beleaguered by accusations of corruption, sent warships to the scene against a backdrop of foolhardy taunts and idle threats against Japan in the South Korean media. Pakistan, too, has of late seemed bent on starting a war with India over Kashmir by smuggling in weapons and making inflammatory declarations.

As in pre-nuclear times, when fighting breaks out there is no great concern on the part of either the protagonists or outside powers to limit its scope. Consequently, infantry clashes can escalate directly to aerial bombing, as in the border fighting last year between Ecuador and Peru, or to artillery barrages against cities, as in the diverse struggles within the former Yugoslavia and the former Soviet Union.

None of these quarrels is new. But while the Cold War induced caution, present circumstances evidently do not. A new season of bellicosity is upon us, and it is unlikely to long endure without serious consequences. Because wars have become less dangerous to fight, the danger that wars will be fought has increased.

When national leaders manufacture or amplify external crises for internal political purposes, as noted above, they rarely intend to start a war. But as each side's gesticulations turn into the other side's perceived threats, confrontations can easily get out of hand. That happened often enough before the Cold War and is now likely to happen again. Indeed, in the case of Ecuador and Peru it has already occurred, not coincidentally when each was in the midst of a presidential campaign.

Cold War Minds

A strategic environment so greatly transformed calls for an equally transformed U.S. military policy. Certainly there have already been important changes. The stock of long-range nuclear weapons has been greatly reduced, and both the defense budget and the number of personnel in the armed forces are considerably smaller than a decade ago. But at a more fundamental level, much remains unchanged and is therefore outdated.

That the end of the Cold War should leave disorientation in its wake was inevitable. Previous great wars entailed strenuous mobilizations, so that in 1918 and 1945 rapid demobilizations naturally ensued once hostilities ended. On both occasions the U.S. military went beyond the steep reduction or outright disbanding of war-inflated forces. It tried to resuscitate prewar routines and customs while attempting to recast doctrines and force structures in light of the presumed lessons of the last war. Thus battleships gave way to aircraft carriers, armored formations became the standard for ground forces, and jet aviation became the norm.

The Cold War required a vast effort, but well short of an all-out mobilization. When it ended, therefore, there was no overwhelming pressure to drastically demobilize. Nor was there any urge to abandon its peculiar habits and institutions. On the contrary, the U.S. military has striven to preserve continuity in all things and has resisted as much as possible the effects of declining budgets.

Cold War military practices and priorities persist in all sorts of subtle ways because they are embodied in the millions of people who make up the military, its civilian bureaucracy and the defense industry, but mainly because they are simply not recognized as products of that era. The Cold War lasted so long that nobody remembers any prewar normality to which the military should revert. Nor are there are any sharply defined threats to which the military can adjust. A deliberate refusal to break with the past is not the issue, nor is the habitual conservatism of military institutions; the issue is the persistence of unquestioned premises. Because all but the youngest officers and virtually all defense officials were educated throughout their professional lives in the strategic culture of the Cold War, its axioms remain embedded in their mentality.

Of these axioms, by far the most significant is the paradox of deterrence: military forces are most useful when they are not used at all. Despite this, the U.S. military constantly struggled throughout the Cold War to maintain high standards of combat readiness, essentially as a matter of principle. But this axiom had a powerful effect on all other core policy decisions—on the sizes, roles, and budgets of the branches of the armed forces. The risk of combat casualties faced by different categories of the armed forces varies dramatically. The prospect of high casualties, which can rapidly undermine domestic support for any military operation, is the key political constraint when decisions must be made on which forces to deploy in a crisis, and at what levels. Yet the distinction between forces that are only theoretically available and those that are in fact politically usable in real-life confrontations is still largely disregarded. The composition of U.S. military forces reflects the lingering priorities of the Cold War, when U.S. forces served primarily for deterrence and self-reassurance. Today, however, the former is largely ineffectual and the latter unnecessary. Calculations of the cost-effectiveness of conventional forces should therefore be governed by their usability. That is far from being the case at present, and the result is a contradictory military policy.

Send Missiles

When senior Pentagon officials and military officers discuss how the United States might intervene in this or that outbreak of violence somewhere in the world, the likelihood of combat and the probable magnitude of U.S. casualties are invariably dominant in their deliberations. Hence the usual recommendation of such conclaves is to avoid armed intervention altogether, except for bloodless visits by American naval forces to nearby waters or perhaps reconnaissance flights, if possible by remotely piloted aircraft. If the situation is seen as requiring more forceful action, a strike by cruise missiles launched by ships or submarines from a safe distance might be suggested. Because of the considerable cost and limited supply of cruise missiles, however, only manned aircraft are suitable if more persistent bombardment is required. Yet the Pentagon is extremely reluctant to allow their use. The difficulty of finding and hitting specific targets, the possibility that stray bombs will kill innocent civilians, and the strength of enemy antiaircraft defenses are the standard objections, invariably coupled with pessimistic assessments of the likely impact on the enemy and his decisions.

In spite of the Pentagon's huge annual expenditure on airpower, many officers and officials endorse the most critical estimates of its worth and discount claims of its efficacy as "the airpower myth." That was certainly the case during the prolonged controversy from 1992 to 1994 over the use of tactical bombing against Bosnian Serb forces. When the strikes were finally carried out last year, their swift technical and political success surprised the Pentagon, for the accomplishments of airpower in the 1991 Persian Gulf War had been attributed to uniquely favorable circumstances.

Pentagon decision-makers rarely propose the use of ground forces, for which the risk of casualties is inherently high because of their proximity to enemy fire. If the introduction of ground forces is nevertheless advocated by State Department or White House officials, military leaders almost always strongly resist it, arguing for demanding preconditions, beginning with the insistence that "vital" U.S. interests be at stake. With the United States now as secure as it can be in a nuclear world, and with its closest allies largely unthreatened, such a precondition is a virtual prohibition. The United States has all sorts of interests that are or might be threatened, but few can accurately be said to be vital—that is, encompassing the country's very survival.

Should that most stringent prerequisite not suffice, however, the military has others. One is that the goal of any military action be precisely and permanently defined in advance, with no "mission creep" allowed—a demand almost impossible to satisfy in this world of human ambiguities and inconstancies. Another is that a swift and decisive resolution to the conflict be assured, a highly desirable aim to be sure, but one that will always depend on what both sides do and how well they do it. Nor can any results be truly decisive for long. With Iraqi President Saddam Hussein still in power and recurrently threatening Kuwait, was the Persian Gulf War truly decisive?

Planning for the Wrong Wars

Yet when senior Pentagon officials and military officers convene to discuss the overall composition of the armed forces rather than their use in combat, the wide variance in the risk of casualties of the different kinds of military forces does not seem to matter very much. To cite the largest differential, Army and Marine Corps troops are the most likely to suffer combat casualties, while long-range missiles are of course immune, and so-called "strategic" bombers expose very few people to enemy attack. If the entire B-2 force now planned were to be deployed in a conflict, the operation would risk the lives of only thirty-two crew members. Yet under current plans, in 2000 the United States would have the equivalent of twenty-nine divisions of ground forces but only modest numbers of cruise missiles, very few standoff missiles for tactical aircraft, and only six wings of long-range bombers, with 130 aircraft in all.[1] Compare the long-term prorated costs: the annual bill for an active-duty armored or mechanized division is almost $3 billion, and a much smaller light-infantry division requires almost $2 billion, while the average annual cost of the costliest bomber wings, comprised of sixteen B-2 bombers, is less than $1 billion. Likewise, for the annual cost of one armored division, the United States could buy more than 2,000 cruise missiles—a truly formidable force, seven times larger than the number launched during the Persian Gulf War.

Ground forces are undoubtedly more versatile than bombers or cruise missiles. Through well-publicized redeployments, bombers can be used as diplomatic instruments during crises, as well as weapons against valuable targets. And cruise missiles have the virtue of being usable in isolation, for one-time strikes. However, none of that compares with the versatility of ground troops across the entire spectrum of conflict, from mere observation for peacekeeping to high-intensity warfare.

Versatility, however, presumes that the ground forces be usable in combat. In reality, political constraints greatly restrict their availability. The best evidence of that, paradoxically, is last year's decision to send 16,000 troops to Bosnia to oversee the Dayton peace accords. Only after five years of intense national debate, amid countless reports of widespread atrocities and exceptionally destructive warfare, was the Pentagon's opposition to the deployment overcome. Even then, very restrictive conditions were imposed: a rigid one-year time limit and an equally rigid troop limit.

No adversary, should any emerge, need fear attacking U.S. troops, or even bothering to attack them, if they will be deployed for such short times and in such small numbers. Thus the deterrent effects normally inherent in a great power expedition—the high risk that attacks against it may well backfire by provoking an expansion of the force and its role was renounced at the start. With that risk removed, the danger to the troops in Bosnia would be correspondingly increased were it not for the time limit, which invites prospective troublemakers to wait a while before acting. That constraint makes it more likely that the expedition will have a violent aftermath, and will thus be seen as futile. Both restrictions may yet prove unfortunate, but under the circumstances they were politically inevitable. They accurately reflect the current underlying reality that U.S. ground forces are not available as instruments of U.S. foreign policy, except under very unusual conditions.

In theory, the lack of obvious "vital" U.S. interests in Bosnia's vicissitudes conditioned the debate and resulted in the ambivalent decision, although the advocates of intervention did make a rather strong case for a wider U.S. interest in world order. In practice, however, the decisive consideration for opponents of intervention was not the presence or absence of U.S. interests but the fear that too many U.S. troops would be killed. The most senior U.S. military officers stated that explicitly in 1992. Remarkably, General Colin Powell, then chairman of the Joint Chiefs of Staff, not only gave background press briefings to that effect, but even published an article in the daily press to argue against any form of U.S. military intervention in Bosnia.[2]

There is clear evidence that the much-cited calculus of U.S. interests was in fact irrelevant to the Bosnia debate. At the very time the Pentagon was successfully resisting any use of force in the former Yugoslavia in the closing months of 1992, it proffered a U.S. expedition to Somalia. Senior military officers were willing to send U.S. troops there because they mistakenly believed that no casualties would ensue in a mission labeled as humanitarian. They were unwilling to send troops or even use tactical airpower in the former Yugoslavia because they feared there would be fighting and casualties. As always, talk of U.S. interests, present or absent, vital or not, was merely part of the rhetorical carapace of policy decisions driven by more compelling motives.

War from Afar

In a world of wars that are less dangerous but much less likely to be prevented, U.S. military forces must once again be kept primarily for combat rather than for deterrent display. Thus the current composition of U.S. forces as a whole, however versatile in theory, is no longer appropriate. What a particular type of force could do in combat—in a theoretical world where Americans sanctioned all types of military adventures—is or should be irrelevant when deciding the actual composition of the armed forces. What counts is not cost-effectiveness in general, but the cost-effectiveness of the military forces and material that can actually be used during a conflict. The two criteria yield widely divergent results because it is invariably expensive to reduce casualties by developing and deploying ways to move personnel and material farther from harms way on the battlefield while maintaining their effectiveness.

U.S. military policy must also prepare for possible drastic changes in the strategic environment, including the emergence of situations that would require the large-scale use of ground forces and the toleration of high casualties. A full range of military capabilities is needed, but that can be assured by preserving capacity for remobilization and by maintaining lower-cost reserve forces. Once the necessary precautions against sudden and powerful new threats are in place, the United States should acquire the military forces it can actually use as instruments of policy. That would be a prosaic prescription—indeed a mere banality—were it not for America's half-century of immersion in Cold War deterrence, during which weapons and forces were most useful precisely insofar as they were not used.

A wholesale recalibration of U.S. military policy is needed to shift money and resources to the forces actually usable, at the expense of the less usable. There is no way of measuring how usable different kinds of military forces are, even in theory. Such a quality is not fixed and inherent, but depends on the perceived political importance of the task at hand, which can change very quickly indeed. On August 3, 1990, President George Bush evoked scarcely any criticism when he ruled out the use of American military strength to expel Iraqi invasion forces from Kuwait. Yet that became the imperative of his administration very soon thereafter. No U.S. forces were usable under the first decision; all nonnuclear forces were equally usable under the second.

What can be measured as a surrogate for political usability is the inherent exposure to casualties of different categories of forces. As a first approximation of what might be called a casualty exposure index, it would be enough to count the personnel in the close-combat echelons of each kind of force. By that measure, for example, armored brigades with their 400 or so tank crewmen and 300 or so riflemen would have a significantly lower exposure index than light infantry or Marine brigades, which have several times as many riflemen and few heavy weapons. Therefore, under current strategic conditions, the use of armored forces would be advantageous, even in terrain and for tasks that would call for infantry forces according to traditional tactical criteria. One lesson of the Somalia debacle is that armored forces nowadays are preferable to light infantry forces in almost any environment, in spite of their tactical limitations. Inserting forces that are theoretically more suitable only to have to withdraw them abruptly because of politically intolerable casualties accomplishes nothing.

Such rudimentary casualty exposure indexes could be made somewhat more realistic by taking into account the proximity of U.S. combat echelons, broadly defined to include the crews of ships and aircraft, to a combat locale, under the reasonable assumption that the closer the proximity, the greater the likelihood of casualties. With that adjustment, for example, the Navy's amphibian and gunfire-support warships, which must come fairly close to shore, would be assigned higher casualty exposure indexes than Navy ships used primarily to launch cruise missiles. Admittedly, complications intrude when a given type of force can be employed for different purposes; most combat aircraft, for example, can carry out both close-support missions against antiaircraft fire and remote attacks with standoff missiles.

Whether adjusted for proximity or not, meaningful casualty exposure indexes could readily be calculated for each type of force. As proxies for political usability, they would define which forces are most suited for current post-Cold War and "post-heroic" conditions, in which the invariable limiting factor for U.S. military operations is Americans' low tolerance of casualties.

In descending order, a rough ranking of usability would begin with unmanned, long-range weapons (notably ballistic and cruise missiles) and proceed through remote forces with small combat echelons, such as air crews that launch standoff weapons, to the least usable forces, the Army and Marine infantry forces whose combat echelons are useful only in close proximity to the fighting. Such a ranking system should become a central criterion of U.S. military policy, as it would further the acquisition of the forces that are less exposed to casualties and therefore more usable in present conditions.

The United States requires reasonably substantial forces in all categories, from aircraft carriers to infantry divisions. But the current inventory of combat forces contains too many manpower-intensive ground units that are highly exposed to casualties and simply unavailable as instruments of foreign policy.

The overall effect of spending too much money on the upkeep of unusable forces instead of merely maintaining a remobilization capacity for them is that Congress now deems an exceptionally rich menu of important technological innovations unaffordable. The list includes the first practical directed-energy, or laser, weapons capable of intercepting rockets and ballistic missiles, which are a scourge from Sarajevo to Israel; stealth aircraft, which are substantially immune to radar detection in most situations and therefore capable of doing much with few fliers exposed to enemy attack and even fewer losses; remotely piloted aerial vehicles, now available only in sample numbers and not yet for strike roles; more and better cruise and standoff missiles; versatile advanced munitions; and all the diverse applications of information technology that only await funding to be implemented, not to mention those that could be developed with more money.

The promise of these innovations is not a stronger United States—it is strong enough—but rather a greater ability to use force remotely, accurately and with discrimination. Tactical bombing, guided and protected by a host of electronic ancillaries and aimed with now-routine precision, proved very effective in Bosnia, notwithstanding the seemingly decisive reasons why it should have failed. So far, however, only fixed or large, easily recognizable targets are vulnerable to remote attack. That may be good enough in classic war situations, as in the Persian Gulf War, but the lower the intensity of conflict, the less can be achieved by attacking airfields, depots, headquarters, or other major targets. The promise of the potential innovations is a greater ability to contend with more elusive enemies in more ambiguous situations.

It is unwise to retard these innovations in the armed forces, but not because dangerous threats to vital U.S. interests are imminent. On the contrary, capital-intensive forces that have the lowest possible exposure to casualties are needed precisely because at present there are no threats that might justify substantial American casualties. The use of military forces will likely continue to be discretionary, as it has been in Bosnia, Haiti, and Somalia, rather than imperative. Some continue to argue against all such discretionary interventions, not coincidentally with the vehement support of senior officers who represent the most manpower-intensive forces. Abstention from all interventions would certainly allow an indefinite delay in the refocusing of U.S. military policy at the expense of those very forces.

There are always strong arguments against any particular U.S. military intervention, and all discretionary interventions can be dismissed as "social work," that is, feel-good endeavors disconnected from core U.S. interests. But what may be true of any single intervention—and was certainly true of the Somalia expedition—is not true of all. If the possessor of much of the world's military power refuses to use it, greater world disorder is only the most immediate consequence. At a time when Cold War restraint has given way to adventurism, if U.S. military power is withheld in one crisis after another, it is bound to stimulate the growth of other military powers. A vacuum will have been created that other countries will fill.

A policy of nonintervention would yield a world not only less stable, but also more militarized. That would certainly affect core U.S. interests, at the very least by damaging economic development and undermining civilian rule, even if no direct threats were to emerge or increase. Hence, the urgency of redefining the priorities of U.S. military policy, to yield forces that can be deployed more readily for discretionary interventions. To fight only when necessity compels is the attribute of small powers. The United States fortunately lacks the classic expansionist proclivities of the great powers of history, but it does have widespread responsibilities that call for appropriate military means.

Notes

1. "Standoff" missiles are air-to-surface missiles capable of attacking enemy targets from beyond the reach of local air defenses and counterattacks, or from friendly airspace behind a battlefield area.
2. Colin L. Powell, "Why Generals Get Nervous," *New York Times*, October 8, 1992.

20

The True Military Revolution at Last

The very success of air bombardment in recent wars has revealed its limitations: in most cases, the maneuver of forces on the ground is essential to make aerial firepower effective. If enemy forces need not concentrate to resist attack from the ground, they can remain dispersed, camouflaged and protected against attack from the air as well. By contrast, if they must gather and deploy to oppose action on the ground, they become correspondingly more vulnerable to action from the air.

At the same time, however, recent wars have exposed the redundancy built into the very structure of U.S. ground forces: they continue to provide their own heavy firepower instead of relying on the proven ability of manned and unmanned aircraft to do the same job far more flexibly and effectively. Redundancy would be no bad thing if it merely meant that the armed forces are more costly than they need to be, for it provides insurance against the vicissitudes of war. But the redundant heavy firepower of U.S. ground forces is not merely costly but also a most severe limitation on their mobility, both strategic in reaching overseas theaters of war in timely fashion, and operational, in moving within any extensive theater of war, as in Iraq.

The mechanized forces of the U.S. Army with their battle tanks and infantry combat vehicles, and even U.S. Marine Corps formations with few tanks certainly cannot be both light and powerful, but it is the artillery that really restricts their mobility, not because of the weapons themselves but rather because of the huge number of ammunition trucks that must follow in their wake. Their volume and weight accounts for the greater part of the logistic load of expeditionary forces, while in combat their mobility is far inferior not because trucks are any slower mechanically than armored vehicles, indeed they are faster, but rather because their advance can be stopped by even by the lightest enemy resistance. Without them, the maneuver forces of the Army and Marines could be deployed far more rapidly to distant theaters of war, and within them they could advance dynamically at their own speed of maneuver. Now by contrast they are restricted to a slow and methodical pace because they cannot far outstrip the long and very vulnerable truck columns that carry the artillery's ammunition. According to a Defense Science Board investigation of the logistic requirements of mechanized units, the single largest consumer of fuel was neither the tank nor the infantry component but rather the artillery's truck element. A negative spiral is at work, because ammunition trucks and their crews require fuel, protection, food, and water, all supplied by truck columns that themselves require fuel, protection, food, and water.

If they relied primarily on air power instead of their own artillery, the U.S. Army and Marine Corps could more fully adapt themselves to today's geopolitical circumstances, in which fixed fronts and continental garrisons have given way to global strategic mobility.

It would be a wonderful thing at the operational level, for then the U.S. Army could advance in depth in a fluid and flexible manner, without running short of firepower at the point of battle.

It would be a wonderful thing tactically, for any squad of the Army or Marine Corps could at any time become the spearhead of an entire offensive in concert with remote firepower against the enemy's vulnerable centers of gravity.

Ground advocates are quick to say that airpower could not do the job—not during the Second World War, not in Korea, not in Vietnam, not even the first Gulf War. But they miss the more important point that airpower has become increasingly effective since its inception one century ago, steadily changing the optimal balance and employment of forces. In no era has that transformation been most evident than in the precision and stealth revolution of the last several decades.

It has always been true that air power has the advantage in concentration, unaffected as it is by land mobility limits that spatially fragment ground forces. That ability to concentrate must be balanced, however, by the simple fact that airpower is condemned to be weak or absent everywhere except in those places where it is planned to be applied. While artillery fires can only be concentrated within the limited effective range of guns or rockets (not much more than twenty miles), airpower available in a theater of war or even globally can quickly be concentrated wherever needed within the limits of aircraft range, which even without refueling invariably exceeds by orders of magnitude the maximum firing range of any ground force weapon.

For all its actual and potential virtues, however, until very recently airpower could not completely replace artillery.

In spite of the notorious inaccuracy of bombing in the early years of airpower, the major obstacle was not a lack of accuracy. Even Second World War dive-bombing could be accurate enough against soft targets, and besides, the first air-to-ground guided missiles were coming into service half a century ago. Originally too unreliable or too costly or both for any large scale use, they eventually evolved into today's very reliable precision-guided weapons which can also be quite cheap.

A more important obstacle than inaccuracy was the chronic lack of continuity of airpower. Artillery can constantly be kept ready to fire on demand, and given enough ammunition can actually keep firing hour after hour, for days on end—given the availability of an almost endless logistics train across sea, air, and ground. Aircraft by contrast cannot be kept constantly overhead ready for action, unless they are very abundant, reasonably close to their bases, and have little threat from enemy fighters or anti-aircraft weapons. Moreover, air operations are frequently degraded, delayed or even interrupted by bad weather, while good visibility from aircraft to target is still required for many forms of air-to-ground attack with infra-red guidance or laser-homing weapons for example. And then of course enemy forces will do whatever they can to oppose the continuity of air operations with anti-aircraft weapons and with their own air forces.

But even continuity is not the obstacle it once was. To begin with, air attacks can now be executed with weapons whose guidance is quite independent of inter-visibility, launched from aircraft flying high over the weather, distant surface vessels, and submarines. As to manned aircraft, with today's landing aids and satellite-referenced navigation, they are much less affected by adverse weather than they once were. Even for the brevity of any one aircraft flight as compared to the continuous persistence of artillery there are remedies, both the old procedure of "taxi-rank" sortie scheduling to keep some aircraft overhead continuously, and the new remedy of long-endurance unmanned air vehicles.

The really severe obstacle to the substitution of ground firepower with far less constraining aerial firepower has not been the lack of continuity or accuracy, but rather the lack of timely knowledge—a matter of data processing, so to speak, and of data transmission. Even if integrated with a most powerful air force, the ground forces could not dispense with their own organic artillery firepower, because they could not rely on air commands and pilots to identify the right targets to attack quickly enough-a matter of mere minutes for a unit about to be overrun, and perhaps not much more to strike at enemy forces on the move. Actually troops on the ground could not even be sure that their own location would be known precisely enough to avert attack by their own air force: "friendly" bombing and strafing was a permanent hazard whenever the close air support of ground operations was attempted.

It is in that respect that there has been a technical revolution, which now awaits structural change to become an operational and strategic revolution—in the collection and processing of timely information on targets and forces, and its secure, near instantaneous transmission to air commands, operational units, and individual pilots. Air to surface guided weapons capable of very high accuracy have long been in service—the first were employed in combat in 1943, and laser-guided bombs were first employed in Vietnam. But it is the information revolution that has made it possible to designate targets just as accurately, and transmit the information quickly enough for timely action.

Although operational and tactical applications of airpower against armed forces in the field are potentially far more revolutionary in their implications, the first results were manifest in the systemic, "strategic" bombardment of Iraq in 1991 These operations were so very different from the strategic bombardment campaigns of the Second World War. As is well known, Baghdad was shut down as a functioning capital city, regime power center, and military headquarter complex in less than 48 hours, while by contrast in Berlin everything critical to the war effort was still going strong as late as January 30, 1945 after years of increasingly heavy bombardment.

Until 1991 therefore, strategic bombardment had been yet another manifestation of mass production and mass warfare with its mass casualties—in the Second World War, the British Bomber Command alone lost more than 51,000 aircrew, and needed hundreds of new bombers each month to keep just over 1,000 ready for action against Germany. The 1991 bombing offensive was radically different, with accuracy in selecting and attacking targets replacing mass, to yield a campaign that resembled a series of commando operations aimed by precise intelligence rather than frontal attacks against the broad array of enemy lines. The total tonnage of guided bombs and missiles delivered by U.S. aircraft throughout the air offensive, from January 17 to February 27, 1991 was only 17,109 tons, an average of 427 tons per day, as against the big raids against German cities in which some 10,000 tons were dropped in one night.

Because the 1999 Kosovo war was fought under the conjoined strategic direction of every member of the North Atlantic Alliance, each of whose governments seemed to have its own shifting opinion of what could be bombed and when, there was no concerted "decapitation" offensive right at the start as in Iraq. Instead there was a torturous progression from symbolic initial raids to the increasingly heavy but not especially focused bombing of one set of targets after another, from weapon factories to major road bridges. Finally, after eleven weeks of air strikes, Serbia's elected President seemingly deferred to the frightened and inconvenienced public and the loss of his crony power base by accepting the loss of Kosovo. Thus in spite of the lack of anything resembling a coherent strategy, air bombardment finally succeeded with no greater ground action than the insignificant skirmishing of the so-called "Kosovo Liberation Army." As in 1991, no extensive destruction was inflicted, as single targets well chosen or otherwise were destroyed one by one, with very little unwanted damage roundabout. Aircrew losses were zero, another first for airpower because in 1991 there had been a few.

In the 2001 offensive that destroyed the Taliban regime of Afghanistan, airpower could not possibly have succeeded on its own. Even if all concentrated targets of any value had been destroyed—ramshackle command posts, a few ammunition dumps and depots, a handful of fighter jets, a malfunctioning radar at Kandahar airport and others such—the Taliban would not have been significantly weakened. Their very backwardness, their lack of structured military organizations, made them almost immune to systemic "strategic" bombard-ment—which could not be usefully directed against the country's miserable civilian infrastructure either. Yet the bombing was perfectly effective all the same, by hitting the Taliban whenever they gathered to resist the forward thrusts of the Tadjik, Uzbek and Hazara militias—who were in turn willing to advance and attack only because the Americans with them could call down very precise air attacks at very short notice.

Although the 1991 Gulf War marked the advent of routine precision in air bombardment, old style unguided "iron" bombs still accounted for most of the tonnage dropped. It was obvious enough that accuracy in hitting targets could only be as useful as the accuracy of the intelligence that selected those targets, which of course required a vast effort to collect, analyze and prioritize information on thousands of separate aiming points. But because all of the "strategic" bombing—as opposed to the improvised tactical bombing of mili-tary forces—was aimed at fixed installation of one kind or another, it could be planned in advance during the five and a half months that intervened between the August 1990 invasion of Kuwait and the start of the air offensive, or rather as soon as the intelligence could be obtained. To be sure, once the bombing campaign started targets were selected day by day by the operational head-quarters of the all-service air commander in Saudi Arabia, but with an overall plan already framed and individual targets already identified. In spite of all the vivid techno-imagery relayed to television audiences, the entire strategic air offensive was directed with much less advanced telecommunications than available today—paper target files, card-index priority lists, telephone land lines and enciphered radio of 1944 vintage would have been quite sufficient. As a matter of scarcely believable fact, daily target lists were indeed sent to the U.S. Navy's aircraft carriers by "hand of officer" in pure 1944 style, to remedy the lack of secure broad-band communications. In the 1999 Kosovo war, guided weapons predominated for the first time, but again the targets were pre-planned and transmitted before take-off, and moreover during the first month of bombing there were so few targets that 1944 procedures would have been more than adequate.

Paradoxically it was only in the 2001 fighting against the utterly primitive Taliban that the full panoply of Information Technology implemented by the U.S. armed forces so far was actually used, and was essential for success. The Special Forces commandos and CIA operators who so impressed local warriors with their seemingly magical ability to summon accurate air strikes against the Taliban, could not have done so without GPS satellite location devices. That equipment moreover was light enough to be carried easily by men on foot, or sometimes on horseback, and very reliable it was too.

As for the aircraft that did the bombing, they could never have been at the right place at the right time with the right weapons without the competent operation of a vast array of computers and electronic data links. These aircraft interfaced with headquarters on the ground—the nearest hundreds of miles away in Saudi Arabia—aboard aircraft carriers and command warships, or built into the aircraft themselves, not just the bombers and fighters themselves but also all the other aircraft that made them effective: radar reconnaissance aircraft with synthetic aperture terrain mapping radar, and moving-target indicators that could spot a single Taliban's Toyota pick-up truck; photographic and electronic intelligence collectors, airborne command posts, and much-needed refueling tankers.

With targets so poorly defined ("low contrast") and constantly on the move, 1944 manual methods could never have ensured the timely take-off of each kind of aircraft, sometimes multiple in-flight refuelings, and the final encounters with elusive enemies. Afghanistan was much too large, too distant from take-off points, the front-less fighting was much too inchoate, and the Taliban were much too dispersed to orbit fighter-bombers overhead in cab-rank fashion for strikes on demand from forward controllers on the ground or flying in light aircraft-the method introduced in the Second World War, routinely used in Korea and still predominant in Vietnam. It might have worked once or twice, if only in daylight, but it would mostly have wasted sorties even as they were urgently needed elsewhere in Afghanistan. As it was, all the complexities of sending out aircraft of differing characteristics and armament on a multitude of specific individual missions were successfully overcome, to yield airpower at its most discriminating and economical.

After the 1991 Gulf War, to some it was still uncertain if warfare had changed in any fundamental way, for the old could still be said to predominate on the new. Some asserted that the 1991 Gulf War was decided by the 100-hour ground offensive rather than the month-long air campaign. This kind of an assertion is an essential contention to defend the status quo, with the vast expenditures of surface forces on armored, mechanized and artillery forces that still very much resemble their predecessors of the Second World War. These weapons cannot absorb more technological advancement than their unchanging configurations will allow-hence while one of today's jet fighters, or guided bombs, is worth dozens of its 1944 predecessors if any comparison can be valid at all, today's very best battle tank could not outfight three 1944 Tigers in close combat.

It is true that while Iraq's air force and abundantly equipped air defenses were almost immediately incapacitated by the disruption of their command and control, the effect of the bombing on Iraq's vast army was invisibly cumulative rather than instantaneous. Nor could precision bombing destroy dug-in Iraqi armored vehicles except one by one, by the direct hits of guided bombs or missiles (less reliably)—either way a slow grinding down much too costly in scarce fighter-bomber missions to defeat an army with tens of thousands of tanks, troop carriers and artillery pieces. That right from the start the mass of Saddam Hussein's armor could not advance into Saudi Arabia to deny ports and airfields to American expeditionary forces, because columns and convoys would have been fatally vulnerable to precision air attacks, was just as true but not so obvious. It was even less evident that once forced into passivity, the Iraqi army in and near Kuwait was increasingly paralyzed by the denial of food, water, fuel and ammunition caused by the bombing of rail and road bridges, ammunition dumps, oil refineries, petroleum product tank farms, and major supply depots. As for General Schwarzkopf's final ground offensive, a prosaic turning movement straight from the rule-book, it was certainly meant in earnest by all who were there, but did not require much veritable fighting. Iraqi troops already immobilized, often hungry and thirsty, diminished by desertions and by the loss of many heavy weapons to air attacks, scarcely resisted the advance of American and allied ground forces around and through Kuwait. Very heavily armored U.S. Army M1 battle tanks advanced unscathed, but so did lightly protected troop carriers, the jeeps of the French Foreign Legion, even the rented cars of adventurous journalists.

After the 2001 Afghanistan war, however, it was no longer possible to deny that a radically new way of fighting and winning had emerged: the Special Forces teams that energized and directed Tadjik, Uzbek, and Hazara militiamen into battle had very little firepower of their own—less than we had in our platoon—yet they were able to employ ample firepower in their operations. All of it was aerial and thus provided remotely without imposing any burdens of conveyance, protection or re-supply on the sparse U.S. presence on the ground—just as well, given Afghan conditions, with no access to the sea, no equipped airfields, vast distances, difficult mountain terrain, and very few roads none of them good. In addition to close air support of unprecedented reliability—past attempts to assist guerillas in this way tended to fail disastrously—there was also real innovation in the more prevalent mission of airpower appropriately postulated as battlefield air operations, in this case the independent air attack of transient targets in the rear, mostly Taliban vehicles. Compared to the vastness of Afghanistan, the forces on both sides were very small, and they had no long road convoys behind them to bring up supplies in the manner of modern armies. In a mostly empty landscape, fighter-bombers could not usefully hunt for targets along the highways as in previous wars from Normandy in 1944 onwards. Yet the Taliban were immobilized by air attacks all the same, because the scattered reports originating from ground spotters, unmanned air vehicles, aircraft with attentive crews, or at night with forward-looking infra red sights and synthetic aperture radars, could all be processed almost instantaneously into coherent information on what was moving, where, in what direction and what speed.

In sum, the war in Afghanistan in spite of its not coincidental brevity and extreme backwardness of the enemy, amounted to a first and exceedingly successful implementation of the new kind of warfare that is now possible, in which movement on the ground is no longer encumbered by the necessities of fire, quite separately provided from the air. And this is truly new, unlike the much-touted "information warfare" that contains not one genuine innovation over the many varieties of electronic spoofing, jamming, disruption and interception of command and communication networks, and the sophisticated counterespionage radio games (*funkspiele*), of the Second World War.

As the currently fashionable term "network-centric warfare" implies, what was demonstrated in Afghanistan was a novel capacity to focus against the enemy the peculiar strengths and skills of very different kinds of units operating under separate chains of command, not as in the past by slow and at times inconclusive staff coordination procedures, but rather by the digital linking of the different data networks, so that all units involved had simultaneous access to the same body of information, from which symmetrical conclusions were naturally drawn given a modicum of strategic direction from the top. This change is of greater magnitude than any merely technical innovation, for to an important extent classic top down hierarchical communications are replaced by almost spontaneous forms of horizontal cooperation.

Under whatever name (I favor information-*based* operations), the new kind of warfare is at least a partial implementation of the broader set of innovations long deemed possible, and long advocated by the veteran Pentagon guru, Andrew Marshall, director of Net Assessment, the so-called Revolution in Military Affairs. That Soviet-sounding phrase is an oblique acknowledgment of its original inspiration, the "Reconnaissance-Strike Complex" proposed by the late Soviet General Staff in the later Brezhnev years. It too was ultimately an attempt to liberate movement from the encumbrances of fire to exploit its full potential for maneuver, while making a much better use of fire by liberating it from the inevitable fragmentation of all forces capable of movement. The system's starting point was the computer-assisted fusion of intelligence from all sources to identify and locate all targets of potential interest. On that basis, the computer-assisted command headquarters would determine priorities among the identified targets, and select the most appropriate means to attack them from the full range of possibilities: ballistic and cruise missiles, manned bombers and fighter-bombers, unmanned air vehicles, tube and rocket artillery, even commando raids. Finally, the system would issue computer-generated orders for each one of the separate but simultaneous attacks of an overall offensive, check to ensure their execution, assess the damage inflicted through more computer-assisted intelligence fusion, and order second and third attacks against insufficiently damaged targets.

This envisaged "Reconnaissance-Strike Complex" was not meant as a mere addition to the Soviet Union's vast array of traditional military forces inherited from the Second World War, which were indeed to be much reduced in size and made much more agile-it is indicative that Soviet commando forces were greatly enhanced in those final years.

Perhaps it was precisely because the Soviet computer industry was so backward that the Soviet General Staff was so innovative in its thinking: it could not achieve the merely incremental improvements that satisfied its American counterparts, who were content to simply add lots of computers to their traditional military forces.

What happened in Afghanistan proves that much more than merely incremental improvements are possible when information technology is used inter alia to substitute precise aerial force application for ground firepower. But that is as much benefit as can be expected from the Revolution in Military Affairs so long as the traditional structure and content of the military forces inherited from the Second World War persists essentially unchanged.

Part 5

Byzantium: Faith and Power

21

The Grand Strategy of the Byzantine Empire

When the Spanish conquerors reached the colossal pyramids and plazas of Teotihuacan, only a few centuries abandoned, they found no one who could tell them anything at all about the awesome sight, which remains a mystery till this day. What could have been Mexico's classical culture—a source of inspiration and reassurance through the ages—had been utterly extinguished, the language, thoughts, and very identity of Teotihuacan's builders entirely forgotten.

Of classical Greece too we would only have the bare stones to look upon in ignorant admiration, if its uniquely creative culture had not been kept alive by the readers, editors, commentators, and copyists of the Roman Empire, until the study of Greek texts was joyfully resumed by the scholars of the Renaissance.

But it was not the western branch of the Roman Empire, commanded from Italy, that assured this most precious continuity. Fatally weakened by the arrival of the Huns in its proximity, increasingly fragmented by Germanic confederates, mercenaries and invaders, nothing was left of its power by the time Romulus Augustulus, last imperial figurehead in the West, was finally deposed in 476. Latin culture was never quite extinguished in the ensuing centuries, but even the language of Greece was forgotten in the western lands, except for a few, isolated ancient cities in the extremity of southern Italy.

Very different was the fate of the eastern branch of the Roman Empire centered on Constantinople—the empire that we call Byzantine by modern habit though it never called itself anything but Roman in laws, edicts, and inscriptions. Having expelled its own Germanic mercenaries and outmaneuvered Attila's Huns in the supreme crisis of the fifth century, the empire resisted each new wave of invaders from the Eurasian steppe, the Persian Empire, the lands of Islam, and the reinvigorated West too for century after century until the Catholic conquest of 1204, even then reviving once more until the final Turkish victory of 1453. Except for the most common texts, and a handful re-translated from Arabic, it was only because the writings of classical Greece continued to be read, appreciated, studied, edited, and recopied in the Byzantine Empire for more than a thousand years that the fragile sequence of manuscripts finally reached the safe harbor of the first printing presses.

This epic of cultural survival, so central to the history of Western civilization, was itself made possible by epic strategic successes. For it was not by mere obdurate resistance that the Byzantine Empire survived, but by a series of creative responses to seemingly overwhelming threats. More than once, successive defeats reduced the empire to little more that a beleaguered city-state; more than once, Constantinople itself came under attack from the sea or by land, or both at once. But time after time, its great walls kept enemy forces at bay while allies were found to attack them, the invaders were driven back, and the imperial power was restored over larger territories than before.

What the East Romans accomplished is known and obvious from the very maps of the empire. But how they did it remains a matter of great controversy, because much of their power derived not from tangible military strength, but from an invisible advantage, the persistent superiority of Byzantine strategy.

What is Strategy?

Much more than sound judgment or competent practice, very different from ordinary common sense, strategy is governed by a peculiar logic of its own:

Men do not understand...[the coincidence of opposites]: there is a "back-stretched connection" like that of the bow...

Thus Herakleitos of Ephesus (c.500 B.C.), thought very obscure by the ancients but for us totally transparent after the experience of nuclear deterrence, whereby the peaceful had to be constantly ready to attack, and nuclear weapons could only be useful if not used. Deterrence unveiled for all to see the paradoxical (i.e., seemingly contradictory) logic of strategy, the "back-stretched" connection that unites opposites. With that Herakleitos, the first Western strategic thinker ("war is the father of all") was finally vindicated, though long before him many a cunning fighter had won by surprising his enemy—a thing only possible when better ways of attacking, hence the expected ways, are deliberately avoided. In that coincidence of opposites, the bad way is the good way precisely because it is bad, and vice versa. Nor is surprise merely an advantage among many, but rather a suspension of the entire predicament of conflict, which is defined precisely by the presence of a *reacting* antagonist who seeks to defeat, evade or deflect all that is done against him. A similar coincidence of opposites is embodied in the Roman precept *si vis pacem para bellum,* if you want peace prepare for war. Almost always content with peace, the Byzantine Empire did so ceaselessly

The modern strategist, Carl von Clausewitz, went beyond the mere re-coincidence of opposites to uncover their processes of reversal one into the other; as for example, on the largest scale: *of victory into defeat*: after its culminating point, victory exhausts the will to fight, overstretches the victorious forces, frightens neutrals into enmity and allies into neutrality; and, *of war into peace*: war itself consumes the means and the will to persist in war, while war losses devalue war-termination losses, thus, e.g., the abandonment of South Vietnam was accepted by U.S. opinion, once enough American lives were lost. As for peace, it undoes over time the preparations that can dissuade war, and also dissolves the fear of war's consequences.

On a lesser scale, Clausewitz showed how the victorious army advancing can advance to its own defeat, while the losing army retreating can gather strength.

And prescriptively Clausewitz offered the solution: stop short of the culminating point, pause, allow the re-establishment of new equilibria (from the acceptance of a new status quo by allies and neutrals, to an army's logistics), and then resume again.

Because the enemy is a reacting being, straightforward actions usually fail; yet "engineering" approaches that treat enemies as inert objects are persistently seductive. When RAF Chief of Staff Charles Portal submitted a mathematically compelling plan on September 25, 1941 that asked first call on all British resources to build a 4,000-bomber force to defeat Germany in six months by bombing forty-three German urban-industrial centers "beyond recovery," Prime Minister Winston S. Churchill rejected the plan, pointing out that if the bombing *did* begin to succeed, the Germans would not passively await defeat, but would instead strengthen their air defenses and disperse their industries, for in war "all things are always on the move simultaneously." Twenty years later, Robert S. McNamara emulated Portal's error with his Mutual Assured Destruction scheme to stabilize deterrence and stop the nuclear arms' race. McNamara's calculation that a reliable ability to destroy half the population and three-quarters of the other side's industrial capacity was ample to deter was unexceptional, but he overlooked the possibility that Soviet leaders might not want what he wanted, i.e., the paralyzed stability of mutual deterrence.

Conflict unfolds at separate levels (grand strategic, theater-strategic, operational, tactical) which interpenetrate downward much more easily than upward. Thus in the Second World War, Hitler's choice of the wrong allies and the wrong enemies at the level of grand strategy could not be overcome by any number of German tactical-, operational-, or even theater-level victories (notably over France, in 1940). Had the D-Day landings been repulsed, Germany would not have won the war but would instead have become the first target of the atom bomb a year later, instead of Japan. As for the latter, given the complete inability of the Japanese to follow through by marching on Washington to impose their peace, the combat success of the Pearl Harbor attack was not even useless: it was counter-productive. Had Japanese pilots failed miserably on that day, evoking ridicule instead of hatred, the outcome of the war would have been the same, but at least the United States might have dealt less harshly with Japan. Again there is a parallel in Sun Tzu: "what is of supreme importance in war is to attack the enemy's strategy; next best is to disrupt his alliances; next best is to attack his army," i.e., the strategic prevails over the tactical.

Practice

Given overwhelming superiority (material *and* moral), wars can be won and peace kept without need of strategy. Antagonists too weak to react significantly are, in effect, mere objects. War may still present huge difficulties, e.g., because of distance, terrain etc. But to overcome physical problems it is not the paradoxical logic of strategy that is wanted but rather the "linear" logic of sound common sense, and of the relevant applied sciences. Hence it is those fighting against the odds, the outnumbered, the beleaguered and the overambitious, who have exploited the logic of strategy in their real-life practices. Naturally, more often than not, the great names of strategy, most notably Napoleon, ultimately failed.

In all their variety, *grand strategies* can be compared by the extent of their reliance on costly force, as opposed to: the leveraging of potential force by diplomacy ("armed suasion"); inducements (subsidies, gifts, honors); and deception and propaganda. The lesser the force-content, the greater the possibility of transcending the material balance of strength, to achieve more with less. During the Cold War, the United States successfully protected many allies with relatively economical forces, little actual fighting, and a constant striving to uphold the armed suasion of nuclear deterrence. In this, Alexander the Great was a precursor, but the Byzantines remain the unsurpassed masters. Before his death while retreating from a foolhardy attempt to invade India, Alexander had already earned millennial glory by conquering Achaemenid Iran, the only superpower for the Greeks. While his tactics were "hard" (frontal attacks by the infantry phalanx, and all-out cavalry charges) Alexander's diplomacy was "soft" and inclusive, as symbolized by the encouragement of Macedonian-Iranian marriages, to win over Achaemenid satraps and vassal-peoples.

The East Roman empire by us called Byzantine was least Roman in its strategy. Successively threatened from the east by Sassanid Persia, the Arabs and finally the Turks, and from the north by waves of steppe invaders, the Huns, Avars, Khazars, Pechenegs, Bulgars, Magyars, and Mongols, the Byzantines could not hope to subdue or annihilate all comers in the classic Roman manner. To wear out their own forces (chiefly of expensive cavalry) in order to utterly destroy the immediate enemy would only open the way for the next wave of invaders. The genius of Byzantine grand strategy was to turn the very multiplicity of enemies to advantage, by employing diplomacy, deception, payoffs and religious conversion to induce them to fight one another instead of fighting the empire (only their self-image as the only defenders of the only true faith preserved their moral equilibrium). Intercepted deep into the steppe by imperial envoys bearing gifts and misinformation, new arrivals were induced to attack the prior wave from the rear, or stand against the next wave, or bypass the imperial frontiers altogether. In this scheme of things, military strength was subordinated to diplomacy instead of the other way around, and used preferably to contain or punish rather than attack or defend in full force.

Other successful territorial empires, in China, India, and Iran followed similar grand strategies, while the Roman, Ottoman, and Spanish empires tended to rely more on force, all three commanding—and expending—the necessary resources. Even so, all three employed diplomacy to intimidate and win over potential enemies, and all three magnified their sphere of control cheaply, through client-states, client-tribes and dependent principalities. For the Romans, the cost of empire increased when garrisoned frontiers replaced the client fringe (by the end of the first century C.E.), increasing much more when a defense-in-depth of mobile armies was also needed (from the third century C.E.), to counter-attack enemies that penetrated the frontiers.

The grand strategy of the British naval ascendancy (fully formed by the early eighteenth century) certainly achieved power greatly in excess of material means. Its essence was to keep continental Europe divided and at war ("to uphold the balance of power" in self-serving British rhetoric) by persuasion, gold, and timely expeditionary interventions to prop up the weaker side. That forced the continental powers to devote their resources to the upkeep of their armies, leaving little for their navies, which the British navy could then economically defeat. That in turn enabled the British maritime empire to exceed its Portuguese, Spanish, and Dutch predecessors and also the French colonial empire, without requiring a vast naval effort: British naval supremacy was actually secured on land, by the balance-of-power policy. In our own time, it was the Soviet Union that for a while acquired power greatly in excess of its economic capacity, by employing ideological propaganda to enlist devotees all over the world and prop up client regimes, deception to mask weaknesses, subversion to outmaneuver opponents, and espionage to transcend technological limits. It was only when the Soviet leadership decided to acquire an actual, material, military supremacy (after the failure of the "Missile Gap" deception and the humiliation of the 1962 Cuba missile crisis) that their ambitions ruinously exceeded Soviet economic limitations.

Other substitutes for force at the level of grand strategy, have included the penetration of enemy societies, and the exploitation of inculcated fears. Exemplifying the former, Genghis Khan's Mongols captured walled cities though lacking in siege-craft because caravan merchants won over by their reliable, cheap protection betrayed the gates of merchants' quarters. The Arab invasion of the Byzantine Empire was likewise helped by dissident monophysite Christians, won over by Islam's promise of religious toleration. Exemplifying the latter, Timur-i-lenk terrorized enemies into pre-emptive surrender by staging spectacular massacres. Hitler's *Blitzkrieg* offensives were likewise preceded by fear propaganda (notably by newsreel) and featured "terror bombing" more demoralizing than physically damaging.

In all their variety through the ages, *military strategies* (comprising the theater, operational, and tactical levels) can also be compared on the basis of a single criterion: their content of circumventing, disruptive maneuver, as opposed to force-on-force, destructive, attrition. The smaller the attrition content, the less material strength is needed to achieve given results. But high-payoff maneuver methods tend to entail proportionate risks. Thus it is the weak and the over-ambitious who have mostly relied on maneuver, while the well-provided through the ages have tended to rely on attrition.

Because of the vast resources secured by their organizational abilities, the Romans could generally afford the low-risk/low-payoff methods they much preferred them. Actually, the entire Roman style of war was positively anti-heroic (when charged with lacking aggressiveness, Scipio Africanus conqueror of Carthage replied "my mother bore me a general, not a warrior"). Relying on the routine skills of well-trained, salaried soldiers rather than the ephemeral fighting spirit of warriors, on sound procedures rather the fortuitous talents of great generals, the Romans preferred to buy off enemies if it was cheaper than fighting them (*not* a decadent late-empire practice); if war still ensued, they preferred sieges to unpredictable battles, and then preferred to end them by starving out the enemy rather than by assault (the legion was a combat-engineer force). Tactically, Roman warfare was mostly pure attrition, with enemies methodically cut down by the relentless advance of armored infantry. It was at the theater level that the Romans relied on maneuver, conquering by the vast encirclements of converging armies on a scale not achieved again till Napoleon. The Ottomans also had great organizational abilities and they too relied on attrition; their *yeni seri* were the first uniformed, drilled, rationed, and professionally commanded infantry since Roman times—complete with the first-ever military bands.

In our days it is the American style of war that has exemplified attrition; sometimes it has amounted to little more than the administration of firepower. Very successful against rigid fronts on land, at sea against both German U-boats and Japanese fleets once means became abundant, sometimes successful in the form of air bombing even before the 1991 Gulf War advent of *routine* precision, U.S.-style attrition only failed badly against guerrillas who stubbornly refused to assemble into conveniently targetable massed formations. But when Americans lacked material superiority, they did not lack for ingenuity; MacArthur's 1950 counter-offensive in Korea with its high risk/high payoff Inchon landings is the very model of maneuver at the theater level.

Maneuver at any level is meant to disrupt and demoralize enemies by cir-cumventing their strengths and exploiting their weaknesses; that is only possible if the enemy's ability to react is negated by surprise, and/or out-maneuvered at each successive stage of combat by more rapid decisions and actions. Hitler's *Blitzkriegen* of 1939-41 achieved results far greater than German material strength. At the operational level, the long, thin deep-penetration columns were theoretically very vulnerable to flank attacks, but instead overrun the enemy forces, supply trains and headquarters caught unprepared in the soft rear of pierced fronts. The Germans had little armor, but enough for tank spearheads to set a rapid pace; they had little airpower, but enough to dive-bomb at critical points to open the way, and to interdict flank attacks. At the theater level, the *Blitzkrieg* disrupted by inducing hasty retreats: advance detachments pushed into the enemy's deep rear would lead to the hurried withdrawal of forces that might have prevailed if left in place. When the Red Army replicated and powerfully outmatched the German method, it did so with less tactical talent but much more real strength.

Deep-penetration maneuver had a long pre-1939 history, from the steppe horse-nomads to Napoleon. Tactically, the horse-nomads fought as they hunted. Enemies were outmaneuvered, trapped and killed as game was, by the arrows of powerful sinew-and-bone compound bows (better than Napoleon's muskets). Able to live off the milk, blood and flesh of their spare horses, with their families mounted also, the horse-nomads had unlimited strategic mobility in grasslands. Attila's Huns first showed what horse-nomads could achieve, if enough of them obeyed a single leader; but it was Genghis Khan who united entire horse-nomad nations to conquer on a Eurasian scale by fast, deep-penetration, all-cavalry advances that overrun enemies before they could muster their defenses. Thus few Mongols defeated many more Russians and Chinese.

Just as the Arab invasions were propelled by a then highly functional religion, whose very rituals taught discipline and drill, and whose tenets positively required war for the conquest of non-Muslims while allowing the incentive of looting, Napoleonic warfare was propelled by a then highly functional ideology. *Liberté, Egalité, Fraternité* attracted volunteers from all Europe, won over many of the educated in enemy societies—and allowed French officers to allow their ideologized men to skirmish ahead without fear of mass desertions. To this, the organizational genius of Napoleon added efficient logistics and entire cadres of excellent subordinates, while his operational genius perfected the converging advance of separate columns that would force battle on a locally outnumbered even if outnumbering enemy.

One of those Greek words that the Greeks never knew, the pan-Western word strategy (*strategie, strategia*, etc) derives from *strategos*, commonly mistranslated as "general," but in historical fact a combined politico-military chief, and thus a better source-word for an activity equally broad. The Chinese achieves the same generality by coupling the ideogram *chan* (indicating war) with further, specifying characters. It remains to be seen if strategy can be broad enough to accommodate the inability of low-birthrate post-industrial societies to either fight wars, or tolerate the chaotic disorders allowed by their inaction. As compared to that quandary, nuclear weapons are merely a technical innovation, which offers an attrition potential that exceeds the culminating point of utility, thereby being too effective to be effective, as Herakleitos might have said.

Through the millennial sequence of downfalls and revivals, there were many innovations large and small, and only one absolute continuity: the Roman empire of the east was not merely Christian by adopted religion, as the Western empire was till it lasted, as the successor kingdoms of Europe also were or would soon become, but rather in its innermost essence. The emperor was not just another Christianized ruler, more or less personally devout, more or less respectful of the prerogatives of the Bishop of Rome, but was himself the secular head of the Orthodox Church. He chose the Patriarch, personally presided over the highest councils of the Church and had his own liturgical role in its ceremonies. Deep religious faith, unquestioning belief in the absolute truth of the Trinity, are essential characteristics of almost every East Roman we know of.

In our own days there is no shortage of passionate religiosity, but no comparable case of an entire political community founded on religion is known to us outside Islam. This central difference between the East Romans and ourselves can never be forgotten by those who seek to understand them. It marks every stage of imperial history, from the foundation of Constantinople in 330 as a Christian city, to the final refusal to sacrifice Orthodox doctrine to seek Catholic help in the last desperate days before the Ottoman conquest of 1453.

Byzantine religion also had another consequence that still affects all who seek to study the empire. It was in the eighteenth century that the modern scholarship contrast to the abundance of sound scholarship on every aspect of pre-classical and classical Greece, and of the Roman Republic and early empire, the Byzantines have been poorly served so far. Of classical Greece and Rome, bookshops everywhere display the three hefty volumes of John Julius Norwich, but their size is deceptive: what is valid in that pot-boiling compilation of obsolete accounts would hardly fill a slim paperback.

The re-naming of the eastern Roman Empire as "Byzantine" –a term invented by sixteenth-century Catholic scholars—was itself almost an insult: Byzantion had been the name of the small Greek city that the emperor Constantine (306-337) turned into his imperial capital, the New Rome. The empire it commanded indeed long retained Roman institutions that changed only slowly and partially through the centuries, and never called itself anything but Roman in its edicts, coins and inscriptions, becoming the Rum of the Arabs and Turks. True, its inhabitants spoke Greek when they did not retain a more local language, but Greek had always been the language of Roman citizens throughout the east. Thus merely to describe it as Byzantine conveys a misleading impression of the Roman Empire of the East.

It was, however, the Enlightenment with Gibbon and Voltaire in the lead to turn, introduced the ill in our dictionaries: see *byzantine* as in maneuvers, machinations, intrigues, and so on. Loathing Christianity as they did, Gibbon and co. denigrated the intensely Christian eastern Empire as an extended degeneration from Roman glories, and its history as a sequence of sordid plots, absurd superstition, bloody usurpations, and shameful defeats. Such was their influence that it was not until this century that Western scholars with Russians in the lead, began to seriously study the history and culture of the Eastern Roman

Empire, and it was not until the 1960s that the reading public at large became interested in the subject.

But the effects of centuries of neglect have yet to be overcome. In contrast to the abundance of good one-volume surveys of classical Greece, starting with H. D. E Kitto's very short, utterly wonderful *The Greeks*, the eastern Roman Empire has been poorly served so far. Bookshops everywhere display the three hefty volumes of John Julius Norwich, but their size is deceptive: what is valid in that pot-boiling compilation of obsolete accounts would hardly fill a slim paperback.

Warren Treadgold's. *A History of the Byzantine State and Society* is in a different class altogether. While fluently written for the general reader—few will tire of its 850-odd pages of text—its coherent account reflects the most up-to-date scholarship, some of it Treadgold's own. In spite of its title, it is definitely an *imperial* history, largely focused on the political and military vicissitudes of the successive emperors down to the last, Constantine XI Dragases (1449-1453) rather than on the evolution of society, religion, the economy, culture or the arts, though there is much about all of them.

Scholars will not scorn this book, because it provides a well-documented overview for their inevitably more specialized research, successfully updating if not replacing George Ostrogorsky's *History of the Byzantine State,* the classic one-volume summary, once read by experts alone, now selling well in bookshops. Many scholars, however, will object to both the fluency and the coherence, not because of any ivory-tower affectations but because of Treadgold's chosen solution for the problem of inadequate sources. Some periods of Byzantine history such as Justinian's sixth century (the reconquest of Italy, his great general Belisarius, his scandalous wife Theodora) are brilliantly illuminated by contemporary writings of Procopius above all, as well as actual documents, archaeology, coins, surviving architecture and art, including the superb and revealing mosaics of Ravenna. For the period on either side of the year 1,000 the sources are almost as good, and for the last centuries they are even better. For other periods by contrast, such as the momentous seventh and eighth centuries, when the empire withstood the impact of the Arabs at the peak of their strength while undergoing important transformations, we only have very scant, unreliable and often contradictory monkish chronicles, no archaeology to speak of, and assorted bits and pieces from the lives of the saints as well as Arabic, Armenian, Coptic, and Syriac texts that only refer incidentally to what was happening in the empire.

Most scholars accept the resulting darkness and limit themselves to the few facts that seem well-documented. Not Treadgold. His declared method—the reader is duly warned, as befits a serious historian—is to boldly leap from one fragment of evidence to the next, in order to produce a coherent account by guessing what he cannot know (he carefully inserts "probably" before each one of his leaps).

The virtue of Treadgold's reconstructions is that they sometimes make sense of isolated pieces of evidence that seemed irrelevant or meaningless to prior historians. Their defect is that they mingle good evidence with bad in the text (though usually separating them in his notes), so that readers are left with an account all too coherent, not necessarily reliable. But there is a sure remedy for that: once their appetite is wetted by Treadgold, readers can turn to other books on specific subjects and periods, and to the sources themselves, such as Procopius who in addition to his excellent military histories and a fascinating survey of Justinian's buildings, all available in good translations, also wrote anonymously *Secret History* which could not be translated in full until quite recently, because of its X-rated version of Theodora's life before she became the most devout of imperial wives.

22

Byzantine Art

Not much late Byzantine art has survived, and of what remains some survives precariously in insecure lands even now, so its keepers tend to be especially protective and averse to lending. Actively revered icons and relics moreover, are wanted for their pilgrim devotees in their respective sanctuaries. Gratitude is therefore owed to the curator Helen Evans and her colleagues at the Metropolitan Museum of Art; they toiled for years to gather works scattered in twenty-seven countries and many more institutions. Even with the Museum's ample resources, prestige and connections, it must have required exceptional tenacity and infinite patience to negotiate with hundreds of high and low officials, all manner of curators, and many men of religion—some known for their liberality and delightful conversation, others for their xenophobia, ignorance and greed (visitors may notice that nothing was contributed by the Athonites for all the riches of the Lavra, Iveron, Hilandar, and Vatopedi).

The first result of these great labors is that important works of art little seen because they are held in unsettled, remote or simply obscure places can be appreciated by a far wider audience than ever before; moreover, many of the exhibits are so poorly lit and displayed in their own abodes that I for one was surprised when truly seeing for the first time works that I should have seen long before, when visiting Macedonian Ohrid, Saint Catherine's monastery in the Sinai and such.

But this exhibition offers much more than a mere gathering of rarities. The urge to include was obviously balanced by inspired selection criteria, for the result is an organic corpus of surviving late Byzantine art that is more than the sum of the parts, while also being broadly representative technically, geographically and temporally.

The starting date of 1261 was over-determined, for it was both the end-date of the previous exhibition ("The Glory of Byzantium") that started with the end

---

Review of the Metropolitan Museum of Art exhibition and catalogue, Helen C. Evans, editor, *Byzantium: Faith and Power (1261-1557)*, (New Haven and London: Yale University Press, 2004).

of iconoclasm in 843, and the natural starting date for Late Byzantium, for it was on August 15, 1261 by our calendar that Michael VIII Palaiologos entered Constantinople in triumph. A presumptively Orthodox, Greek-speaking emperor of the *Romaioi* once again ruled the new Rome after the disastrous Catholic interregnum of the Western "Latins." The eastern Roman Empire that expanded in the sixth century, scarcely survived the calamitous seventh, recovered to expand once more by the eleventh, that collapsed in 1204 only to be resuscitated once more, now entered its final two centuries diminished in territory to western Anatolia, Thrace, parts of northern Greece and Macedonia.

Yet contrary to the black legend of feeble decadence, Empire was no misnomer till the next century's loss of fertile western Anatolia. For as soon as it recovered Constantinople, Michael's domain resumed its place as the most powerful single state in the entire Christian world. More than any other, the Byzantine state had educated administrators and clerks who could effectively extract tax revenues, as the lieges of western monarchs could not. It had an advantage in conducting foreign relations because its officials knew more of the past and of the present world; Michael VIII kept dangerous Catholic and Muslim invaders at bay by successfully recruiting allies as diverse as the Mongol khan Hulagu, destroyer of Abbasid Baghdad, and Peter III of Aragon. It *controlled* its own church as no western kingdom did, whose better educated priests and monks were in demand by other Orthodox churches, adding substance to the nominal ascendancy of the patriarch of Constantinople. And finally it had the politically useful prestige of a residual, if waning, superiority in scholarship, many crafts and the arts. But of course all the advantages listed were actually cultural in their different ways, and this gave strong incentives to Byzantine secular and ecclesiastical leaders to sustain learning and the fine arts, even as their power and revenues declined. That is why even the remnant we have testifies to the rich artistic production of an ever poorer state, though of course Byzantine art was increasingly produced outside its boundaries, some in the sub-Byzantine Despotate of Epirus and the Trebizond enclave, in Greece and the Near East, much more in the mainly Slavic lands converted to Orthodoxy, the "Byzantine Commonwealth" of Dimitri Obolensky.

For Byzantine religion, art and culture were far more successful conquerors than any emperor, and the visitor to the exhibition soon encounters Bulgarian, Serb, Armenian, Russian, Macedonian and Moldavian or Romanian works that are purely Byzantine in every way—and then those in which syntheses with more autochthonous or indeed western elements are emerging. It is one of the distinct merits of this exhibition that it illustrates so well this historical process, which has not yet ended insofar as Orthodox ecclesiastical art and architecture persist from Vladivostok west to San Francisco, and from the White Sea islands down to Australia, always retaining an immediately recognizable "Byzantine" look, and not necessarily contemptible because of it.

Therefore it must have been difficult indeed to set an end-year. The second fall of Constantinople and the final end of the Roman Empire in 1453 would have been a perfectly logical choice. But also rather foolish, not just because there was a Byzantium after Byzantium in the aforementioned "Commonwealth," but also because its culture was never more consequential than during the ensuing century, when texts edited by Byzantine scholars and a handful of teachers opened the door for the Western rediscovery of classical Greek ideas, with revolutionary consequences that have not ceased to reverberate. So a century of prolongation at least was in order, and it really matters not that 1557, the particular year chosen, is justified by the introduction of the endlessly unfortunate yet irresistible term Byzantium for the Eastern Roman Empire by the librarian Hieronymus Wolf, who with his employer the banker Anton Fugger started the publication of Byzantine historical texts.

All categories and media are represented including the least transportable, such as the fragment of a thirteenth-century fresco from the Gradac monastery removed to the Belgrade National Museum, which shows a very handsome mature male head ("of an apostle"). Another fragment of a fresco of the same period originally from the church of the Epirote village of Voulgareli near Arta, lent by the Byzantine Museum of Ioannina, depicts the betrayal of Judas by juxtaposing at right angles the vividly expressive heads of the two protagonists. This tells us how accomplished the art of a rural church could be, no doubt because of urbane patronage—a Theodoros Tsimiskis depicted in the narthex with his wife Maria may have been a senior officer of Nikephoros I, a Byzantine ruler independent of the Byzantine emperor, as Despot of Epiros).

The Byzantine taste for portable mosaics allows a rich representation of that more commonly immobile art, ranging from a severe Virgin-the-mother (*hodegetria*) with a small-man child from the Academy's museum in Sofia, to a far more accomplished fourteenth-century mosaic diptych undoubtedly made by the palace workshop in Constantinople. Lent by Santa Maria del Fiore in Florence, its twelve scenes of feast days are peopled with exceptional finely formed figures. Another striking mosaic is a Saint John Chrysostom with wisdom's elongated forehead from the Dumbarton Oaks collection in Washington, DC, in which that master of eloquence is depicted as sadly silent. And it is to silence that one is reduced by the two diametrically opposed faces of Christianity that can be contrasted most powerfully within yards of each other in this exhibition. Both mosaics are dated to the early fourteenth century. One, probably removed from Saint Catherine's monastery in the Sinai (it has a painted St. Catherine of Alexandria on the back) and lent by the Basilica of Santa Croce in Gerusalemme of Rome, is set in the center of a much later reliquary case. This masterpiece of expression that elevates an iconographic convention, shows the bust of the naked and dead Christ upright in a sarcophagus, with the head lolling despondently over overlapped nailed hands, in the liturgically fashionable pose of defeat and humiliation (*e akra tapeinosis*, the *imago pietatis* of the Latins). The other mosaic lent by the Hermitage is a miniature of a young, good looking and alert Saint Theodore Stratelates, in which that soldier-saint, much needed to defend the failing empire, holds spear and shield ready for combat in the splendid blue, red and gold of marble, jasper, lapis lazuli, stone and gilded- copper tesserae. Its 9 centimeters by 7.4 that can easily fit into a pocket—I cased the joint, try it not—would be enough, if nothing else remained, to validate the overall conclusion with which one leaves the exhibition—that the art of the late Byzantine Empire really was *very* good.

Yet the valiant Saint Theodore is outmatched by a much less colorful late thirteen-century mosaic from Dumbarton Oaks, an incomplete (because of damage) rendition of the often depicted Forty Martyrs of Sebasteia (Pontic Sebasteia, with its cold mountains, not the Sebaste of warmer Samaria). As described in homilies by Basil the Great and Gregory of Nyssa, and venerated on March 9 of the Julian calendar, they were Roman soldiers who could not be stoned—bouncing back, the stones wounded the persecutors—and were therefore driven onto or into a wintry lake or pond to freeze to death if they would not renounce Christianity. Martyrs will very soon ascend to heaven and must therefore be indifferent to earthly suffering. Not these forty muscled men in loin cloths, still with their strong soldiers' bodies but now in varied poses of acute distress. Of course as martyrs in good standing it is not their own insignificant pain that makes them suffer, but the torments endured by their comrades— so there is no screaming or crying but only deep, silent sorrow for what they see and indeed feel, pressed as they are against one another in a useless quest for warmth. An evocation of intense comradeship as well as faith, the Forty Martyrs were much produced to serve the cenobitic market; this rendition differs only in its sublime quality, for aided by the very smallest half-millimeter tesserae, the artist endows each martyr with his own distinct expression of the common suffering, and indeed distinct personality. The other icon of the forty martyrs of Sebasteia in the exhibition, painted in Saint Catherine's monastery where it remains, has interesting colors and is complete with the missing bathhouse that was to tempt waverers, but naïve in composition.

Metal work is broadly represented in many coins, seals more poignantly (each a reminder of documents lost, Byzantium being so ill-documented), some medals, a gold signet rings, a bell and numerous revetments for icons, as well as embossed, engraved, repousse and chased book bindings, large and small reliquaries and caskets. One perfectly preserved early fifteenth century and plausibly Trapezuntine casket in gilded silver and niello from Saint Mark in Venice, shows four martyrs, Aquilas, Eugenios, Canidius and Valerianus on either side of an enthroned Christ. They are earnestly praying for the heavenly intercession that the doomed enclave ruled by *the Megas Komnenoi* ("the empire of Trebizond") certainly needed. The detail is very finely detailed in the drapery on the bodies especially, but it is craftsman's work withal, for no artist would replicate five identical faces, awarding youth to Aquilas by merely omitting the beard of the other four. In spite of their own repetitions, one does not feel that two of the liturgical implements included in the exhibition should be consigned to the same side of that notoriously undemarcated border: a gilded silver ritual fan (rhipidion) from St John's monastery in Patmos, donated by prince Stephen of Moldavia to an Athonite monastery in 1468, and plausibly credited to the "Saxon" metal workers of Transylvanian Hermannstadt (now the almost German-free Romanian Sibiu), and another even later Serbian rhipidion from the Belgrade Serbian Orthodox Church Museum. One is stellar in outline and the other is circular, both incorporate medallions, both are very finely made with the first in intricate, filigree-like wire work, but it is their inexpressible artistry that strikes the viewer.

A fourteenth-century reliquary arm of Saint Nicholas in sheet silver from the Armenian Catholicosate in Lebanon's Antelias is a bit of problem, because while the medallion on the hand that shows the saint is characteristic and as original to the piece as the inscription of the katholicos Konstandin of the Armenian year 774 (whose inception in 552 yields our 1326, not the 1325 of the catalog), the strikingly naturalistic hand must date from the distinctly post-Byzantine reconstruction of 1926.

Relics were important indeed. Every saintly limb and organ but one could aid not only salvation but earthly power also—Constantinople was long defended by the arm of St John the Baptist now in the Topkapi. Armenian Cilicia certainly needed protection in its precarious slice of south-east Anatolia where it faced attacks from both the Seljuks of Konya until their demise and the expansionist Mamluks of Egypt. But in this case the saintly arm was conscripted to face enemies at home: Konstandin mentions and thus legitimizes his rulers as "Oshin and his son Levon," except that this was the usurping regent Oshin Count of Korykos, neither son of his predecessor King Oshin I who died in 1320, nor the father of young Levon the fifth, son of the King Oshin, upon whom the Count forced his daughter as a wife. The exhibition includes an earlier (1274) and not especially attractive illuminated Gospel from Armenian Cilicia commissioned by a "Marshal Oshin," who was Levon's ancestor.

The largest of the metal exhibits is a circular chandelier rig for both candles and oil lamps meant to illuminate a dome ("*choros*") from Munich's Museum fur Vor-und Fruhgeschichte. Eleven feet in diameter and fifteen feet high, it is assembled from 1,105 cast copper-alloy pieces. While the work is rude if not quite mass-produced, it is impressively evocative in its place within this most artfully arranged of exhibitions.

Stone carving is better represented than one might expect in both capitals and reliefs from the Istanbul Archaeological Museum, the Louvre and elsewhere, although a very handsome work did not have to travel far, for it belongs to the Museum's own collection: a thirteenth-century (the design suggests) marble relief of a devil-fighting griffin within a foliate circle, set in turn within a square frame that.

There is woodwork also including iconostasis doors from Novgorod, but the most affecting exhibit in that medium is the richly carved coffin-shaped and coffin-sized reliquary in scarlet red of the Serbian ruler Stefan Uros III (1321-31), who achieved further promotion after death when awarded sainthood in his successor's reign. Then the body was exhumed and transferred to the reliquary made in the Decany monastery in Kosovo, where it safely remained through centuries of Ottoman rule and subsequent mayhem and to which it must return, within easy striking range of church-burning Albanian-Muslim mobs. Very little Byzantine wood-work has survived of course, in some part perhaps because flames so often attend religious strife; co-religionists are content with looting and killing.

Materials hardly more resistant than wood are also well represented, not only stucco, gesso, steatite (magnesium silicate ceramic), earthenware ceramics bone and ivory but also sumptuous ecclesiastical cloths both woven and embroidered. Carefully differentiated silk robes, some of whose patterns reflected Chinese influences that had originally arrived through the Khazars, were badges of rank in the imperial palace and therefore naturally in the church also. While there are even more luxurious examples, the two fourteenth-century broad-sleeved caftans (*sakkoi*) exhibited are of the highest rank and fit for Patriarchs. One from the Vatican in blue silk with embroidery in silver, gilt silver and colored threads, shows an assembly of angels and saints in the front, and a transfiguration in the back; another from the Kremlin museum with much more gilt thread, much reworked and further decorated in Russia with pearls, offers a quick guide to orthodoxy in pictures and texts that present and elaborate scenes of the life of Christ—Isaiah and Ezekiel each have a panel to speak their lines. Among the many woven and embroidered *epitaphioi* with the usual body of the dead Christ (they were primarily used for the "burial of Christ" ceremony), the probably misnamed silk "epitaphios with Maria of Mangop" made in the Monastery of Putna in northeast Romania to which it still belongs, attracts particular attention. Of the Byzantine imperial Palaiologos family, Maria was wife to Stephan the Great ruler of Moldavia (1457-1504), and died young in 1476 just when he was at his most successful in resisting the Ottoman advance, earning his soubriquet. She is depicted in emerald green, lying dead with eyes shut against the scarlet rectangle of the *epitaphios* whose edges are inscribed all around in gold wire and gilded silk thread to form the text in Old Church Slavonic. What is so striking aside from the startling colors, is that Maria is in a broad Byzantine court dress that looks decidedly Chinese as well it might—but so does her face! Stephan's brilliant career incidentally, recently resumed very successfully upon his elevation to sainthood by the post-Ceausescu Romanian Orthodox Church in 1992. His feast day is July 2

There is paper and parchment, starting with the very first item, a gold and ink and tempera full-length portrait of the crowned, sceptered and gowned Michael II Palaiologos (1391-1425) set in the text of his funeral oration for his brother Theodore, Despot of Peloponnesian Morea, complete with complaints of Latin treachery; and there are illuminated pages from secular as well as religious texts—some very attractive such as the very fine plant pictures in a *Materia Medica* of Dioskorides.

This is altogether fitting because of the central importance of Late Byzantine textual scholarship in launching the sixteenth-century Western intellectual revolution that preceded all the others. Except for a few long-translated Greek classical texts, and a handful of scientific works re-translated into Latin from the Arabic, it was only because a wide range of secular texts (pornographic poems included) continued to be read, copied, edited and elucidated by (mostly ecclesiastical) Byzantine scholars that the fragile sequence of manuscripts finally reached the safe harbor of the first Western printing presses. As late as the mid-fourteenth century, the most famous Western scholar of the day, the poet and inveterate book collector Petrarch (1304-1374) did not have even one Greek text in his famous library. When a Byzantine envoy gave him a copy of Homer, basic schoolboy reading in Constantinople, Petrarch was much frustrated by his inability to read it. The remedy came with other Byzantines who came to teach, starting with Manuel Chrysoloras whose 1397 inauguration of the first regular lectures on classical Greek in Florence make that year a fundamental date in Western cultural history. The Dioskorides is apposite: it was almost certainly copied in the *scriptorium* of the famously rich library of the Prodromos Monastery of Pera, and is lent by the Seminario Vescovile in Padova, where Europe's most tolerant university sheltered from the Inquisition by Venetian power became the prime destination of Byzantine and simply Greek students and scholars.

But naturally it is icons that are preeminent in the exhibition, both in the broader and older sense of any devotional image (from *eikon*, simply image) and in the more recent and narrower sense of a painted wooden devotional panel, mostly in tempera—pigments suspended in egg yolk. Many visitors no doubt make their way to the Museum anticipating an encounter mostly or even only with Byzantine icons.

That is fair enough because of their centrality for the Byzantines that inevitably followed from the utter centrality of religion in their lives, and the extreme importance of images in their devotions. Officially God's prohibition of graven images as per Exodus 20:4 was accommodated by insisting that there was no image-worship (*latreia*) but only reverence (*dulia*), such as might be given a king (the Virgin Mary rates *hyperdulia*). That indeed was how the inconoclastic controversy had been settled long before—but the inconodules cheated through the category of *acheiropoieta*, "[images] not made by human hands." These are not merely symbols of that which is to be worshiped because they can work miracles in themselves, including their own miraculous reproduction; of these the most important is the *Mandylion*—the face and neck of the living Christ impressed on a towel that he himself sent to the worshipful of Edessa in Osrhoene in lieu of his own visit.

The first icon is a "Commonwealth" product par excellence, a late thirteenth-century Serbian Peter and Paul from the Vatican Treasury in an appropriately rich frame encrusted with colored stones. There is a conciliatory political message in this painting sent to Rome: while the small figures on either side supplicating the apostles above them are the Orthodox kings Milutin and Dragutin, their mother the Roman Catholic Helen of Anjou is shown between them bowing to a Roman Catholic bishop.

Next comes a bit of curatorial virtuosity—the reunion of three long-separated fourteenth-century icons commissioned by the well-connected and twice-married Maria Angelina Doukania Palaiologina. They were gifted to, and probably made in Meteora: two of them lent from where they have always remained, the Transfiguration monastery in Meteora, and the third—a diptych of the Virgin and Christ with saints all around them set in luxuriously bejewelled gilt silver casings—from the Diocesan Museum of Spanish Cuenca.

All these have their merits but this eye at any rate was much more taken by the subsequent mid-fourteenth century Moscovite Boris and Gleb from St. Peterburg's State Russian Museum. There is no individuality in their expressions, but the two handsome figures, impressively tall in luxurious princely clothes and fur-rimmed hats, and armed with both short crosses and long swords to defend Russia from infidel invaders, are wonderfully colored in scarlet, blue, gold, and more. There are many such—the cult of the two sons of Vladimir, first Christian ruler of Kievan Rus', who were murdered by the pagan Svjatopolk and whose sainthood was promoted by their brother Prince Iaroslav the Wise, outlived the demise of Kievan Rus' and prospered throughout the Russian lands. An earlier Boris and Gleb from Novgorod in the exhibition is equestrian and was sumptuous even before the much later silver revetment was added.

A three-scene register icon from Novgorod dated c. 1475 of the praying Virgin—but she is shown only in two tiny boxes—has no better faces but again has wonderful colors and composition. It depicts the possibly legendary 1170 siege of the city-state of Novgorod by the city-state of Suzdal, with a dynamic cavalry battle in the low register, more cavalry attacking the wall (with accurately depicted compound bows) in the middle register as well as potentates parlaying on horseback, and an assembly of worshipers and saints in the upper register, with the city on the left and a monastery on the right.

The late Byzantines were more Marian than most Marian Catholics, so the virgin mother-of-god (*hodegetria*) is present in many versions, and while there is no temporal evolution to illustrate, there is everything else from differing configurations (*glykophilousa*, *pelagonitissa*, *kykkotissa*, *dexiokratousa*, *kardiotissa*) and different origins to simple artistic individuality. Macarius the ordained monk signed c.1421 an anxiously tender Virgin in browns from the Museum of Macedonia in Skopje whose infant Christ twists his head back to look at us, a striking composition. Byzantine Virgins traveled far whether looted, imported or imitated, the latter being well illustrated by a Madonna and child from Siena's Pinacoteca Nazionale attributed to the Badia a Isola painter (fl. 1290-1320) that follows Byzantine iconographic conventions in exact detail.

By contrast, another *hodegetria* also painted in Siena in 1262 (*Madonna and Child with Two Angels*) also from Siena's Pinacoteca attributed to the painter of the San Bernardino Madonna, has the configuration and the details but also a different (proto-Sienese?) coloration. The Madonna of Breznice from Prague's Narodni Galerie (although "the people" have formally given it back to the Breznice Catholic parish church) dated 1396 again follows the configuration but is otherwise wonderfully original as well as very attractive indeed, both in being a sort of collage with parchment and linen, and in the drapery and even more in its colors, the faces of both mother and child being decidedly brown; in the Virgin's halo the Song of Songs is quoted "nigra sum sed Formosa," so the color was deliberately dark, for the reason stated in the back of the panel, that the work was to resemble another Virgin held in Bohemia painted by Saint Luke himself.

Finally after so many Virgins, Giovanni Bellini's c.1475 Virgin and child from Washington's National Gallery is reached, which owes something to Byzantium but whose Madonna is an actual woman actually looking at us, even if the child is still a little man. Byzantine painting was good, but with Bellini we enter another level of art when it comes to Virgins. That is not necessarily the case with other motifs. In a group of exceptionally attractive icons lent by Saint Catherine's monastery in the Sinai, there is an expressive thirteenth-century Saint Theodosia in a striking dark cape, and the beautiful thirteenth century Archangel Gabriel in green tunic and gold and red himation that is reproduced in the catalog cover and exhibition posters, as well as a "c. 1280s" (?) two-sided icon with a crucifixion on one side, and an *anastasis* on the other. With the crusaders, Western paintings and even Western painters had reached the Byzantine sphere, and specifically Western iconographic details aside (Aaron standing alongside the rising Christ wears the *Rosh Tefillin* of a Rheinland rabbi), there is an overall Western element in two very successful syntheses, with excellently balanced colors and vivid expressions. The crucifixion is highly symmetrical, with grieving Mary and pensive Saint John on either side of a muscular but sorrowfully dead Christ eyes closed, with blood spurting out from the spear wound in the chest. The *anastasis* has a very interesting composition too, but it is this crucifixion with its blood spurting from the chest that was destined to have an exotic iconographic career, for it is now encountered in vivid part-indigenous colors as the product of Peruvian and other Spanish colonial and Latin American painters. So the Western synthesis with Byzantium would inspire other trans-cultural encounters.

That was also true of the Mandylion—the neckless face of the bearded, long-haired, living Christ impressed on a towel—although the influence in that case went strictly east to west. The original towel gifted by Christ himself was extorted from Edessa (Turkey's Urfa) by the Byzantines in 944, after their historical re-conquest of the city from the Arabs, and traveled first to Constantinople where it was eventually lost in the mayhem of 1204, but the image was by then diffused in the Christian world. Byzantine emperors were devoted to Christ needless to say, but they relied chiefly on the motherly indulgence of the Virgin Mary for protection, so the Mandylion did not become as great a focus of official ceremonies as icons of the Virgin also "not made by human hands". But the Mandylion aroused popular devotion that extended far beyond Byzantium. The so-called "Holy Face of Laon," still kept in the Cathedral, still an object of pilgrimage, is certainly an impressive thirteen century Slav work (it is inscribed in contemporary Slavonic) but anonymous, while a slightly east-Asian Russian Mandylion lent by the Tret'iakov may well be the famous 1447 work by the ordained monk Serapion from the northern town of Veliky Ustiug (who did not paint but merely reproduced the image not made by human hands), for it was removed from Veliky Ustiug in 1964, at the very end of the actively atheistic and culturally centralizing phase of Bolshevism.

The influence of Byzantine painting in the West during this period was first constrained by the theological divide, and then naturally diminished; but in the geographic sphere of orthodoxy, religious practice ensured its prolongation, albeit with an ever greater local or at least localized content. Of that imperceptible progression, the very exemplar is the work of Andrei Rublev, here associated with the painter Daniil (who did not share his very early and very great fame) in the twin icons of John Chrysostom and Saint Gregory lent by the Tret'iakov but originally from the iconostasis of the Uspenskii Cathedral in Vladimir. Both are wearing elegant long robes accented with brocade effects as well as the characteristically bold black and white crosses. Both definitely express individual faces, just as both are an individual's work of art, and that too marks a transition.

* * *

The beautifully printed catalog of 676 foot-high pages seemingly free of misprints, replete with invariably well-reproduced illustrations, and incidentally a real bargain at its New York prices, is abundantly prefaced by a statement in both Greek and English from B, that being the official signature of Bartholomew, Archbishop of Constantinople, New Rome and Ecumenical Patriarch, by notes from the generous sponsors, by a foreword from the Museum director Philippe de Montebello, New York City's cynosure in spite of the offending *particule*, by six pages of acknowledgments to all who lent, or allowed the lending, or persuaded others to lend, two pages listing the lending institutions and collectors by country (Macedonia being saddled with the odious FYR to assuage Greek obsessions), and three pages listing the contributors of the item-by-item catalogue entries, some curators, keepers and conservators with a merely antiquarian knowledge of their own holdings, others historians of art and culture. Accordingly, these item-by-item contributions vary from cursory factual notes to significant short essays.

And all that still leaves room for a substantial body of articles, starting with an historical introduction by the curator of the exhibition and editor of the catalogue, Helen C. Evans. It is followed by the few pages of Alice-Mary Talbot, in which that most distinguished Byzantinist offers contemporary perspectives, some Byzantine and others of visitors. The one objection that could be advanced to these well-written summaries of late Byzantium which efficiently include all the essentials, is a familiar one: just because *we* know that Constantinople finally fell in 1453 and that the Roman empire of the East was utterly extinguished, it does not mean that pessimism was the only possible attitude, that decline and fall had to be accepted as inevitable, or were so accepted. Nor would such a refusal necessarily imply a lack of realism, as Alice-Mary Talbot writes of the Patriarch Antonios IV's c.1393 rebuke of the Grand Prince Basil I of Moscow for failing to remember the Emperor in the prayers. True, by then the Empire was reduced to peninsular and insular fragments, with Constantinople itself surrounded by the victorious armies of Bayezid I, the great Ottoman conqueror. It was as bad in 626, when Constantinople was besieged by the formidable Avars, their numerous Slav subjects and the all-conquering Sasanian Persians, yet the Empire had survived and soon regained its lost lands. And of course the Empire had disintegrated by 1204, only to be revived once more. So Antonios IV along with others may still have hoped—and not fecklessly but with good reason as it happens, for Bayezid I did not conquer Constantinople, but was himself totally defeated by the completely unexpected irruption of the Mongol-Turkic armies of Timur, Tamerlane Tamburlaine, who crushed Bayezid's forces at Ankara in July 1401. With that, the long siege of Constantinople was instantly lifted, lost positions were regained, and Antonios IV's successor Matthew I could enjoy all the Patriarchical dignities while Bayezid was supposedly raging in a cage in Timur's camp. Pessimism there was, but to create art there had to be a sort of optimism also.

One of the articles is in the nature of a testimony, by his Eminence Archbishop Damianos of Sinai, Faran and Raitha, Abbot of the Greek Orthodox Monastery of Saint Catherine in the Sinai, the oldest place of Christian worship in continuous use according to Damianos. He recognizes the merits of scholarly appraisals and aesthetic appreciation, but presents another view of icons as powerful cult objects—once bitterly contested doctrinally but now seemingly simply accepted by contemporary Greek orthodox prelates: "The Icon as a Ladder of Divine Ascent in Form and Color". Damianos also writes of his own monastery in a way that no outsider could–and the place is certainly an extraordinary apparition deep in the desert mountains, and filled with artistic treasures.

Specialists will have to comment on the specialistic articles such as Jannic Durand's "Precious-Metal Icon Revetments," but all are accessible. In their different ways all can serve to disenthrall the general reader from the Vasari version–no, it did not all start in Florence, it had started before.

23

Byzantine Court Culture

It is uncontroversial that during much of the period 829 to 1204, the Late East Roman Empire, which we diminish with Du Cange's irresistibly convenient label "Byzantine," was a very successful administrative structure. Until overrun by the Fourth Crusade in 1204, it was able to extract enough revenue which was used with enough efficiency to equip, supply and pay armies and fleets powerful enough to contend with a multitude of dangerous enemies, Western, Bulgar, Slav, Muslim, and the latest invaders from the steppes.

At the same time, our sources depict a palace life largely filled with elaborate ceremonies, elaborately ridiculed by the invidious but indispensable eyewitness Liutprand, who was to be happily echoed by Enlightenment and many post-Enlightenment writers down to Arnold Toynbee, who dismissed the imperial ceremonies as useless, silly, ludicrous, and portentous in his late (1973) and eccentric tome on the Emperor Constantine VII Porphyrogennetos. By then, however, Toynbee had left East Roman studies entirely unattended for a decisive half century, during which they had finally been rescued from the Enlightenment's worship of pagan antiquity and its obloquy of all things Christian by a growing band of scholars: Russian proto-Russianists seeking roots, reformed classicists venturing beyond golden ages, and medievalists broadening their horizons.

One of their prime tasks was precisely to reconcile the paradoxical conjunction of this long-lived militancy and its ornate ceremonialism, especially for the Macedonian dynasty (867-1057) distinguished for much of its existence by both formidable effectiveness and extreme ceremoniousness. Much was quickly achieved once the ban was lifted, and readers could already find in George Ostrogorsky's fundamental *History of the Byzantine State* (1940) documented explanations of how outer forms promoted concrete aims, how imagery, props and ritual were employed to enhance the emperor's authority, how ceremonies communicated a disciplined leadership by visible deed. Above all, until the late eleventh century, the court functioned as an open, indeed two-track meritocracy: the highly talented could rise to administer the empire regardless of their origins, by way of classical scholarship or even the eunuchs' domestic service. Thus peasants' sons routinely entered the ruling class, powering the state with their raw ambition.

By 1994, when the authors included in this book gathered to present their papers, that work had been accomplished, allowing them to pursue more recondite preoccupations than to refute the misrepresentations of Enlightenment scholars.

The empire's greatest source of strength was its persistent ability to enlist religious devotion in its constant struggle for survival. The emperor not only provided the armies that defended the church that provided the gateway to salvation, but he also headed that church. There has been endless controversy on just what that meant, contemporaneously between Patriarchs and Emperors, more recently among historians of both. Was he substantive head of the church, as was the Pope in Western Rome (the "Caesaropapism" thesis), a merely nominal head, as is the Queen of England of the Church of England, or something in between? George P. Majeska fittingly opens the volume with a careful examination of the emperor's ritual role in the Church of St. Sophia on three occasions: coronation, dominical festivals, and the annual Holy Saturday censing of the sacred vessels. His aim is to define the emperor's exact status in the liturgies. Finding him to be both priest and congregant, Majeska concludes that the ambiguity was purposeful: not a priest-king, he is not just a congregant either, for he officiates along with the prelates as Elizabeth II does not, and that makes him *a* priest as well as the king—not a useless attribute for one seeking to evoke all possible sources of loyalty.

Constantine's choice of a site for his new Rome was altogether too perspicacious from the viewpoint of modern archaeologists: the place never fell from favor to become a desolation which could be dug up at will. The construction boom he unleashed has continued ever since with only a few decades of interruption now and then, greatly impeding archaeology, which has so far contributed relatively little to our knowledge of Constantinople. A.R. Littlewood's attempt to reconstruct imperial gardens—a habitual adjunct to palatial projections of power—suffers accordingly. In a neighborhood where Assyrian conquerors boasted of cutting down other rulers' gardens, and Achaemenid rulers boasted of having planned and planted their own (our paradise is their "walled garden" *pairidaeza*), a proper emperor could not get by with just palace edifices and no palace gardens—and game parks too (a key status symbol for eastern rulers as for Colombian *narco-traficantes*). Littewood duly cites many a literary reference—satisfying us if not himself, for as an historian of gardens rather than of East Rome he wants to know what they actually contained, and looked like. In Pompeii, enough of the detail complete with seeds has been recovered to have allowed the planting of genuinely Roman gardens—not a likely prospect in crowded downtown Istanbul.

Elisabeth Pilz can summon paintings to illustrate the ample literary evidence mustered in her "Middle Byzantium Court Costume," even though it is not always clear which picture pictures which costume—of which there were a great many, including the pearl- and jewel-studded *Loros*, worn by the emperor himself on high religious occasions, and the luxurious silk *Skaramangion*, worn by high officials on many occasions in designated colors (some were issued as pay along with gold coin). What is clear is that costumes and changes of costume played an essential role in the ceremonial choreography of the palace, sometimes to dazzle with gold and purple, sometimes to affirm religious humility (e.g. the Emperor's ultra-plain *Himation* on Good Friday), sometimes to denote changes of rank (e.g., the *Pelonion* worn exclusively by the eparch at his promotion), but always to send precise signals while detaining attention by a constant alternation of visual effects.

The grisly severed hands, odd bones and others such that confront modern tourists in their eye-level glass boxes when they look down from the over-the-altar Lorenzo Lotto they have come to see in some Italian church, i.e., the entire saints' relics phenomenon, has long been de-coded as a prime instrument of institutional aggrandizement. Instead of attracting just the locals as any church could do, relics could attract out-of-area devotees, gaining ecclesiastical prestige and lucre. In the lively relic trade, quotations for bits of saints went up and down, values reflected localized enthusiasms, recognizable limbs always outsold fragmentary tissue, and while the ultimate blue chip was a splinter of the True Cross, a well-preserved arm or leg that could be attributed to a first-league saint were very highly rated as well.

The title of Ioli Kalavrezou's essay on imperial ceremonies and the cult of relics: "Helping Hands for the Empire" tells it all, though hands were not enough: arms, legs, hearts, noses, and indeed everything except for you-know-what were much needed for the churches of Constantinople (though the arm of St. John the Baptist, stolen from infidel Antioch in 956 and received in Chalcedon by the royal barge with Patriarch and Senate in attendance amidst candles, torches and incense, ended up in the Great Palace—the emperor wanted that ultra-prime catch for himself). For Constantinople's great defect as a locus of religious prestige was its lack of antiquity as compared to Rome, Antioch, Alexandria and of course Jerusalem. Relics were the only remedy. Kalavrezou's investigation of the frustratingly fragmentary evidence begins by citing an estimate that (at the peak?) there were more than 3,600 relics of about 476 different saints, including the aforementioned arm now encased in silver but unworshipped in the Topkapi), before examining a few in detail to show just how they did their job of attracting loyalty by interposed holy object.

Annemarie Weyl Carr briskly defines icons as portable devotional panels in her complementary essay on their nexus with court culture. Not all icons were equal; most were mere paintings of use as props in liturgies whose sanctity had to derive from the word or an associated relic, but some were miracle-working, i.e., holy emanations in themselves, whose possession obviously conferred lots of authority. With its rich inventory of super-icons even too-new Constantinople could be a plausible holy city in the eyes of foreigners, especially converted Bulgar, Kievan, Serbian allies/enemies, enhancing its imperial master's standing by rubbed-off holiness, a very useful adjunct to armies and fleets not always sufficiently powerful. But in this essay the other side of the coin is explored, the uses of icons not by the whole vis-à-vis outsiders but by emperor versus his courtier high officials (his servants, true, but also his best-placed rivals), by courtiers in trouble, and by contending factions.

Alongside super-icons there were super-edifices that generated megawatts of sanctity from their form, decor, or just their ancient associations—as plain Nativity and messy Holy Sepulcher did and do. Saint Sophia famously achieved that effect from day 1 by pure form. Procopius tells us that its first visitors felt that they had stepped off the street into heaven's antechamber when standing under the upper cupola, which seemed to float in the air above, illuminated as it was by the invisible windows that pierced its recessed supporting ring. William Tronzo explores the theme by examining the case of the Capella Palatina, a bit of a stretch for this volume, given that the chapel-cum-reception hall was chartered (in 1140) by the Norman Roger II for his palace of Palermo, never a center of Byzantine culture. Tronzo dutifully reports that it has been dismissed as "derivative" and "unoriginal" but claims that the Capella Palatina offers an instructive perspective on contemporary Byzantine practice, for while its mosaics were made by craftsmen themselves Byzantine or Byzantine-trained (eastern Sicily was then still very Greek), the treatment of the ruler-Christ nexus is radically different, as is the overall style. The outright Christomimesis of Roger II is certainly a striking departure from Byzantine humility: granted, he felt on top of the world at the time—Pope Innocent II had just recognized his kingship *de jure* notwithstanding the great Norman crime of leaving Sicily's Moslems and Jews unmassacred—but it was a bit much to have himself depicted looking just like Christ opposite the real thing, and standing just a head lower. Tronzo's claim of stylistic difference is amply warranted—there are important Islamic elements (including protruding *muqarna* vaults) and Norman ones too of course, but by the same token they scarcely relate to anything East Roman. (Tronzo mercifully does not report that the Capella Palatina, as the entire Normal Palace, is now the headquarters of the Regional government of Sicily, whose misfeasance, malfeasance, and non-feasance unfold under its mosaics—devastatingly beautiful in their free forms and brilliant colors—in fact the cited author who used the words derivative and unoriginal deserves the rack: it is worth walking all the way to Palermo just to see the green peacock mosaic under which the Region's bureaucrats pass their idle days).

Oleg Grabar offers another distant but more persuasively relevant perspective in his "The Shared Culture of Objects." The objects in question are treasures and gifts, and the sharers are Byzantines (and other Christians) as well as Muslims, as is the pre-1071 source, al-Qadi al-Rashid Ibn al Zubayr of Fatimid Cairo, author of *The Book of Treasures and Gifts*, a compilation of 414 accounts of valuables received, looted or inherited. One of the earliest refers to a gift package from Emperor Maurice (582-602) to the Sassanid Khosro Parviz—all raw materials, silver, gold, precious stones, silk, necessarily unrevealing of style or culture. But the great many gifts sent by Romanos Lekapenos (post 920) to Caliph al-Radi are carefully described in an accompanying letter, e.g., item: "another gilded bucket studded with precious stones; item: a heavy battle-axe with a head of gilded silver inlaid with precious stones.... In 1053 Michael VI stayed well away from buckets to send more lively merchandise to the Fatimid caliph al-Mustansir: Turkish slave boys and girls, partridges, peacocks, cranes, aquatic birds, ravens and starlings; huge bears that played musical instruments; Saluqi hounds.

Grabar's key point is that courtly appreciation of beautiful objects of value transcended both religious and cultural boundaries; he cites the limiting case of the Byzantine-made cup in the San Marco treasury which combines "perfectly clear but meaningless Arabic letters with perfectly clear but iconographically senseless classical figures."

George T. Dennis contributes briefly and most usefully on the themes and purposes of imperial panegyrics. For speakers they afforded the opportunity to display learning, political orthodoxy and mastery of much-prized rhetorical techniques, all qualities that could elicit imperial job offers or outright pay-offs; with due caution, speakers might also insert policy suggestions amidst their oodles of praise. For emperors, panegyrics could provide propaganda support against enemies within if not the un-Greek without. For both, as well as for audiences at large, they affirmed a profoundly reassuring sense of cultural continuity, going back through Libanius et al. through master-rhetoreticians Hermogenes and Isokrates to Homer himself (always read, always quoted). In so doing, panegyric also differentiated those able to appreciate its metaphors and allusions from barbarians outside as well as "ditch diggers and tavern-keepers" inside the frontiers. Dennis deviates at one point to note that strict adherence to hallowed rhetorical rules, and the required boatloads of flattery did not wholly preclude factual information of historiographical value, e.g., on the innovative use of stone-throwing machines, and possibly the counterweight trebuchet by John II Komnenos (1118-1143) according to his panegyrist Nikephoros Basilakes (Dennis has enriched us with his indispensable editions of Byzantine military manuals).

Paul Magdalino's "In search of the Byzantine courtier" actually finds two: the late ninth century (b.) top official and writer Leo Choirosphaktes, best known for his preposterous epistolary attempts to entrap Symeon of Bulgaria into making unrequited concessions by sheer orthographic trickery (*pace* Gibbon et al. a most unrepresentative parody of Byzantine diplomacy) and the twelfth-century scrounger, social climber and jobless/moneyless snob Constantine Manasses, author of assorted literary flatteries of the rich and famous. Before focusing in detail on his two unlovely exemplars—he could have chosen nicer guys—Magdalino notes the interesting contrast between the pan-Western notion of "court," whence courtly, courteous, courtier, courtesan, and the much less resonant *aule* likewise a physical metaphor for a social phenomenon but which yielded none of the derivates above except the late and rare *aulikos* (only common in modern Greek).

I believe that much more than words are involved in the difference. Magdalino does not, instead opining that court culture was simply taken for granted in palace-dominated Constantinople. But his list of defining traits ("the acute sense of hierarchy, rank, and proximity to the ruler; the ethos of attendance, service and reward; the cult of luxury, exoticism, delightfulness, and play...") misses a crucial element much-present in medieval and early-modern Western courts, but normally absent in the imperial palace: autonomous potentates whom the ruler keeps near himself not just to obtain deference and service but also to watch and control as closely as possible. Emperors had to contend with usurpers frequently enough, but if in the palace at all, the latter were his dependent servants until they made their move. Western kings by contrast worked, played and prayed with dukes and such around them who had their own lands, revenues, men and formal local powers too—till centralizing royal bureaucracies eventually flattened the lot into mere wealth if that. A constant if latent tension was thus the hidden mainspring of medieval and early-modern Western courtly life, giving it an edgy liveliness that could at times set the stage for the bloody games of musical thrones that Shakespeare made the most of. *Aule* did not, say, a Plantagenet court make. It was evidently the central purpose of Byzantine ceremoniousness to suppress the very atmosphere that could made contemporary Western courts both livelier and deadlier.

In their important essay on the sociology of the Byzantine court, the late, much-missed Alexander P. Kazhdan and Michael McCormick begin by carefullly differentiating between (1) aristocracy; (2) ruling class; (3) elite and (4) courtiers, before themselves taking a stab at the court/*aule* problem—except that they prefer *to palation*, so describing once again a mere edifice. Next they ask how many courtiers could be so counted, citing a budget-based estimate of just over two thousand in circa 842; a spatially-based maximum of 2,900—the calculated capacity of the galleries of St. Sophia where all the courtiers periodically assembled; and the number 1,600, derived from the Emperor's banquet guest lists for the twelve days of Christmas, minus the 216 indigents who were Christianly included, and minus an allowance for high officials repeatedly invited. They cautiously conclude with a range between one and two thousand men, women not being invited.

After counting everybody, the authors differentiate between them, beginning with Persian, Armenian, Varangian and Latin bodyguards, certainly important but not culturally. The *philoi*—the emperor's friends who shared his dinner and breakfast tables—were that and more, being charter members of the elite, as opposed to aristocracy or ruling class or courtiers in general. A group as close to the Emperor but otherwise very different was the *koubouklion* (one of the countless Greek-twisted Latin words in the Byzantine lexicon): the eunuchs of the bedchambers originally but far more widely powerful at times. The castrated allowed a palace government to mix administration with domesticity without risk of adultery. That was their lesser virtue, not necessarily of consequence. Their supposed greater virtue was their supposed freedom from paternal temptations to transfer the emperor's treasure or even his power to their own kin. That only worked reliably with foreign eunuch slaves, if then. Foreign eunuchs being in short supply, local boys were castrated precisely to rise high enough to enrich their families. That they did as leading officials, prelates and even patriarchs, and military commanders. One eunuch born of a peasant family, John Orphanotrophos, achieved far more than that, successfully maneuvering the empress Zoe into marrying his brother, who ruled well enough for a while as Michael IV (1034-1041).

The authors report that more is known of eunuchs than of the hierarchy of the palace clergy, though they duly figured in the Christmas banquet lists. Patriarch, metropolitans and their staffs were all definitely members of the elite, but they were not courtiers as the priests, deacons, sub-deacons and *psaltai* of the palace certainly were. The civil servants of the "sandaled senate" were of the elite if senior enough but not aristocrats, and only the highest ranking can be classified as courtiers. The banquet lists suggest a total of 168, who might perhaps be deemed the equivalents of the administrative class of the British civil service, for the empire had many more officials at large. Also given the honor of a seat at one of the last of the Christmas banquets were the *diaitarioi*, the servants of the imperial palaces who did all the carrying and fetching but also the tailoring, goldsmithing and such. They were scarcely courtiers in a Western sense but of the court nonetheless and surely an important slice of society in Constantinople.

As for women, they were included out to use the immortal phrase, for sexual segregation was the norm. That did not mean an atomized isolation: *De Ceromoniis* depicts the empress as head of "the court of the women." As in much later times, their status was of course entirely derived from their husband's rank—one reads of *patrikia, protospatharia, kandidatissa*—the *frau herr doktor* and *frau oberst* of their day.

Kazhdan/McCormick have more to say all of it interesting before they reach their conclusion: the ceremonial apparatus was a "magnificent tool for the control of an ambitious ruling class." How exactly? By detaining physically (attendance was compulsory), by conditioning psychologically (the anxious wait for advancement induced dependency), by deliberately contrived insecurity: in addition to the scheduled palatine and religious ceremonies set by the calendar, courtiers were routinely summoned to attend functions that followed an often stately and always specified protocol, yet were only announced the afternoon or night before for the morrow. Once in his set place—to which he might have desperately hurried from afar—the courtier in his specified robes might find himself promoted, demoted or the humiliated witness of a rival's elevation. Nothing in the progression of seemingly frivolous and fatuous elaborations that fills the pages of *De Ceromoniis* betrays such seriously manipulative purposes—except the explicit, detailed provision for last-minute ceremonies, and that is quite enough.

The suggestively-named Nicolas Oikonomides offers more precise measures in his "title and income at the Byzantine court." The Emperor was served by officials, not landed magnates as in the West; they were paid annually in cash (the *roga*) except for minor added perks, not in kind as in the "store-house" empires of earlier antiquity and post-Tetrarchic Rome; and the highest officials were paid by Himself in person, to better remind them whence their income came from. On March 24, 950 Liutprand was present when Constantine VII Porphyrogennetos literally handed over the *roga* in the Great Palace. The Rector was first in the queue though not the best-paid: he got four *skaramangia* as well as a heavy bag of gold; next the top army officer, the *domestikos* of the "schools" (elite units) and *droungarios* of the fleet, came up to the table, both needing help to drag away their heavier bags of gold. And so it went on, down to the officials who received 320 grams for their year of service. There is a surprising abundance of information about salaries if not total revenues and spending; Oikonomides makes the most of it to explore the economy of the country as well as public finance. Taxes were supplemented by voluntary capital contributions—irreversible investments: rich individuals could buy honorific imperial sinecures for a lump sum, which yielded a modest return (2.31 percent—3.47 percent) by way of the *roga* prescribed for the office. That was less than the standard interest return of 6 percent, but bought a title and possibly Senate membership as well. Moreover, additional payments could earn a very handsome 9.72 percent return. The system of course has been much and widely, and perversely survives still in the ambassadorships that U.S. Presidents give away for campaign contributions, the state not benefitting at all.

Byzantium was not unchanging: all of the above relates to the Tenth century. By the Eleventh, inflation and devaluation—a.k.a. a "gold shortage"— pushed up (real) interest rates from 6 to 8.33 percent. Imperial revenues were compromised: salaries were cut, taxes increased, and the *roga* return on contributions diminished. High officials had to have high pay. When that could no longer be supplied, the logical alternative was aristocratic government by magnates rewarded with donations of land, fiscal revenues, or both. That was the solution of Alexios I Komnenos (1081-1118) father of Anna of the hagiographic *Alexiad*, who thereby degraded the meritocratic empire into a quasi-feudal one —if I may dare to use that scorned term. Oikonomides would no doubt protest such a crude simplification, and deserves to be read in full, indeed beyond the limits of his short presence in this volume.

Everyone knows about the artificial tree with its artificial singing birds that stood in the throne room with its automatic lions. That sets off James Trilling, elegantly enough ("Daedalus and the Nightingale: art and technology in the Myth of the Byzantine Court") but his is a reverie, not analysis that one may summarize. Too predictably Catherine Jolivet-Levy's "Presence et figures du souverain a Saint-Sophie de Constaninople et l'eglise de la Sainte-Croix d' Aghtamar" is all disciplined analysis: the aim is to supplement the scant evidence on how emperors and kings were portrayed in the ninth to twelfth centuries (Ravenna serves gloriously for its period; but only fragments of the mosaics of Constantinople survive). One solution is to go just beyond the empire to examine the decor of a smallish but most remarkable Armenian Church, built between 915 and 921 by king (?) Gagik Arcruni, tributary to the Caliph as his artists were largely tributary to Byzantine masters; and the Capella Palatina is also looked at. It is all very interesting by way of comparative art-history but the author concludes by noting the political purpose and how it was achieved: the iconographic program was to assimilate the sovereign to the holy by suggestive biblical analogies, as much or more as by direct juxtaposition (Roger II's cruder method).

Henry Maguire fittingly closes the volume by examining a wide range of visual evidences for the relationship between the two courts of the Christian Empire: the court of the emperor in Constantinople, and the heavenly court above. Each was headed by a supreme being: god over all creation, emperor included of course; the emperor over all men. Not merely God's anointed choice among other mortals—as per Jewish kings and thus all Western monarchs so long as monarchy was in earnest, the emperor was the very image of god on earth, a much grander claim. Exactly as his counterpart of China did, the Emperor benevolently recognized all foreign rulers who humbly accepted his supremacy. Thus Michael VII Ducas (1071-78) presented enamels to the Magyar king Geza I, now decorating the Hungarian crown, one of which shows Geza looking up reverentially at Michael, just on the reverse the archangels Michael and Gabriel look up at Christ, whose own arched enamel exactly replicated Michael's. An illuminated manuscript illustrates a still greater claim for Nikephoros III Botaneiates (1078-81): one image shows him as altogether larger than two court officials on either side of him; another places him between the archangel Michael and St. John Chrysostom who float precisely at his own height and are depicted in his own dimensions—moreover both look at the emperor who is himself looking at us. One court was decisively above the other but that did not exclude all sorts of interpenetrations: when archangels appear in earthly contexts, they not only wear court attire, or military dress, but that of eunuchs too. As for the emperor, he is still that in the heavenly court, for he wears his own costume up there too.

Much is to be learned from images, but in one crucial respect almost *all* the images evoked in this volume, many actually reproduced if only in black and white, seriously misrepresent the Byzantine court. The themes of most mosaics and paintings were necessarily Christian or at least biblical. But devotion to the Trinity was almost matched by the veneration of Homer, often memorized in extenso. There was much praying but also much reading. It was not only religious faith that was enlisted to support fighting morale and political resilience, but also intense pride in the great inheritance of learning and literature, in Greek at least. Religion pervaded the life of the court but so did a pagan culture that remained vibrant and creative if much less visible to us.

Part 6

Amazon Misadventures

24

Drugs, Crime, and Corruption

When the Bolivian narcotics police stopped us to search our jeep, my wife and I were driving down from La Paz on our way to the Amazon. We were therefore entering rather than exiting the coca-growing area, and would hardly be smuggling the stuff to its source. I therefore asked the police what they were looking for. "*Precursores*" they said, the chemicals used by the barrel to convert coca leaves into concentrated paste. The search was clearly a useless formality: no worthwhile amount of the suspect chemicals could possibly fit in our jeep. There was no point in complaining, and in any case we did not mind the break after the hair-raising descent from 15,000 feet by narrow, unpaved track. Then, a canvas-covered truck came down the road. The driver briefly stopped to hand over a tightly rolled newspaper to one of the policemen, and sped off. As he did so, a canvas flap opened in the wind to reveal large yellow barrels. The American with the patrol, dressed up in Vietnam War camouflage with a Department of Justice-Drug Enforcement Agency badge pinned to his breast pocket, did not react when I sarcastically congratulated the policemen on their assiduous interest in reading the latest news from the capital.

Having spent a grand total of ten days in Peru, Richard Clutterbuck includes a section on the bribery of Peruvian army officers in one of the four chapters on that country (2.5 days of on-scene research per chapter). In it, he calculates that in 1994 the two-star general in command of the Huallaga valley—Peru's major source of coca paste—could earn six years' worth of salary from a single US$ 15,000 "facilitation" fee for allowing one light aircraft loaded with paste to take off, and there were several flights per night. In a later chapter, on the world-wide distribution of cocaine, Clutterbuck presents a table showing how the price per kilo increases stage by stage from the Peruvian paste exporter ($4,000 per kilogram) to the London street dealer ($100,000/kg) without tumbling to the obvious conclusion: if $4,000/kg merchandise can corrupt Peruvian army

Review of Richard Clutterbuck, *Drugs, Crime, and Corruption,* New York: Macmillan.

officers, how corrupting is the importer's $ 40,000/kg cocaine or the distributor's $ 60,000/kg ?

Perhaps HMS Customs and all British police-persons are immune. But in the United States, hundreds of small-town sheriffs in areas where drug flights are wont to land have in-ground swimming pools with all the trimmings in their backyards; uncounted thousands of plain policemen add greatly to their retirement savings, more DEA agents than the one I encountered in Bolivia are routinely paid by both sides, while district attorneys, federal prosecutors, and judges too have been engulfed by corruption. In a trade whose major protagonists routinely travel about with attaché cases filled with neat bundles of $100 bills, many if not most encounters with the law go no further than the separation of the attaché case from its owner.

Nor is it likely that, in the whole world, only U.S. law-enforcers and Peruvian Army officers can be bribed (Clutterbuck's $500 billion per annum for all drugs world-wide is perhaps an over-estimate, but not absurdly high). It is more reasonable to assume the exact opposite, that corruption is roughly as widespread as the attempt to police the drug trade. It is only rarely, however, that dealings so inherently discreet come to the surface. In Mexico, clamorous murder trials have incidentally revealed that the drug trade was efficiently protected by high officials of the Salinas government; in Budapest, any tourist can see Lebanese money-changers at work in the heart of town, entirely unmolested by seemingly oblivious policemen as they turn local-currency drug revenues into dollars; in both Karachi and Bombay every child knows that the biggest drug dealers are as immune from the local police as Al Capone ever was in Cicero; nor are Paraguay and Thailand the only countries were known drug bosses can serve as cabinet ministers, or where cabinet ministers serve drug bosses more or less openly in exchange for votes and cash.

That is the first effect of drug prohibitionism on the workings of police forces, courts and governments world-wide: a tide of corruption at every level, from street cops to cabinet ministers. With it, there comes a degree of incapacitation, for those who protect the drug trade for their cut of its routine profits, cannot dutifully pursue all the other crimes that traffickers occasionally indulge in, from armed fights over sources or markets to over-eager debt collection. But mostly the trade prospers peacefully enough—in Beverly Hills, as in Mayfair and Via Montenapoleone, it is downright genteel

The second effect is to enormously increase the work load of police forces, courts and prisons worldwide. That sellers can often purchase immunity is of no help to those buyers who steal, housebreak, rob, pimp or prostitute themselves to pay for their drugs (though the trade would hardly be so prosperous if it did not have a great number of gainfully employed or even affluent consumers for whom drugs are not more than a minor luxury). In the United States, the entire criminal justice system is notoriously and grossly overloaded by the annual intake of hundreds of thousands of such demand-side offenders, in addition to the handful of supply-side importers and wholesalers, and huge numbers of street dealers. Under the new "three strikes and you are out" federal law that the world's greatest democratic politician recently saw fit to sign, life sentences are now mandatory for third convictions, even for simple theft. That law should gradually transfer hundreds of thousands of non-affluent habitual users to federal penitentiaries. But it seems that not enough is being done: the head of the Drug Enforcement Agency has recently announced that the Agency will now focus much more than before on marijuana. That is undoubtedly a shrewd bureaucratic move: it expands the DEA's customer base from a mere four million or so cocaine, crack and heroine users to the tens of millions who sometimes use marijuana. In few countries do puritanism and bureaucratic urges so fatally converge to maximize the criminalization of society by drug prohibitionism, but everywhere the futile comedy is daily played out as police forces proudly announce arrests and seizures that keep drugs expensive, thus ensuring the abundance of drug-related thefts, housebreakings and robberies.

But there is also a third effect, on the largest possible scale. It was the American-inspired "French Connection" struggle against the Marseilles heroin labs that shifted the business to Sicily, enormously increasing the Mafia's revenues and power. It was the American-supported struggle against cocaine production in Colombia that induced both the Cali and Medellin cartels to provide seeds, loans and technical aid to the ex-villager urban slum dwellers of Lima who returned to the land to grow Peru's coca (a rare example of successful foreign agricultural aid, Prof. Bauer please note). And it was the American-lead harassment of Peru's growers and traffickers that made Bolivia a major exporter of paste (the legal, domestic trade in unprocessed leaves is far less profitable). Most recently, the damage inflicted on the Medellin cartel has primarily served to expand the market of the Cali cartel. The U.S. tax payer has therefore successively enriched the Sicilian Mafia, many Peruvians, many Bolivians and lately the Cali cartel, and instead of receiving a cut, even had to pay for the DEA's inflated budget.

It would be very odd if great believers in the power of the invisible hand somehow believed that only in the case of drugs demand will not evoke supply, ensuring that there is never true suppression, but only displacement. Of course it is no such delusion that propels America's blatantly futile yet widely destructive "war on drugs," but rather the puritan urge to punish whatever can be punished by first being de-legitimized, including of late cigarettes and rich foods (by medical intimidation) nude bathing (by County laws, in Florida) and office hanky-panky (by easily successful sexual harassment law-suits). What is truly odd is that only in the Netherlands for all its own puritan antecedents is the totally exploded theory of drug prohibitionism (repression reduces crime) openly resisted by a rival theory of monitored toleration, which does assuredly minimize the collateral criminality of poor buyers. That cops world-wide should be unmoved by the Dutch experiment is perfectly understandable: it greatly reduces work-loads, personnel expansion, promotions—and bribes. That politicians worldwide should be just as indifferent, is no mystery either, for it is very hard to be anti-prohibitionist without appearing to be pro-drugs. What does require explanation is the conspicuous silence of intellectual leaders. Of the many who will readily address all other societal questions, only a handful are willing to oppose the theory, practice and consequences of drug prohibitionism. What does require explanation is the conspicuous silence of intellectual leaders. Of the many who will readily address all other societal questions, only a handful are willing to oppose the theory, practice and consequences of drug prohibitionism.

One exception is Richard Cluttterbuck, even if his status as an intellectual leader is dubious—unlike his fully established reputation as one of the British Army's intellectuals-in-uniform, before his retirement while still rather young yet already in the rank of a major-general (the Army's lingering reputation for anti-intellectualism is grotesquely out of date). Since then, Clutterbuck has pursued a three-part career in the American style, combining straight-academic university affiliations, professional consulting work for commercial as well as government clients, and a great deal of writing, including no fewer than sixteen books on every form of violence except conventional warfare: terrorism, guerilla, riots and revolutionary politics, large-scale crime and "industrial conflict" including the media coverage of the same. All his books seem to have a mixed reputation among specialists. Unfailingly sensible and well-informed, often shrewd, Clutterbuck is as careful in presenting his often recondite facts as he is relentlessly unoriginal in their interpretation. Perhaps the phenomena he has chosen to study contain no great abundance of profound truths that await discovery, but certainly he has not uncovered them.

In this bad good book—crudely written, poorly organized yet filled with useful facts, simplistic in many of its particular analyses, yet both original and very persuasive in its conclusions—Richard Clutterbuck has chapters on producing countries (Bolivia and Colombia as well as Peru, but the Golden Triangle and the "Golden Crescent" of Afghanistan, Iran and Pakistan only rate a single chapter along with the Turkish and West African transit routes); on the different drugs (cocaine, crack, heroin, cannabis and the synthetics); on money laundering and the largely futile attempts to stop it, by controls that greatly complicate honest transactions; on the United States, on the Mafia, on drugs and crime in Russia and Eastern Europe; on Italy and Germany as markets and the Dutch experiment, and finally on the United Kingdom in detail with separate chapters on drug trafficking, law-enforcement, and the mixed record of suppression and medicalization. It is only after all these meanderings through far away countries of which he knows little, and through all the clichés of the subject familiar from countless newspaper stories (expendable Nigerian condom couriers, BCCI, big-deal police ops that leave no dent in the traffic, etc.) that Clutterbuck comes to his conclusions.

It is then that hurried excursions through many subjects abruptly give way to a methodical and logical progress through the alternatives, whereby decriminalization is carefully distinguished from de facto tolerance, legalization per se, and legalization under licensing, with each judiciously weighed in its costs and benefits. Clutterbuck then presents the arguments against licensed legalization, but that is the alternative he finally and most persuasively recommends. In arguing that the United Kingdom should be the "test-bed" for his remedy, he points out that Britain is still island enough to confer adequate isolation from continued prohibitionism elsewhere (Zurich's "needle park" experiment was swamped by out-of-town consumers, as the Netherlands' success is diminished by drug tourists and their suppliers). In the same judicious way, Clutterbuck draws parallels with the licensing of alcohol while noting the differences, and his explanation of how the system could work in practice is convincing. In the United States, Newt Gingrich has recently surprised some of his more fervid admirers and shocked not a few by recommending even harsher repression or else legalization. So perhaps there is hope after all.

25

Trinidad

Trinidad, Bolivia, in the tropical lowlands of the Beni below the Amazon, was not even our destination. We were only driving to Trinidad to leave it again, by way of the road to Santa Cruz de la Sierra—a real road that, not paved of course because tropical Bolivia does not run to paved roads, but literally a highway, raised over the swamps with upcast from the drainage ditches on either side to stay dry enough for wheels even during the rainy season. That was the glorious prospect that awaited, if we ever made it to Trinidad, except that we were not normal human beings in need of going from A to B but venturing travelers, who had come specifically to see the animal wonders of the flooded plain. So for us the Trinidad-Santa Cruz highway should have been no promise at all, for it would mean the end of our adventure. But that was before we run into trouble. And so it was that having flown from Washington to Miami and from Miami to La Paz, to then drive down from the Andes along the precipices of the Yungas road—voted the world's "most terrifying" by the *Lonely Planet* editors—we finally reached the flooded plain only to discover that we were very eager to leave it again.

We had come to see animals, and see them we did: alligators and snakes, giant lizards and giant rodents, birds of every hue and size, Amazonian wolves, were all around us in great profusion, just as Pedro Sarmiento had said in La Paz. But Pedro, just back in the capital after five years in the Beni, had also said that we would never make it to Trinidad. An *inferno!* was how they cursed the endless track through the lowlands, though it was not hell that came to mind. There was no burning heat, and with cascades of rain every few hours, and black clouds gathering beforehand that obscured the sun, it was not even warm. Instead it was wet, wet from above and wet below. Here and there the red-earth roadway had withstood the rains, but for the rest it was only a ribbon of watery mud that marked our route, and that too was frequently interrupted by streams of muddy water flowing in from the rain-swollen swamps on either side.

Some really were streams, visibly shallow and easily crossed by the high-built Japanese jeep we had rented in La Paz. Others were more like torrents, much wider, much faster and also certainly deeper—but how deep? We could not tell by looking at the muddy water, nor could we risk sinking our jeep by simply driving in. So my son Joseph, or his college roommate Benjamin who had joined him for the unlikely combination of an exciting winter vacation with dad, or I, had to wade in to test the depth with a stick. I have a photograph of Joseph standing knee-deep in the water, which seems attractively blue. That is most peculiar because we both remember it as brown. But what mattered would not have photographed anyway: the water was alive with darting fishes of all sizes, and we knew that there were snakes in it, and alligators, and much larger caimans. It was only the fishes that worried us—piranhas are abundant in the Beni—until we saw a very poisonous green mamba nicely curled on the jeep's front winch.

After successfully crossing dozens of streams, several torrents, and one full-blown river, it happened: six-foot Joseph reached the far side with the water still well below his waist, but when we drove in after him, the jeep slid sideways into deeper water, and stopped. The rushing torrent must have dug out a hollow that Joseph had eluded. After trying and failing to climb out by sheer engine power in ultra-low gear, it was the turn of the winch. The trick was to run the engine fast, so as to keep charging the battery that the powerful electrical winch could drain in minutes. The other trick was to find a sturdy tree on the far side to loop the wire around, within its fifty-foot length. At that point we were crossing a vast grassland, with few large trees but there was a candidate—a good yard into the swamp. Somebody would have to wade in, clearly a job for dad, who much preferred to be bitten himself (the mamba had just made its appearance) than return to Washington with Joseph or Ben on his conscience. It was then that Oscar arrived.

That part of the Beni is almost uninhabited, and we had seen no humans along the way since passing a three-hut village hours before. But there he was, a young fellow in ragged trousers turned up to his knees, bare feet, a torn shirt, and a small bag over his shoulder. Oscar—or Ohcar, as he later pronounced his name in the s-less dialect of the lowlanders, had clearly decided to earn our instant gratitude. Saying not a word, he quickly crossed over to seize the end of the wire from my hands, waded into the torrent again towards the obvious tree, and astonished us by leaping over the bushes to dive at the trunk, looping the wire around it in one swift movement.

There was no time for introductions. Winch controls in hand, with Joseph now in the driver's seat to rev up the engine, I turned the switch only to find that the jeep would not budge. I tried again, and again, each time the drum would start turning, and then stop. The slope was just too steep, the jeep too deeply dug into the mud. Soon it was all over, the engine had seized, and the battery was exhausted. Such things can happen anywhere, and are sometimes seriously inconvenient if there is no cellular phone at hand with which to immediately summon help, and no public phone in sight. In the Beni it is not the absence of telephones that is the problem, but the absence of anyone to call. In the largest villages, there is some sort of police post, but the policemen have no vehicles, or telephones for that matter. There are of course no garages or tow-trucks to call, and even if we could have somehow sent a message to San Ignacio de los Moxos, the only village before Trinidad, nobody there would have been mad enough to attempt the drive. In the meantime, the light was failing, it would soon be dark, or rather pitch black in that moonless time, and the water seemed to be rising.

There we were, exactly where we had wanted to be, in the flooded plain. But to leave had suddenly become our only aim in life. Oscar had been walking ahead of us when he heard the engine straining and turned back, hoping for a ride. It now seemed that we would be joining him on his walk to San Ignacio, some eighty miles away. It would have to be a non-stop slog—the Beni is one of the few places left in the world where it is not *only* the animals that are endangered, and once we left the jeep we would have no safe place to sleep. For the rest, there was no problem because we had a hand-pump water filter guaranteed to keep out bacteria, some dry biscuits, a few high-tech fruit bars, two tins of corned beef and besides, young alligators are easily caught.

Oscar had a better idea. The endless grassland and swamp all around us showed no signs of habitation, but he was sure that there was an *estancia* nearby, where they might have a tractor. Where is it? Further up the road. How far? Not far. I tried to ask how many kilometers away, but kilometers meant nothing to him. So we set out him and me. It was soon too dark to see as far down as my feet and my feet were often in the water. I had thick-walled boots on, and nothing to worry about. When I stepped too near an alligator, it slapped me with his tail in bolting away, but it was too small to hurt, and I was concentrating on keeping up with Oscar who was much faster in his bare feet. After a while I heard Joseph's voice and by the time we saw the oil lamps of the *estancia*, they had caught up with us—they had decided that dad should not be out at night on his own.

There is some relaxed cattle ranching in the Beni. Humped Brazilian Zebus are let loose in as much land as the owner can afford to fence in (the wire costs more than the land), and the herd's natural increase over what the jaguars eat is culled once in a while for the meat markets of La Paz, Cochabamba or Santa Cruz. All are far away, transport costs are huge, and Zebu meat cannot compete with Argentina's superlative beef on export markets. There are no luxurious ranch-houses on the Beni's *estancias* or any real houses at all, just a few huts, perhaps with a generator for a few light bulbs, radio and VCR. So it was in the one we came to, but there was also a shed with two bulldozers and a tractor. The tractor was OK, just what we wanted. The bulldozers were another matter. No cattle ranch needed them, and no Beni rancher could possibly afford one, let alone two. Their presence could mean only one thing. The *estancia* was being used to fly out cocaine paste, the bulldozers were there to flatten airstrips before landings, and then to slight them after take offs, so that they would not show up on American satellite pictures, attracting a visit by the U.S. Drug Enforcement Agency's helicopters with its load of trigger-happy Bolivian auxiliaries.

It was the last place where prudent *gringos* should wonder into. Six or seven youngsters, pure-blood Moxos by the looks of them, were the first people we saw in the faint light of a weak bulb dangling outside the main hut. They were shy but friendly enough—when I told that them that we needed the tractor to pull out our stranded jeep, some promptly went over to the shed to get it going. But then two older men in their forties appeared, their bosses. Neither was a native, nor were they friendly. One was sinister and very silent, offering no reply to my greeting. The other was sinister and less silent, for he flatly refused to send out the tractor. It is late. We are tired. Come back tomorrow, maybe. We could be busy. His striving for a dismissively sarcastic tone was entirely unnecessary: Bolivians are famous in Latin America for their formal good manners (even policemen say *buenos dias* before saying anything else), and the man's original refusal, abrupt and unapologetic, was quite enough to express extreme hostility.

It was then that Oscar chose to whisper in my ear that the *estancia* belonged to the brother of the mayor of San Borja. I had thought that he was just passing through, but evidently he knew all about the area, too much for my taste just then. The Beni's miniature version of Medellin and Cali, where the cocaine-paste millionaires build their mansions, San Borja has an evil reputation for violence in tranquil Bolivia (the *Lonely Planet*: pass through if you must. Do not linger.) Joseph has mainly studied medieval history at the University of Rochester and is a very gentle soul for all his six feet of muscles. But when I told him to unfold his leatherman as I was doing, and do as I did if I did it, he nodded and got ready.

At that point, it was important that neither man be allowed to enter the hut, where they undoubtedly kept their weapons—every adult in the Beni has a shotgun, and these two particular adults would have had shorter weapons too. I was not worried about the young Moxos—they seemed far from happy with their bosses, and eager to help. The speaking one kept saying no, I kept insisting, and both San Borja gentlemen soon realized that they might be standing there all night. We would not go away, and they would not get to the hut. When the speaking one changed his tone, to complain once again that he was too tired, but without the sarcasm of the first time around, I offered him forty dollars, a princely sum in Bolivia. He asked for fifty. I agreed, but told him that he would get nothing if we reached the jeep too late—the water was rising, thick clouds made the night utterly black, and to dive into the muddy torrent to look for the winch drum amidst plenty of reptile company was unthinkable.

It was a fast ride back, all of us—Oscar, Joseph, Benjamin, the Moxos, cling-ing to the tractor driven by the speaker, while the silent one rode the engine as if it were a horse. And it was a fast job to drag out the jeep still only half submerged, and the engine promptly jump-started with one pull of the tractor. The silent one squeezed in the back seat with Oscar, Joseph, and Benjamin as we drove back to the *estancia*.

I had been grateful to Pedro for having found such a splendid jeep for us in a country full of ancient wrecks, a brand new upmarket model, with a powerful engine and very comfortable too. But now I regretted his choice. There was a good $40,000 of vehicle in it, plus whatever we had in cash, which could not be a small amount in country where all must be paid in cash. We were heading back to the *estancia* where $50 were to change hands—but why only $50? The tractor was steadily gaining on us, we could not speed on the muddy track without risking a slide into the swamp. They would get there before us, and the speaker would get to his gun. After turning to glance at him, receiving the answer of a millimetric nod, I was utterly certain that Oscar would do his part, by keeping the silent one now wedged in next to him on the back seat from doing any harm, once we got there. Nor would the young Moxos help the speaker, of that I was almost certain. But they would not side with us either. A shotgun would not do it, him being alone and outnumbered, but in San Borja they go for automatic weapons, AKs, M.16s, Brazilian copies of HK sub-machine guns, Uzis, and just one of them goes a long way. It was another moment to regret that I had brought Joseph with me.

Within minutes it was all over. When we followed the tractor into the front yard of the *estancia*, dozens of men, women and children were milling about in the glare of our headlights. Throughout Bolivia, people commonly travel by hitching rides atop of the cargo on normal commercial trucks, whose drivers charge half the equivalent bus fare. The *flotas*, the "fleets" of the cooperatives that run old U.S. school buses on standard routes, charge some of the lowest per-mile fares in the world but even that is too much for most Bolivians, who eat what they grow, gather, fish or hunt, and can rarely sell any spare food for cash. In the Beni, however, the *Flota Yungena* is chronically unreliable during the rainy season. So the crowd that had piled out of a full-size Scania truck and a Toyota jitney to await the morning light was a mixed bunch, with some almost middle class by Bolivian standards, men wearing shoes, women in store-bought clothes, who would have paid the bus fare had there been a bus running.

That, as well sheer numbers, had turned the OK Corral into a social gathering. While the two gentlemen of San Borja ruefully stood about, now reduced to a silent wait for the promised fifty dollars at best, I talked with the drivers and the more assertive travelers. They were all from San Ignacio, they were going to the capital, to La Paz, at least three days away even during the dry season. How long to San Ignacio? Not long—it took us six hours, it will be less for your strong car. Water? Plenty, but all shallow, nothing that will stop you. Our car had to be pulled out of the last *rio*, I said. We know what is ahead, that is why we stopped here for the night. Tomorrow, after the sun rises, the truck will pull the Toyota through. There is nothing so difficult for you on the way to

San Ignacio. And from there to Trini? I asked—that is how Oscar called it. No idea, sorry. Maybe the road will be passable tomorrow or in a few days, but we ourselves came this way because even if one makes it through the mud all the way to the river bank in front of Trini, the rafts of the *cooperativa* cannot cross the Mamore'—too many giant tree trunks rushing down in the flood, the current is just too fast. Always at least half a mile wide, the Mamore' which flows into the Itenes along the Brazilian border, which flows into the Madre de Dios, which flows into the Madera which flows into the Amazon, was more than two miles wide when we eventually crossed it, on a raft of giant tree trunks pushed by a dugout canoe with an outboard motor. By then the current had slowed, and only the shallows on the edge of the flood threatened to leave us stranded.

Beni protocol allows for the unceremonious exchange of nakedly practical information in forced road-side encounters, but once it becomes a conversation one is supposed to go through introductions, and to share food and drink if the hold-up is long enough. That is how it had been when we had to wait for many hours before a gigantic land-slide on the Yungas road. By the time a bulldozer came along to ram through a passage (as the only passage into the lowlands and onto Brazil it has the privilege of a road crew) we had enjoyed many a joke, learned much about what waited ahead from an intrepid *Flota Yungena* driver, and found dinner companions in a Bolivian couple brave enough to risk the journey down to the foothills in an ancient Volkswagen. They were headed for the market town of Caranavi, still two thousand feet above the flooded plain, and tried hard to persuade us to stay there with them in the town's exceptionally pleasant inn, instead of descending any further. Go in the summer, the man said.

I could not have been more grateful to the San Ignacio travelers, I knew that they would have preferred to talk on into the night rather than face bedless sleep on the bare ground, or whatever berths their vehicles offered. But for us it was time to go. Even if it turned out that we would have to drive back from San Ignacio, we might find beds there in the meantime, in the village *hostal* or *residencial* (the word hotel has not been devalued in Bolivia, it promises proper rooms, with running hot water). And we would come back in daylight, and much better prepared. Earlier, I had asked Benjamin to have fifty dollars ready. He passed me a single $ 50 note folded over many times into a tiny perfect square. I silently gave it unopened to the speaker—the other one had said not a word even when riding with us—and off we drove into the night towards San Ignacio de los Moxos, known for its friendly Indians, and a lagoon where in the dry season the thirsty *garzas* (Ibis, herons, flamingos?) stand toe to toe along the water's edge, next to sleepy alligators and huge turtles. Oscar came with us, naturally.

26

The Sane Cow Syndrome

At the Wye plantation on the eastern shore of Maryland, the Department of Agriculture of the University of Maryland raises beautiful Black Angus cattle with all the latest equipment and best techniques. Although its own output now consists of bullocks and breeding cows, it serves as a model for what the trade calls "cow-calf operations," to produce beef for the table rather than milk. It is indeed a model of its kind: corrals, chutes, catch-pens all seem brand new because they are so perfectly maintained, with everything neat, clean and freshly painted. The results of the best Maryland raisers are impressive: 90 percent of their cows produce a calf each year, and steer are ready for sale by their eighteenth month at the latest, at impressive weights. I went there to find out how my entirely primitive Bolivian ranch might be improved—only 60 percent of our cows give birth in any one year, and our steer grow so slowly that we must keep them for thirty months to achieve worthwhile weights for the market. Cattle is capital, and was indeed its very first embodiment, yielding the interest of its offspring. The higher the birth rate, the higher the rate of return, if costs are equal. And time is money with cattle as with any other form of capital: a steer sold at thirty months earns less net revenue than one sold after eighteen months at equal weights, prices and costs–just how much less depends on the interest cost of waiting, which exceeds 12 percent per annum in Bolivia. All in all, the numbers I was shown at Wye showed that there was much to be improved in our ranch.

The Maryland experts were much interested in how we ranch and sell our cattle, given the 200 roadless kilometers to the nearest town. They were eager to help. Our humped Nelor cattle, a Brazilian breed evolved from Brahmans originally brought from India by the Portuguese, conceive by the fifteenth month or even earlier, give birth after nine months of gestation, and can become pregnant again a few weeks later, just like the Wye cows. But our fertility rate is so much lower, I learned, because if cows and bulls are left to commune according to their desires, many cows resist impregnation each and every year, much preferring to raise their calves for six months at least before becoming pregnant again. Artificial insemination is the remedy. In Wye, all cows ready to breed back but not visibly pregnant are tested with sonograms by the resident vets, and those carrying no embryo are separated from the herd to be frequently tested with a thermometer inserted into their vaginas, until oestrus is detected. At that point, the frozen semen of prize bulls is defrosted and injected, with the procedure repeated until sonogram results are positive.

With our cattle dispersed over seventy-eight square miles of savanna grasslands interrupted by islands of tropical forest, we cannot emulate any of those practices. With one-by-one animal husbandry impossible, our cows and bulls are left to graze and procreate on their own except for the few days a year when our eight cowboys, their older children, the manager and myself round up all the cattle we can find to corral it for counting, the branding of yearlings, castration, foot-and-mouth vaccination, the feeding of a vermifuge, and fumigation against external parasites. During the long rainy season, when swollen streams, enlarged lagunas and swamped pastures drastically limit movement even on with our sturdy *criollo* horses, we do not even know where our cattle is much of the time, let alone which of our heifers is ready for impregnation. In any case we have no sonogram machines or the electricity to operate then, our cows are too wild to be tested for estrus with a thermometer, and we cannot preserve semen for we have no refrigeration. The only way we can increase the fertility of our cows—the key to our entire profitability for we have no dairy cattle—is to provide enough bulls. In Wye, they keep a few "clean up" bulls with their 170 cows to complement artificial insemination, but we have forty bulls for each lot of 500 cows, deliberately selecting smaller-framed animals because young heifers flee from the very large bulls that win prizes—heavy and slow, they seem to enjoy standing around looking impressive, but mount few cows and only earn their keep with extracted semen. Our calves are also born smaller of course, but that is no disadvantage at birthing time, when our heifers easily drop their young without any help at all, let alone the pulling chains, winches and risky caesarians used by cattle raisers in all advanced countries.

There was one consolation in my failure to learn anything useful about fertility. Our procreation costs start and end with our bulls, bought at four hundred dollars each–and we can eventually recover more than that when we sell them for meat in their eight year, for middle-aged bulls easily put on weight. At Wye by contrast, as in commercial cattle-raising venture in Europe and the United States, high fertility does not come cheap. Sonogram machines, veterinary care, even the semen at $30-40 a shot are all very expensive, and there are many more abortions and dead births when cattle is bred for size, to jump-start the race to the market. Doing my sums, I discovered that for us a 60 percent live birth rate was better than 90 percent in spite of all the extra bulls we also have to keep, simply because of the vast difference in the cost of keeping animals in the first place.

In almost every cow-calf operation in Western Europe and the United States, cattle cannot feed itself year round on green pasture. Only hobby farmers with few cows and much land have the ten acres or so of decent land per head that is needed–and even they must usually provide baled hay during the coldest winter months when grass stops growing. With all the better land in Europe and North America taken up by intensive or arable farming that inherent productivity or subsidies make more profitable, almost all commercial cattle raisers must complement whatever green pasture they have with hay and other feeds at a cost of roughly $250 per year per head on average–it makes little difference if they buy the hay ready-baled or grow it themselves, with tractors, harvesters, fuel, fertilizer, weed-killers, and pesticides. The left-over straw of cereal crops and other roughage that may cost little or nothing is also fed to cows, but lactating and pregnant cows and those fast-growing steer must also be fed more costly, more protein-rich concentrates, such as maize, oats, barley, grain sorghum, wheat, beet-pulp, oilseed or soybean meal, molasses, synthetic urea and, until recently, processed animal offal including the sheep brains that lead to present difficulties. Our cattle by contrast, eats only the natural grasses of the savannah, picking and choosing among different plants at different times of the year to find all the nutrition it needs, except for salt with mineral additives that costs us $3 per head, per year.

We can afford to keep both all those extra bulls and the 40 percent of our cows that fail to give birth in any one year, because each steer we sell can pay for the salt of eighty-three heads. With feeding costing us 1 percent of what cattle raisers in Europe or North America must pay, their animal husbandry holds no lessons for us. True, we must keep our steer for thirty months before they are ready for the market, but that only costs us $7.5 in salt as opposed to the $375 or more in hay and concentrates eaten by a Maryland or British steer by the time it is ready for sale at eighteen months. Of course there is the interest on delayed revenue to be reckoned as well the much lower weight of our steer, but given our abundance of grass it simply does not pay for us to minimize time and maximize weight at high cost, let alone fatten our animals in feed lots with expensive concentrates and supplements.

In other words, while European and North American cattle raisers pay their dues to the corporations that supply them with everything from tractors and fuel to bagged concentrates, we pay our dues to nature by accepting its pace and limits. So far that has been a rewarding choice: our return on cattle capital exceeds 30 percent, more than twice what North American and European cattle raisers can expect, though their corporate suppliers fare much better of course. The profitability of the entire sector is so tenuous in the United States that many ranchers only stay in business because they are not in business at all, but rather keep their ranches for pleasure and display, 'a la W. Bush or CNN's Turner, losing money each year which they bill to the taxpayers by way of loss credits against the earnings of their real trade. Recently "buffalo," that is, bison ranching became fashionable in the tax-loss crowd, though it was attempted by some desperate cow ranchers as well, who discovered that costs are even higher—not least for steel-tube fencing—and profits even lower. Among the dwindling band of genuine ranchers, a great many are consuming their capital year by year, by accumulating mortgages against their land. As the number of independent ranchers and farm-based cattle raisers continues to decline in the United States, as it would in Europe but for subsidies, they are replaced by large-scale corporate operations, some immense, but they too are not faring well.

All that frantic productivity is thus an attempt to offset miserable margins with sheer quantity, which in turn drives down prices, reducing profitability even more. During the last two years, we have sold finished steer in the border town of Costa Marquez, in the back of Rondonia, one of Brazil's least developed areas, at prices ranging from $1.05 to $1.45 per kilo, measured at 50 percent of live weight ("pencil shrinkage"), only a few cents less than the price to be had in Chicago, for animals on which far more money has been spent. But then if Amazonic ranching were not so inherently profitable, Amazonic forests would not be endangered (for the record, we preserve our forests intact; our land in San Joaquin province is on the very edge of the uninterrupted rainforest that begins just across a ten-mile lake, but is still mostly savannah grassland that was never de-forested).

But at the Wye plantation I also learned something else, or rather saw it while we were conversing. It was the veterinary chart of a large cow-calf operation, with separate rows for pneumonia, diphtheria, infectious bovine rhinotracheitis, parainfluenza-3, bovine viral diarrhea, bloat, three kinds of clostridial infections, coccidiosis, pinkeye, cancer eye, footrot, actinobacillus lumpjaw, hard lumpjaw, acidosis, laminitis, nitrate poisoning (from heavily fertilized pasture) and many more conditions. Treatments were also listed with antihistamines, dexamethasone, epinephrine, sulfa boluses, dimethyl sulfoxide, nitrofurazone and novalson as well as several vaccines, vermifuges, fumigants, homely iodine and castor oil, and many, many applications of antibiotics—a long list of them, starting with penicillin and going to LA-200 and others equally obscure to me.

The reason I found this chart startling—though I later learned that it reflected normal conditions throughout Europe and North America—was that in our ranch we get by with one vaccination, two vermifuge doses, and two fumigations per year, all done by ourselves for there is no vet within reach. How could it be, I asked, that the Wye cows needed all those medicines, and the frequent services of veterinarians? The experts immediately pointed out that only the largest cattle raisers and feed-lot operators had full-time vets on staff as they did, while most raisers only called them in now and then, because they could apply most treatments themselves. But yes, a great variety of medicines was indeed essential, for otherwise cattle would die of disease. They estimated that veterinary care and supplies added some fifty dollars per head per year to the average cost of upkeep.

We too lose cattle to disease as well as to jaguars, maned wolves and ana-condas (yes, they can swallow a newborn calf), but our combined losses have been running at roughly 1 percent per year. No, I was told, it was nothing like that: without several specifics and lots of antibiotics, cattle raisers would lose a great many heads, and in feed-lots mass deaths would be inevitable for infections spread immediately among animals kept within inches of each other. Again, I asked why cows in salubrious Maryland—or England for that matter—were so much more vulnerable to disease than our cows which live in the intensely tropical Amazon basin, dense with every form of life including a myriad of micro-organisms, internal and external parasites, and blood-sucking vampire bats that incidentally carry all manner of diseases.

I received two answers. The first was that our slim Nelors, while much less productive of meat and useless for milking, were resistant to disease because they were the offspring of natural selection undistorted by veterinary interventions, rather than cattle systematically bred for productivity alone. The second answer, however, was the more consequential: unlike us or pigs who can eat anything organic animal or vegetable, except for grass and wood because our stomachs cannot break down cellulose, bovines are pure herbivores. Their four-part ruminant stomachs break down the cellulose in grass that we cannot digest to extract all the proteins, vitamins, minerals and calories they need. Conversely, cattle can-not easily digest proteins, beyond the tiny amounts consumed by the microbes in their first stomach or rumen which break down cellulose. Yet for the sake of rapid weight-gain and rapid procreation, European and North American cattle is fed with cereals and all those other concentrates that contain even more protein, as well as pre-bloom alfalfa hay which is itself 16 percent protein. One result is that European and North American cattle raisers are always in danger of losing their animals to bloat, a foamy gas build up in the rumen that presses against the lungs with a suffocating effect. Trocars are kept in hand to puncture the rumen in emergencies, while more normally anti-foaming agents are used.

The other results of feeding proteins to herbivores are much less dramatic, altogether more prevalent, and of far greater significance for human health: chronic diarrhea and acidosis, which hardly ever kill cattle outright but which disrupt their immune systems, exposing them to all the diseases I saw on the Wye chart, and a few more besides.

To put it plainly, nearly all beef cattle in Europe and North America is per-manently unhealthy, and only survives in its chronic state of low-level sickness with large amounts of antibiotics. Because they are cheap and induce water retention that increases weight, antibiotics are just the thing for cattle raisers and feed-lot operators—whose animals could not survive a week without them. For those who eat the resulting beef no ill consequence need follow individually, although I myself am nauseated by the idea of eating the meat of sick animals pumped full of antibiotics and assorted medicines–since visiting Wye , I eat only Argentinian beef when I can get it, and my own when in Bolivia.

Public health, however, is another matter. At a time when old diseases such as TB are reappearing, and wounds and fractures are once again followed by stubborn, even lethal infections because many bacteria strains have become highly resistant to antibiotics, their use in mass quantities by cattle raisers adds to the problem. Until recently, it was thought that humans cannot absorb antibiotics from cooked beef, but research prompted by BSE has incidentally disproved that reassuring belief. One result is that those who eat beef may be spared an infection now and then; another is that they too are contributing to the extinction of vulnerable bacteria strains, and their replacement by increasingly resistant strains.

The much larger issue is the entire logic of European and North American beef production in its present form. Tens of millions of heads of cattle are raised in spite of the lack of anywhere near enough green pasture for them. In Western Europe, subsidies provide an incentive to raise beef cattle even without any pasture at all, or almost none, as in Tuscany for example whose Chianina breed —the source of much-celebrated *Fiorentina* steaks—is the largest of all cattle breeds, but where meadows are a rarity among all those vineyards and villas. When I questioned the systematic use of antibiotics by the entire industry of both continents, the Wye experts replied that without them there could only be grass-fed beef, of wonderful taste as any visitor to Argentina can attest, but too tough for palates used to the very soft flesh of grain-fed animals, further softened by immobility in feed lots and by antibiotics. But their stronger retort was that beef fed on grass alone would be necessarily scarce, and expensive. It could no longer be an everyday food for virtually everyone, but only for the affluent, and only an occasional treat for the poor or parsimonious. Yet at the same time cardiologists unanimously assert that most people in Europe and North America eat far too much beef—that it *should* be an occasional treat rather than an everyday food, which many indeed eat twice a day.

The veterinary profession has therefore systematized, indeed normalized the raising of unhealthy cattle to achieve the very abundance that makes people unhealthy. In its rarity, BSE is only an extreme consequence of feeding animal proteins to herbivores that cannot eat even alfalfa in any quantity without ill effect, let alone sheep brains. If the unending BSE drama finally attracts public attention to the habitual malpractice of cattle raisers industry, we may yet see North American and European herds reduced to their naturally fed size, that small fraction of present numbers for which green pasture can be provided year round. And if that supply is insufficient, the pampas and savannahs of South America can provide all that is needed, my ranch too of course with its beautiful Nelors.

27

The Good in Barbed Wire

Barbed wire is important in my life—the cattle ranch I run in the Bolivian Amazon could not exist without it. In Britain as in other advanced countries, it is mostly fences of thin unbarbed wire enlivened by a low-voltage current that keep cattle from wandering off, but in the Bolivian Amazon they have no electrical supply to transform down, and in any case the cost, over many perimeter miles, would be prohibitive and the upkeep quite impossible. Ours is a wonderful land of lush savannahs and virgin forest, but it is just not valuable enough to be demarcated by anything more expensive than strands of barbed wire held up by wooden posts driven into the ground.

Invented and patented by Joseph F. Glidden in 1874, an immediate success in mass production by 1876, barbed wire, first of iron and then steel, did much to transform the American West, before doing the same in other prairie lands from Argentina to Australia. Actually, cheap fencing transformed the primordial business of cattle-raising itself. Solid wooden fences or even stone walls can be economical enough for intensive animal husbandry, in which milk and traction as well as meat are obtained by constant labor in stable and field to feed herbivores without the pastures they would otherwise need. Often the animals are tethered or just guarded, without any fences or walls. But in large-scale raising on the prairie or savannah, if there are no fences then the cattle must be herded, and that requires constant vigilance to resist the herbivore instinct of drifting off to feed—and also constant motion. As the animals eat up the vegetation where they are gathered, the entire herd must be kept moving to find more. That is what still happens in the African savannah of the cattle herdsmen, and what was done in the American West as in other New World prairies, until barbed wire arrived to make ranching possible.

One material difference between ranging in open country and ranching is that less labor is needed, because there is less need for vigilance within the

---

Review of Reviel Netz, *Barbed Wire: An Ecology of Modernity*, Wesleyan University Press.

fence. Another measurable difference is that cattle can do more feeding to put on weight, instead of losing weight when driven from place to place. But the increased productivity of ranching as opposed to ranging is actually of an entirely different order. African herders must be warriors to protect their cattle from their like as well as from the waning number of animal predators, but chiefly to maintain their reputation for violence which in turn assures their claim to the successive pastures they must have through the seasons. It was almost the same for the ranging cowboys of the American West, and while their own warrior culture was somewhat less picturesque than that of the Nuer or Turkana, it too was replete with the wasted energies of endemic conflict over land, water and sometimes even the cattle itself. Ranchers are not cream puffs either, but they can use their energies more productively because in most places—including the Bolivian Amazon for all its wild remoteness— their fences are property lines secured by the apparatus of the law, which itself can function far more easily among property-owning ranchers than among warrior nomads and rangers. Skills too are different. African herdsmen notoriously love their cattle to perdition but their expertise is all in the finding of pasture and water in semi-arid lands, as well as in hunting and war, and they are not much good at increasing fertility, and hardly try to improve breeds. It was the same in the American West, where the inception of today's highly elaborate cattle-raising expertise that makes red meat excessively cheap had to await the stability of ranching, and the replacement of the intrepid ranger by the more productive cowboy.

Barbed wire is important therefore, and the story of how it was so quickly produced by automatic machines on the largest scale, efficiently distributed to customers necessarily remote from urban centers, marketed globally almost immediately, and finally used to change landscapes and societies, is certainly very interesting. But for all this, the reader will have to turn to Henry D. and Frances T. McCallum's *The Wire That Fenced the West* rather than the work at hand, in spite of its enthusiastic dust-jacket encomia from Noam Chomsky ("a deeply disturbing picture of how the modern world evolved"), Paul F. Starrs ("beautifully grim") and Lori Gruen, for whom the book is all about "structures of power and violence." The reason is that Reviel Netz, the author of *Barbed Wire: An Ecology of Modernity*, prefers to write of other things.

For Netz, the raising of cattle is not about producing meat and hides from lands usually too marginal to yield arable crops, but rather an expression of the urge to exercise power: "What is control over animals? This has two senses, a human gain, and an animal deprivation." To tell the truth, I had never even pondered this grave question, let alone imagined how profound the answer could be. While that is the acquisitive purpose of barbed wire, for Professor Netz it is equally—and perhaps even more—a perversely disinterested expression of the urge to inflict pain, "the simple and unchanging equation of flesh and iron," another majestic phrase, though I am not sure if equation is quite the right word. But if that is our ulterior motive, then those of us who rely on barbed- wire fencing for our jollies are condemned to be disappointed, because cattle does not keep running into it, suffering bloody injury and pain for us to gloat over, but instead invisibly learns at the youngest age to avoid the barbs by simply staying clear of the fence. Fortunately we still have branding, "a major component of the culture of the West" and of the South too, because in Bolivia we also brand our cattle. Until Netz explained why we do it—to enjoy the pain of "applying the iron until—and well after—the flesh of the animal literally burns," I had always thought that we brand our cattle because they cannot carry notarized title deeds anymore than they can read off-limits signs. Incidentally, I have never myself encountered a rancher who expensively indulges in the sadistic pleasure of deeply burning the flesh of his own hoofed capital, opening the way for deadly infection; the branding I know is a quick thrust of the hot iron onto the skin, which is not penetrated at all, and no flesh burns.

We finally learn who is really behind all these perversities, when branding is "usefully compared with the Indian correlate": Euro-American men, of course, as Professor Netz calls us. "Indians marked bison by tail-tying: that is, the tails of killed bison were tied to make a claim to their carcass. Crucially, we see that for the Indians, the bison became property only after its killing."

We on the other hand commodify cattle "even while alive." There you have it, and Netz smoothly takes us to the inevitable next step:

> Once again a comparison is called for: we are reminded of the practice of branding runaway slaves, as punishment and as a practical measure of making sure that slaves—that particular kind of commodity—would not revert to their natural free state. In short, in the late 1860s, as Texans finally desisted from the branding of slaves, they applied themselves with ever greater enthusiasm to the branding of cows.

Texans? Why introduce Texans all of a sudden, instead of cowboys or cattlemen? It seems that for Professor Netz in the epoch of Bush II, Texans are an even more cruel sub-species of the sadistic race of Euro-American men (and it is men, of course). As for the "enthusiasm," branding too is hard work, and I for one have yet to find the vaqueros who will do it for free, for the pleasure of it.

By this point in the text some trivial errors occur, readily explained by a brilliantly distinguished academic career that has understandably precluded much personal experience in handling cattle. Professor Netz writes, for example, that "moving cows over long distances is a fairly simple task. The mounted humans who controlled the herds —frightening them all the way to Chicago...." Actually, it is exhausting work to lead cattle over any distance at all without causing drastic weight loss—even for us in Bolivia when we walk our steer to the market, in spite of far more abundant grass and water than Texas or even the upper Midwest ever offered, at the rate of less than nine miles a day to cover a mere 200 kilometers, instead of several times that distance to reach Chicago. Used as we are to seeing our beautiful Nelor cattle grazing contentedly in a slow ambling drift across the pastures, it is distressing to drive them even at the calmest pace for the shortest distances; they are so obviously tense and unhappy, and of course they lose weight with each unwanted step. As for "frightening them all the way to Chicago," that is sheer nonsense: nothing is left of cattle stampeded a few days, let alone all the way to Chicago. Unfortunately, his trivial error makes it impossible for Netz to understand the difference between ranging and ranching that he thinks he is explaining.

All this and more besides (horses are "surrounded by the tools of violence") occurs in the first part of a book that proceeds to examine at greater length the cruelty of barbed wire against humans. He starts with the battlefield—another realm of experience that Netz cannot stoop to comprehend. He writes that barbed wire outranks the machine gun in stopping power, evidently not knowing that infantry can walk over any amount of barbed wire if it is not over-watched by adequate covering fires, and need not waste time cutting through the wires one by one. Nowadays well-equipped troops have light-alloy runners for this, as other purposes, but in my day, our sergeants trained us to cross rolls of barbed wire by simply stepping over the backs of prone comrades, who were protected well enough from injury from the barbs by the thick wool of their British battle dress— because the flexible rolls gave way of course.

Perhaps because the material is rather directly derived from standard sources, no such gross errors emerge in the still larger part of the book devoted to the evils of the barbed wire of the prison camps, and worse, of Boer War British South Africa, Nazi Germany and the Soviet Union (Guantanamo no doubt awaits a second edition). It is reassuring if not exactly startling to read that Professor Netz disapproves of prison camps, concentration camps and extermination camps, that he is not an enthusiast of either the Soviet Union or Nazi Germany, while being properly disapproving of all imperialisms of course. But it does seem unfair to make barbed wire the protagonist of these stories as opposed to the people who employed barbed wire along with even more consequential artifacts such as guns. After all, atrocities as extensive as the Warsaw Ghetto with its walled perimeter had no need of barbed wire, any more than the various grim fortresses and islands in which so many were imprisoned, tortured and killed without being fenced in.

There is no need to go on. Enough of the text has been quoted to identify the highly successful procedures employed by Reviel Netz, which can easily be imitated – and perhaps should be by as many authors as possible, to finally explode the entire genre. First, take an artefact, anything at all. Avoid the too obviously deplorable machine gun or atom bomb. Take something seemingly innocuous, say shoelaces. Explore the inherent if studiously unacknowledged ulterior purposes of that "grim" artifact within "the structures of power and violence." Shoelaces after all perfectly express the Euro-American urge to bind, control, constrain and yes, painfully constrict. Compare and contrast the easy comfort of the laceless moccasins of the Indian— so often massacred by booted and tightly laced Euro-Americans, as one can usefully recall at this point. Refer to the elegantly pointy and gracefully upturned silk shoes of the Orient, which have no need of laces of course because they so naturally fit the human foot—avoiding any trace of Orientalism, of course. It is all right to write in a manner unfriendly or even openly contemptuous of entire populations as Professor Netz does with his Texans at every turn ("ready to kill…they fought for Texan slavery against Mexico"), but only if the opprobrium is always aimed at you-know-who, and never at the pigmented. Clinch the argument by evoking the joys of walking on the beach in bare and uncommodified feet, and finally overcome any possible doubt by reminding the reader of the central role of high-laced boots in sadistic imagery.

That finally unmasks shoelaces for what they really are—not primarily a way of keeping shoes from falling off one's feet, but instruments of pain, just like the barbed wire that I have been buying all these years not to keep the cattle in, as I imagined, but to torture it, as Professor Netz points out. The rest is easy: the British could hardly have rounded up Boer wives and children without shoe-laces to keep their boots on, any more than the very ordinary men in various Nazi uniforms could have done such extraordinary things so industriously, and not even Stalin could have kept the Gulag going with guards in unlaced Indian moccasins, or elegantly pointy, gracefully upturned, oriental shoes.

Part 7

Economics

28

The Russian Mafia: Does It Deserve the Nobel Prize in Economics?

It is now conventional wisdom that "mafyia" extortion and official corruption of every sort are inflicting much damage on the Russian economy. In a widely cited estimate, crooked officials and plain gangsters are said to have sent some US$100 billion into their foreign bank accounts since 1990, thus depriving the Russian economy of much more hard currency than the sum total of post-1990 Western aid. Countless newspaper articles have profiled the unappealing beneficiaries of the new economic order, from violent thugs with platinum-blonde molls and BMWs who do their showing off in restaurants, to sleek ex-officials in Armani suits with Vienna bank accounts, Manhattan apartments and good friends in the Kremlin who show off in *New York Times* interviews.

Far more numerous are the less obviously criminal and much less glamorous "biznessmen"—thousands of them—who traffic in state-owned raw materials diverted for entirely private export, who help thieving state managers transfer public property to personal ownership, who collaborate with foreign adventurers to smuggle consumer goods in and weapons out, or who simply buy and sell without bothering to pay taxes. Most visitors to Russia have encountered specimens of the type in the hotel lobbies that are their favorite places of business; some earn just enough to get by from day to day while waiting for their big hit, but quite a few have become very rich, very quickly.

There is no doubt that the pervasive criminalization of the Russian economy imposes real costs. The purchasing power of an impoverished population is further reduced, because Mafia "protection" fees increase prices. Efficient private-enterprise firms suffer from the unfair competition of less efficient rivals backed by corrupt officials. And, as anywhere else, tax evasion must ultimately be offset by inflationary money printing, or higher taxes inimical to growth. Moreover, the intense popular resentment of both gangsters and tycoons certainly threatens Russia's economic liberalization very directly: at the next opportunity, a majority of the electorate may decide to vote for go-slow Communists, or even hard-line Stalinists—though even they could only stop further privatizations, not reverse the process.

The political threat is real enough, but in purely economic terms the conventional wisdom is all wrong. To begin with, it overlooks the natural evolution of the capitalist animal. The fat cows that populate advanced economies—stable, highly capitalized firms which offer good employment, pay their taxes in full, invest in new plant, develop new technology and contribute to charities and culture—were not born as such. It was as lean and hungry wolves that they originally accumulated capital, by seizing profitable market opportunities—often by killing off competitors in ways that today's anti-monopoly commissions would not tolerate—and by cutting costs in every way possible, not excluding all the tax avoidance they could get away with. But when countries and their economies undergo truly drastic transformations, as Germany, Italy and Japan did because of the destructions of the Second World War, and as Russia is now doing, conditions are too harsh even for wolves. Only ruthless hyenas can survive and prosper in the chaos of thoroughly disrupted economies, by trafficking in whatever can be profitably sold legal or otherwise, by buying up valuable real estate for pennies from desperate owners or corrupt officials, by the improvised manufacture of sub-standard products for deprived consumers, or by the simple theft of abandoned, semi-abandoned, or just poorly guarded public property.

Many of the dynamic industrial firms that now fill the landscape of Emilia-Romagna, most Japanese real-estate fortunes that long ago diversified into industry and finance, and not a few of the businesses that propelled West Germany's rise to prosperity, had their start in the immediate post-1945 year. It was by black-marketeering, predatory buying, sub-standard manufacture, and efficient stealing (but the polite expression was to "organize") that the hyena-entrepreneurs of those days accumulated the capital that enabled them to become honest wolves, and eventually productive cows. Legend has it that many of Emilia's metal-working firms were first equipped with tools and machinery looted from a Werhmacht ordnance-repair train abandoned in April 1945 near Piacenza. In Japan, old people still vividly recall some of today's tycoons in their original incarnations as dance-hall operators, gambling masters or purveyors of GI luxuries diverted from PX shops. In the German case, the persistence of the GI market after 1945 made the ownership of night-clubs and outright brothels, as well as black-marketeering, the prelude to many a business career. Had the respective police forces been effective enough to round up all the hyenas and lock them up, the economic recovery of West Germany, Italy and Japan would have been much slower, and many of the successful entrepreneurs of the 1950s and 1960s would never have been able to get their start.

All this is true of the Russian economy—only more so, because in its case even simple theft could be highly productive. The still intact Soviet Union produced, per capita, more electricity than Italy, more steel than the United

States, more mineral fertilizer than Japan, more tractors than West Germany, and far more cement than France.

As the same time, the Soviet standard of living was almost incomparably lower than those of France, Italy, Japan, West Germany or the United States. Statisticians quarreled over the numbers in trying to come up with numerical comparisons but in truth they were entirely meaningless: a number representing per-capita income is worthless when much patience or ingenuity were needed to get even a bit of butter, and it took special connections to be able to buy a decent pair of shoes.

The too-obvious explanation of the huge gap between impressive production figures and the poverty of everyday life was the huge cost of Soviet military ambitions, by then in the final stage of baroque excess. Much steel did go into the making of tanks and warships, and cement too was consumed in huge amounts to build gigantic underground command centers, as well as more mundane airfields, missile silos, and more. But what about the agricultural tractors and fertilizer, in both of which the Soviet Union out-produced not only West Germany and Japan but also the United States, France and Italy? Neither were claimed by the military for their own use in any significant quantities, yet all those tractors and all that fertilizer did not finally produce enough grain for home consumption, let alone the sort of export surpluses that France and the United States must dump on world markets. By the highest estimates, the military used up some 30 percent of the Soviet Union's GNP, but the gap between basic inputs and outputs actually useful to the Soviet population was much greater.

As everyone knows, the real explanation for the gap is that by 1989 the Soviet economic system was no longer just inefficient: in many ways, it was positively destructive. Perfectly good Uzbek cotton which had real value—it could be sold on the world market—was made into shirts so poorly cut and of such ugly colors that not even Soviet consumers would buy them. Hence all the spinning, weaving, dyeing, cutting and sowing actually removed value from the raw material, turning virgin cotton into the equivalent of scrap rag for paper-making. The same was true of leather, wool and synthetics, of wood and structural plastics, and of all sorts of other inputs that went into Soviet light industry.

Likewise, steel and cement not reserved for military use that ended up in Soviet building projects were, in effect, lost for several years because the pace of construction was so extraordinarily slow. Quite a lot was lost for ever, as unsheltered cement bags solidified and steel rods rusted away.

Above all, by the 1980s Soviet agriculture had become a more costly luxury than the armed forces. While the Soviet army at least kept its tanks in service for twenty years or so, Soviet state and collective farms ruined many tractors, reapers and combine harvesters of near-Western quality in less than one year, because of the lack of maintenance, or simply because they were left out to rust in the open all winter long. Likewise, truckloads of fertilizer simply dumped on fields actually reduced the output of crops.

Given such a counterproductive system, simple theft can be highly productive. It definitely increased the overall standard of living of the Soviet Union. Cotton, as other light-industry raw materials diverted from official channels, could be made into useful products by domestic or illegal craft work. Construction materials, stolen from the interminable official projects, provided the means to build many houses and dachas with illegal or do-it-yourself labor. Gasoline, removed from state trucks that often drove about uselessly, could provide much-needed fuel for private car owners. And it was with stolen fertilizer and farm tools that the tiny private plots produced so much of the Soviet Union's food supply.

Inevitably, thieves and final consumers could only be brought together by a functioning illegal market, which in turn could only be operated by criminals who were sufficiently organized to do the job, namely the Mafia. Because bureaucrats and policemen had to be paid off at every stage of acquisition, transportation and distribution, it followed that the mafia had to collect "protection," its own unofficial taxes. It was that crypto-capitalist system that emerged in view fully ready to function in sector after sector, in place after place, as the liberalization progressed. Many if not most of the Russians who bitterly complain about the Mafia had greatly relied on its indispensable services during Soviet times.

True, by now almost half of the economy has been privatized. But that leaves the other half in state ownership—and much of it remains so counter-productive that theft can still increase Russian living standards. Moreover, many state firms have only been privatized very nominally—they are still run by their old managers, in the old inefficient ways.

It is also true that Mafia extortion practiced against private shops and stalls adds no value, but merely redistributes income from many, mostly very poor, consumers to fewer, richer gangsters.

But in one crucial respect organized crime remains a very beneficial force: it is the only counterweight to the great number of firms, backed by corrupt officials, which now engage in ruthless monopolistic practices.

At the local level, ex-Soviet officials who now own shops, restaurants, hotels, and workshops do not hesitate to use their old Party connections to drive competitors out of business—by arranging the imposition of huge taxes and fines, hygiene inspections, or arbitrary administrative rules. In such cases, there is almost no possibility of obtaining redress from the overburdened Russian courts, which have barely started to deal with commercial and fiscal matters. Only the local criminal mafia may be able and willing to resist the ex-Party mafia, for a price of course.

On a larger scale, genuinely private industrial firms—usually joint-ventures with foreign partners—are now often confronted by the extortionate pricing of officially-backed suppliers, especially for natural gas, oil, coal and electricity. While liberalization has created many natural monopolies, there is still no functioning anti-monopoly system, nor any mechanism to regulate utility prices. Again, the only possible counter-weight is organized crime. In one case, an important industrial firm in a rather remote location was confronted by a sudden 500 percent increase in gas prices. With immediate closure as the only possible alternative, the enterprising foreign manager on site who had once worked in Sicily, turned for help to the local mafia, which in turn threatened the gas-company officials with serious bodily harm, eventually persuading them to accept a tolerable compromise, including a cut for themselves, of course.

Normally, without need of much violence, local mafias act in many places and many ways to resist the excessive concentrations of economic power brought about by government corruption, or rather by the prevalence of under-the-table joint ventures between Russian government officials and the new private firms. They are, in effect, competitors which use physical force, or more often just the threat of force, to usefully offset monopolistic market power in a still lawless economy.

Nor is Russia unique in deriving a broad economic benefit from organized crime. Colombia, Peru and Bolivia all receive much hard currency from the drug trade, but because the accompanying lawlessness inhibits economic growth, the three countries might be better off without it. By contrast its Yakuza gangsters have certainly been of great economic benefit for Japan. So highly organized that at least one gang has more than 20,000 registered members, and that most have overt street-level offices, the Yakuza collect protection money from bars, gambling dens, massage parlors and brothels. But it is their role in the construction industry that is vital for Japan's economy. Because of the extreme fragmentation of land ownership into a huge number of tiny house plots, developers usually find it impossible to legally buy sites big enough for apartment houses or office buildings. Only with the help of hired gangs and their colorful repertoire of threats and vandalism can house-owners be persuaded to sell, even at very high prices. Many of the modern buildings one sees in Japanese cities could never have been built without Yakuza help, which is just as essential for the Japanese construction industry as ferro-concrete.

One day, Russia will acquire a functioning system of commercial law, administrative and fiscal courts that can actually protect citizens from the exactions of arbitrary, corrupt government officials, and even anti-monopoly safeguards. Only then will it be safe to unleash the police against the mafia, to stop the social and political damage it is certainly inflicting. In the meantime, it is the only force interposed between the new economic powers and the defenseless consumers and entrepreneurs of Russia.

29

The Secret the Soviets Should have Stolen

Over the past decade, the world has witnessed an astonishing display of the power of innovation. As the Internet rose from obscurity to become the focus of a new electronic age, thousands of firms—entire new industries—sprang up, generating astronomic wealth for their founders.

Now an even greater power is at work: creative destruction. The luckless entrepreneurs, fired employees, and impoverished shareholders of companies in decline or collapse may be excused for seeing only the bleakness of the situation. For all their pain, however, this is the essential prelude to a new wave of creation. Free-market capitalism promises wealth—not happiness, and least of all tranquility. The disruption of human relations is one of the inevitable consequences of rapid economic change, upward or downward.

That rudimentary idea was very clearly explained back in 1942 by the great economist Joseph Schumpeter. Nevertheless, it remains poorly understood by bankers, businessmen, and even economists, while politicians routinely vow to deliver booming growth and unchanging family values at the same time. For creative destruction is not just an unfortunate side effect of free-market capitalism; it is the very engine of capitalist prosperity. Unprofitable methods, firms, and industries must be left behind in order to release resources for new enterprises. Otherwise, there can be no economic growth beyond that which accompanies the expansion of the labor force, the discovery of additional natural resources, and the opening of new external markets.

It's a cruel process, and a wasteful one. The unemployed are not immediately absorbed by rising firms—indeed, some never are. Expensive machinery ends up as scrap. Costly buildings are abandoned or demolished. In the wreckage of shut-down startups lie billions of dollars misspent on everything from software to corporate logos.

And all this is inherent to free-market capitalism. An economic system that always functions in perfect equilibrium—in which there is no unemployment and nothing is junked—will be inferior in the long run to a system that is never in equilibrium. As Schumpeter tried to explain, investment is not enough. There has to be disinvestment as well.

Creative destruction is the capitalist secret that was never uncovered by Soviet spies. They were always trying to steal the latest technologies from the West; they would have served their masters better by bringing back a copy of Schumpeter's old book. With its overstaffed factories, antiquated machinery, and outdated goods, the Soviet Union eventually became a monument to the inadequacy of investment alone.

For, contrary to legend, the Soviets invested heavily in new machinery. As devoted as they were to the arms race, they poured capital into their factories and farms, strangling the supply of consumer goods to do so. Along with massive capital investment, there was abundant new technology—more of it bought than stolen, and much of it developed by Soviet engineers, who were world leaders in metallurgy, among other fields.

With its vast resources and well-educated populace, the Soviet Union had nearly everything needed for prosperity. All it lacked was a means of driving unprofitable factories, farms, and shops out of business, freeing up their labor, capital, and real estate for better uses. A brand-new automobile plant would be imported from Italy, complete with assembly lines, hand-tools, and training. But right alongside that plant, where modern cars came off efficient production lines, other plants turned out ancient models with ten times as many employees. There was innovation aplenty, but there was no way for it to spread, because the up-to-date plant lacked the power to invest more capital and hire more workers; both had been pre-assigned. With no competition, obsolete factories stayed in business forever. There was no junked machinery, and there was no unemployment. But the overall result was to leave the population in poverty, squandering the world's largest store of natural resources along with immense amounts of capital and the skills and talents of a vast labor force.

Japan, oddly, now finds itself in a strikingly similar predicament. A decade ago, when its great boom ended in a stock market and real estate crash, Japan could have quickly re-launched its economy with a brutally fast liquidation and an interval of bankruptcies and high unemployment. But that is not the Japanese way.

Unlike Americans, most Japanese expect the economy to serve society, not the other way around. Considering themselves very prosperous already, they could see no grounds for imposing the misery and humiliation of unemployment and financial ruin on many of their fellow Japanese, merely to hasten the arrival of an even higher level of national prosperity. Accordingly, the Ministry of Finance was far more tolerant of lending to insolvent companies than our Federal Reserve would ever be. In turn, Japanese companies balked at the mass firings that have become so common among troubled—and even not-so-troubled—American companies. They relied instead on natural attrition by retirement to correct, however slowly, for the over-staffing of the boom years.

There is a world of difference, of course, between the old Soviet Union and present-day Japan, with its great manufacturing base and its eleven trillion dollars in personal savings. Now that the Soviet system has departed and far more timid forms of socialism are on the ropes, however, the Japanese rank among the world's leading guardians of security and stability. Of the advanced industrial nations, they stand at one end of a spectrum of controlled capitalism, which, broadly speaking, is also the system that produced America's great postwar boom. In the United States, meanwhile, controlled capitalism has yielded to turbo capitalism—a lifting of social and legal restraints that is widely believed to have set the stage for a breathtaking economic revival.

Along with a new wave of creative destruction, however, turbo capitalism has led to levels of anxiety and distress we would not have countenanced in the 1950s and 1960s. The economic miracle of the 1980s and 1990s was accompanied by a fraying of community and family ties, a readiness to consign the care of elderly parents and small children to paid strangers, and the application of market values to such institutions as hospitals, publishing houses, universities, and botanical gardens. Perhaps most shocking of all—to a Japanese sensibility, at any rate—is our steady drift toward towards preindustrial extremes of inequality.

The Japanese, with their warm and cuddly and morally principled caution, have avoided a great deal of human suffering, but at a steep economic cost. Along with excess employees, they have held onto excess facilities and product lines. Even failing companies were unable to jettison their unprofitable parts because Japanese banks, instead of forcing them into bankruptcy, kept them going with further loans, year after year. Carrying too many non-performing loans on their books, Japan's banks are powerless to lend elsewhere, and with unemployment never higher than 4.5 percent, there is no great supply of eager labor for new businesses.

Ten years after its crash, the Japanese economy is still stagnating at zero-growth or less—a great warning to the United States as it faces a downturn and possible recession after the longest boom in its history. Here, too, many companies over-invested, and most households over-spent, accumulating the heaviest debt burden on record—more than 120 percent of average household income. Interest rates and taxes are both now being reduced to help the moderately and immoderately affluent alike—the untaxed, no-credit poor get nothing. That will make the inevitable liquidation less painful and slower, ensuring an equally slow recovery.

Turbo capitalism is not the end of history. Humans surely have it in them to evolve a system better able to sort out the social and emotional as well as purely economic effects of its actions. But a quick look around suggests that we haven't found such a system yet.

30

The Gospel According to Greenspan

A fanatical religion has swept the United States and Europe in recent years: central bankism. Its high priests, Federal Reserve Chairman Alan Greenspan and his European counterparts, believe in a devil and are dedicated to the struggle against it—in this case, inflation. Common sense suffices to oppose high inflation and to fear hyperinflation as the death of currencies, but it takes the absolute faith of religion to refuse even very moderate inflation at the cost of immoderate unemployment and economic stagnation, as the Europeans have been doing, or at the cost of slow economic growth for years on end, as in the United States.

Like many religions, central bankism has its sanctuaries, and these inspire as much awe as any great cathedral—from the majestic Bank of England to the Greek temples of the Federal Reserve in Washington, from the solidity of the Banque de France to the massive modernity of Germany's Bundesbank. In these sanctuaries the pontiffs constantly strive to assert their independence from secular politicians, mere mortals voted in and out of office by the ignorant masses. Although, like other public officials, they receive their salaries from the taxpayers, central bankers claim the right to ignore the public will. They invariably remain in office for terms of papal length often prematurely renewed for fear of disturbing financial markets. And when these high priests do at last retire, they are frequently elevated to financial sainthood, their every fleeting opinion reverentially treasured, their candidacy for any position of special trust eagerly accepted, their very names talismanic, as with Paul Volcker on Wall Street and far beyond.

Because their power derives largely from their supreme command of the crusade against the devil of inflation, central bankers naturally see his insidious presence everywhere. Very often, they detect "disturbing signs of incipient inflation," or even "alarming warnings of mounting inflationary pressure" in output, employment, and wage statistics that many respected economists view with equanimity or find downright reassuring. True, every time new statistical indicators are published, there are calls from some quarters for slightly lower interest rates to achieve a bit more growth, but such outbreaks of heresy are easily quashed by the high priests.

Simple, definitive proof of the doctrinal supremacy of central bankism can be found in the fact that any policy initiative branded as "inflationary" is usually rejected out of hand. By contrast, the term "deflationary" has no resonance at all. Although it is occasionally used as a purely technical term to express falling prices, deflation might more properly be used to describe what the central bankers have given us: overrestrictive fiscal and monetary policies that strangle growth, policies that in the 1930s brought about the Great Depression, political chaos, dictatorship, and war. Inflation harms the instrument of money while deflation has an immediate impact on people, denying them the opportunity to work and earn, and to buy goods and services, which would allow others to work and earn. Indeed, in the United States, central bankism has resulted in falling real wages; although unemployment at the end of 1996 remained at 5.3 percent, more than half of all American jobs pay less now in constant dollars than they did twenty years ago. No wonder, as President Clinton keeps boasting, millions of new jobs keep being created (a quarter of a million were created last December alone): American labor is so cheap.

Of course, it is true that real incomes and real wealth cannot be created by printing money, that inflation hurts the poor disproportionately as well as rich bondholders and everyone who lives on a fixed income. Inflation benefits smart speculators and all who are already wealthy enough to own real estate and other marketable assets. It is also true that, if unchecked, inflation naturally accelerates into hyperinflation, which not only destroys currencies but also degrades economic efficiency.

Inflation, then, is bad; and hyperinflation, very bad indeed. But it is just as true that deflation is bad and that hyperdeflation is disastrous. In economic theory, deflation should have no consequences at all, because any increase in the value of money can be nullified by a compensating reduction in wages. In practice, however, prices resist going down, and very few employees anywhere at any time accept wage cuts without the most bitter resistance—even in the United States, with its mass immigration, increasingly unfavorable labor market, and weak unions. Contrary to theory, then, deflation starves economies; with deflation, moreover, people feel poorer and spend less simply because the nominal value of their houses and other assets is falling. Inflation and deflation should therefore be viewed as equally objectionable; they should resound in our ears as equivalent evils, like flood and drought. It is the greatest triumph of central bankism that only inflation is viewed as sinful.

How did the ascendancy of the central bankers come about? How did the employees of one public institution assume a priestly status, becoming more powerful in many ways than prime ministers or presidents? One heard very little about them in the three postwar decades of rapid economic growth, sharply rising incomes, and widening prosperity. Only during the thirties, not coincidentally the years of the Great Depression, were they as prominent as they are now. A world in crisis followed with bated breath every pronouncement from the lips of the Bank of England's Montagu Norman, Germany's Hjalmar Schacht, and their lesser colleagues on both sides of the Atlantic. With tragic consequences for millions of American families, and far more terrible repercussions in Europe, governments almost everywhere accepted the central bankers' remedy for the Depression, which was to deflate, deflate, deflate, by cutting public spending and restricting credit. One result was that Hitler's rise to power was accelerated by mass unemployment.

We now know that the central bankers were completely wrong. The only way to restart the stalling economies of the thirties was to start the chain reaction of demand by sharply increasing government spending, never mind a bit of inflation. Had the big boys of the world economy led the way, by inflating and by importing first, to generate more demand for their own exports, everyone would have come out just fine. But only a few adventurous souls, and only one reputable economist, John Maynard Keynes, dared to contradict what seemed to be common sense, and even they were hesitant. The central bankers, by contrast, were utterly certain that they were right, just as they are now; and they gave exactly the same advice that they are giving now, the only advice central bankers ever give: tighten credit, restrict spending, hold back demand.

Another reason for the rise of central bankism as the prevailing wisdom of the age is institutional: while the value of money is protected with fierce determination by the central bankers, industry and labor have no such exalted defenders, only mere governments and parliaments now greatly inhibited by the decrees of central bankism.

Like all religions, central bankism demands sacrifices from the faithful. Catholics, Jews, and Muslims have it rather easy by comparison: central bankism resembles the Aztec faith in its demands for human sacrifice. So far, we have yet to see central bankers climb pyramids to cut out the palpitating hearts of young men and virgins with obsidian knives, but not a single one of them hesitates to impose levels of unemployment that year after year deprive millions of young people of the opportunity to start a career. Indeed, the central bankers have all the moral certitude of the Aztec priests. Gathered together last August with their host Alan Greenspan, in Jackson Hole, Wyoming, the central bankers congratulated themselves at length on their success in reducing inflation by keeping real interest rates high; they did not pause to deplore miserable growth rates. As it is, the estimated 1996 growth rates for the G7 countries (the United States, Canada, Britain, France, Germany, Italy, and Japan) average out at 1.8 percent, which guarantees rising unemployment simply because both the size of the labor force and its productivity are increasing somewhat faster. Still, in Jackson Hole the central bankers competed for the prize of calling for the lowest inflation rate.

France was the surprise winner of this deflation Olympics. Untroubled by an economy not merely stagnant but in rigor mortis, with a level of unemployment—above 12 percent—unseen since the Great Depression, the French were enormously proud of their amazingly low 1.3 percent inflation rate, a full 0.2 percent below Germany's! It was as if the defeats of 1870 and 1940 had been undone.

Indeed, there was heady talk of ascending to the paradise of central bankism: a zero inflation rate. It would only be a matter of eliminating budget deficits by scrapping more welfare programs, and of maintaining interest-rate discipline, orders easily handed down from the magnificent heights of Jackson Hole to the vulgar crowd of Europe's 18 million unemployed.

As for Alan Greenspan, he has nothing whatsoever to worry about, because in the United States, slow growth (just over 2 percent annually), a 5 percent unemployment rate, and falling wages are all now accepted as perfectly normal, or even as good news. The stage has been reached in which any spurt of faster growth, any fall in unemployment, is very bad news indeed for Wall Street and for all of us, because it will only lead the Federal Reserve to increase interest rates in order to "cool down the economy."

In fact, nobody knows the exact rate of unemployment below which wages start rising, pushing prices upward. Economists continue to debate the issue, but the Fed takes no chances. Greenspan invariably errs on the side of caution: a million people can lose their jobs because higher interest rates might, perhaps, keep inflation at one-tenth of one percent below what it might have been. But the central bankers decree: in the name of the holy struggle against inflation, the public must be willing to sacrifice.

31

The New Bolshevism

The great scientific discovery that gave us penicillin was achieved by Fleming for one reason alone: when his routine cultivation of bacteria for an experiment failed because some mold contaminated the petri dish, he immediately realized that it was not his original experiment that was important, but rather the "disturbance" that ruined it. Once he focused on the mold, it was a straightforward deduction that it produced something that could kill bacteria, an antibiotic.

Likewise when we consider the protests of the Seattle WTO meeting, the key is to isolate the important phenomenon from all the confusion. What is important is not the violence, which was the work of a tiny number of cultists, followers of an anarchist guru, and not the failure of the WTO conference itself, which is the normal result when big international conferences are organized too quickly to respect an arbitrary date. It was not even the unexpected dimension of the protest that is significant. Rather, it was rather the *incoherence* of the protest that is truly significant.

The politicians, bureaucrats and businessmen believe that the Seattle demonstrations are only a "disturbance" because environmentalists, trade-unionists, and protectionists are too diverse to form a coherent opposition to globalization in their respective countries. They are missing the point: what is significant is precisely the fact that they offer only one truth and only one model, while there are many different reasons to oppose globalization.

Two generations ago, it was the Bolsheviks who proposed a single Leninist model for all industrialized countries, from Japan to Belgium (it was not until much later that the Communist model was proposed for pre-industrial countries as well). The Bolsheviks ignored all differences of size, culture and religion, all differences in social, economic and political structures: they were convinced that their model could be and should be imposed everywhere.

Today, the new Bolsheviks are the advocates of "turbo-capitalism," who believe that all economies should be opened to all forms of competition by privatizing everything, abolishing all economic regulations, and removing all barriers to international commerce. Again, fundamental differences between countries are being ignored. The privatization of public services, for example, works very well if there is a dynamic and fearless anti-monopoly unit of government constantly attacking emerging monopolies, like the U.S. anti-trust office is now destroying the power of Microsoft. Then we see services improve and tariffs go down.

But without that counter-force, public services become private monopolies that make a few people very rich and impose high costs on the entire economy. Such was the case in England with water and railway services, and worse still in Italy, where one man was allowed to monopolize the private television industry—to the unending amazement of the world. Likewise, the deregulation of the financial sector works very well if there are modern laws to prevent abuses of power and a highly motivated financial police with powerful computers and talented professionals. In the United States, this is the Security and Exchange Commission, which destroyed not only the billionaire banker Michael Milken but countless stock exchange manipulators and corporate barons. Half the top men in the City of London would be in prison if they operated on Wall Street. As for Milan's CONSOB, it is decidedly improved from the past, but it has a very way to go before Italian small investors will be protected from corporate manipulations.

In other words, the Ferrari engine of a fully privatized, deregulated economy also requires powerful brakes. Yet recent years have seen the promotion of free markets without any real effort to create equally dynamic controlling institutions. In Britain, Bill Gates would be Lord Gates of Windows, far more untouchable than Prince Charles. A French Microsoft would be a sacred institution and the anti-monopoly official who dared to start a case against it would find himself on a one-way flight to the Indian Ocean island of Reunion. In Russia he would have his own offices in the Kremlin, with an open door to Yeltsin. In Italy he would buy himself three or four political parties to become the prime minister of his own coalition.

The large question that globalization specifically raises, is nothing less than the relationship between culture and commerce. To stop European subsidies for wheat production would not only help the wheat farmers of Argentina, Australia, India, and the U.S. but would also stop the destruction of the environment in northern France and elsewhere in Europe. To open the heavily protected Japanese rice market on the other hand, would destroy the entire culture of rural Japan with its festivals and folklore—in other words the *Japanese* part of Japan, whose industrial areas are nothing but a local version of undifferentiated modernity. Because the Japanese operate their economy to sustain their society and not the other way around, they correctly think that it is idiotic to destroy what they value most for the sake of a minor increase in efficiency.

Just like the old Bolsheviks ignored all structural differences between countries in their insistence that only state ownership of everything would eliminate economic inequality, today's turbo-capitalists do they same when they insist that all trade barriers are inefficient, that a globalized world economy would be much more productive, and that all impediments to free trade should therefore be abolished. But this final proposition is a giant non sequitur, because impediments to trade may protect not only inefficiencies but also national cultures and societies. To ignore this possibility is to equate kleptocratic African trade barriers with the tariffs that protect the livelihood of millions of European and Japanese farmers and much traditional culture and to conflate the regulatory protection of tiny, very privileged minorities with the labor laws that are moderating the real-wage reductions that global competition is imposing on millions of European industrial workers.

That was the real significance of the Seattle demonstrations: through their very diversity, they exposed the one-model extremism of the new Bolsheviks, who would sacrifice everything for the sake of efficiency—failing to see that even the model, deregulated American economy relies on its functioning governmental institutions.

LaVergne, TN USA
19 January 2010
170530LV00004B/84/P